ECONOMIC GROWTH & DEVELOPMENT

ECONOMIC GROWTH & DEVELOPMENT:

A MATHEMATICAL INTRODUCTION

PHILIP A. NEHER

Associate Professor of Economics, University of British Columbia

John Wiley & Sons, Inc.
New York · London · Sydney · Toronto

Copyright © 1971 by John Wiley & Sons, Inc.

All rights reserved. No part of this book may be reproduced by any means, nor transmitted, nor translated into a machine language without the written permission of the publisher.

Library of Congress Catalogue Card Number: 73-123742

ISBN 0-471-63100-0

Printed in the United States of America

10 9 8 7 6 5 4 3 2 1

To My Parents

PREFACE

This book evolved from an economic growth and development graduate seminar at the University of British Columbia. The participating graduate students were keen on the subject but their academic preparation was uneven. Many of them were not familiar with the elementary theory of production and most of them had not been introduced to economic dynamics. As a result, it seemed useful to devote the first few seminars to an introduction to economic dynamics at the elementary level and to review production theory. Since the requisite material was scattered throughout the available literature, it appeared useful to gather together the bare bones of it in the form of lecture notes, which were distributed prior to seminar meetings. This procedure seemed to facilitate the communication of basic ideas and paved the way for the discussion of current topics in growth and development. This book is an expansion of those lecture notes.

I assume that the student has been introduced to calculus and has studied elementary price theory. Since many undergraduates fall into this category, the book could be used in some undergraduate courses in intermediate macro theory, mathematical economics, and growth and development. I hope that first-year graduate students will find something useful in it as well.

The growth of two basic single-sector models is explored: a neoclassical model of an advanced economy and a dynamic model of a primitive economy. These basic models are introduced early in the book by using familiar graphic techniques. Mathematical methods are used in subsequent chapters to illuminate the models. Other chapters deal with special topics, including an introduction to intertemporal efficiency.

I have attempted throughout the book to keep the mathematics as simple and intuitively appealing as possible. My aim has been to use mathematics to illuminate the structure and dynamics of the models, and mathematical rigor has often been sacrificed toward this end.

My intellectual debts are obvious from the footnotes. I am thankful to George Borts, Martin Beckman, Jerome Stein, and Ryuzo Sato for my early appreciation of economic dynamics.

Franklin Fisher and Karl Shell were kind enough to read the manuscript, and they made many suggestions that improved the presentation. My colleague, Keizo Nagatani, gave invaluable advice on Chapter IX. Since I have not always heeded the advice of these gentlemen, they are not responsible for errors or omissions.

I am grateful to the University of British Columbia for its support; to Sally Bate and Donna Hepple for bearing the final typing burden; and to my students for their forbearance. My wife, Judith, contributed moral and editorial support throughout the project.

Philip A. Neher

University of British Columbia, 1969

CONTENTS

One

ECONOMIC GROWTH, ECONOMIC DEVELOPMENT, AND ECONOMIC MODELS — 1

Dynamics and Economic Models — 1
A Theory of Growth — 3
The Time Path Solution — 5
Statics and Dynamics — 7
Exercises — 10
References and Suggestions for Further Reading — 10

Two

PROPORTIONAL GROWTH — 11

The Constant Proportional Rate of Growth — 11
The Derivatives of the Growth Path — 15
The Equation of Proportional Growth — 16
Proportional Growth and Natural Logarithms — 19
A Recapitulation — 21
Exercises — 22
References and Suggestions for Further Reading — 22

Three

AN INTRODUCTION TO GROWTH IN AN ADVANCED ECONOMY 25

Introduction	25
The Production Function	26
The Saving and Investment Function	30
The Population Growth Function	33
The Equilibrium Rate of Growth	35
Net National Product and its Distribution	36
A Single Technological Improvement	38
Continuous Technological Improvement	42
Increases in the Saving Ratio	44
Decreases in the Rate of Population Growth	46
The Sources of Growth	46
The Case of Fixed Proportions	47
Exercises	49
References and Suggestions for Further Reading	50

Four

AN INTRODUCTION TO GROWTH IN A PRIMITIVE ECONOMY 51

Introduction	51
The Production Function	52
The Population Growth Function	53
The Equilibrium Rate of Growth and the Distribution of National Income	58
Improvements in Technology	60
A Decline in the Propensity to Proliferate	63
A Fall in the Death Rate	64
Exercises	66
References and Suggestions for Further Reading	66

Contents xi

Five

THE CONSTANT RETURNS TO SCALE PRODUCTION FUNCTION 67

- The Function 67
- The Marginal Products of Capital and Labor 75
- The Elasticities of the Wage and the Interest Rate 88
- The Elasticity of Substitution and the Elasticities of Factor Rewards 92
- The Average Products of Labor and Capital 98
- The Shares of Output Imputed to Labor and Capital 102
- A Recapitulation 103
- Dynamic Production Relations 104
- Exercises 106
- References and Suggestions for Further Reading 107

Six

TECHNOLOGICAL CHANGE 109

- *Introduction* 109
- *Technological Change and the Passing of Time* 111
  - The Growth of Marginal Products 111
  - The Growth of Output 116
  - The Hicks Measure of Bias and the Growth of Marginal Products 117
  - The Growth of Average Products 124
  - Changes in Relative Shares 124
  - A Recapitulation 125
- *Labor Augmenting Technological Change* 125
  - The Growth of Marginal Products 125
  - The Growth of Output 131
  - The Growth of Average Products 133
  - Neutrality as Defined by Harrod 133

xii Contents

Changes in Relative Shares	137
A Recapitulation	137
A Comparison of Hicks Neutral and Harrod Neutral Technological Progress	137
Exercises	141
References and Suggestions for Further Reading	142

Seven

GROWTH WITH TECHNOLOGICAL CHANGE — 143

Comparative Dynamics	143
Technological Change in an Advanced Economy	148
Continuous Labor Augmentation	148
Continuous Improvement with Bias as Defined by Hicks	155
A Single Improvement	156
An Explicit Solution	160
Technological Change in a Primitive Economy	173
A Single Improvement	173
An Explicit Solution	177
Exercises	181
References and Suggestions for Further Reading	182

Eight

BALANCED AND UNBALANCED GROWTH — 183

Introduction	183
One Variable	184
Existence, Uniqueness, and Stability of Balanced Growth Paths	184
Disequilibrium Growth in an Advanced Economy	187
Low-Level Equilibrium Traps	189
A Saving Trap	189
A Population Trap	191

Two Variables	193
Systems of Equations	193
A Model of Explosive Growth	199
Exercises	205
References and Suggestions for Further Reading	206

Nine

AN INTRODUCTION TO THE THEORY OF OPTIMAL ECONOMIC GROWTH — 207

Optimum Points	207
Profit Maximizing	207
The Golden Rule	209
Optimum Paths	216
A Turnpike	216
Optimal Growth Paths—The Basic Model	222
The Euler Equation	222
Control Theory	240
Optimal Growth Paths—Extensions of the Basic Model	243
Exercises	253
References and Suggestions for Further Reading	254

Ten

GROWTH IN AN OPEN ECONOMY — 257

The Balance of Payments	257
Growth in the Domestic Economy	260
Growth of National Wealth	262
Growth with Capital Movements	266
An Explicit Solution	273
Foreign Aid	278
Exercises	281
References and Suggestions for Further Reading	282

Eleven

A SIMPLE TWO-SECTOR MODEL OF GROWTH IN AN ADVANCED ECONOMY — 283

The Model — 284
   Production Conditions — 284
   Resource Constraints — 285
   The Factor Markets — 285
   National Income Accounting — 287
   The Demand for Final Products — 288
   A Graphical Solution of the Static Model — 288
   The Dynamic Problem — 294
Comparative Statics — 295
   The Capital-Labor Ratio and Factor Prices — 295
   The Interest Rate and Factor Prices — 300
   Relative Shares and Factor Prices — 301
On the Uniqueness and Stability of Growth Equilibrium — 303
Exercises — 308
References and Suggestions for Further Reading — 308

Twelve

UNDERDEVELOPMENT AND ECONOMIC DUALISM — 311

An Interpretation of Economic Dualism — 311
The Dynamic Core of a Developing Economy — 313
   The Setting — 313
   Growth with Constant Technology — 314
   A Single Technological Improvement — 316
   Continuous Technological Improvement — 319
Exercises — 320
References and Suggestions for Further Reading — 320

INDEX — 321

ECONOMIC GROWTH & DEVELOPMENT

Chapter One

ECONOMIC GROWTH, ECONOMIC DEVELOPMENT, AND ECONOMIC MODELS

Dynamics and Economic Models
A Theory of Growth
The Time-Path Solution
Statics and Dynamics
Exercises
References and Suggestions for Further Reading

DYNAMICS AND ECONOMIC MODELS

It has been said that economic models are caricatures of economic reality. (likeness exaggerated) Just as a good cartoon caricature efficiently conveys essential features of a person's character, so a good economic model cuts through to essential relations in economic systems.

Models are conceptual frameworks that set out the variables of concern and specify how they are related. They are indispensable in economic analysis because human economic behavior is so complex that we cannot hope to understand it in detail. If that were our immediate goal, economists would have given up long ago the task of achieving any understanding whatever of economic behavior. To understand anything at all, we must reduce the complexity of the real world to manageable dimensions. But in simplifying, we run the risk that important variables and relations are discarded so that relatively trivial ones remain. This is bad theorizing. An economist who stresses the role of apple prices in determining the demand for sirloin steak, while neglecting the price of round steak, has probably erred.

Models can be implicit or explicit. Implicit models are often found underlying the literary work of economic historians and institutionalists who undertake to understand the links between historical events and to expose the intricate fabric of institutional arrangements. Implicit models seldom spell out precisely what is assumed about human behavior, what the critical variables are, and precisely how they are related. As a consequence, the implicit theorist can range widely, grappling with ill-defined subject matter and, hopefully, obtaining new insights.

Explicit models may be literary, but more often they are set out in symbolic form. Behavioral assumptions and technological constraints appear explicitly, usually in the form of equations. This facilitates a check to see if there are enough equations to determine the specified number of unknowns. It enables a critic to perceive quickly the assumptions being made. Finally, it facilitates the logical process whereby the consequences of the assumptions are worked out by the theorist.

Explicit theorizing is becoming more popular in economics because, increasingly, we want to specify economic relationships, the implications of which are not intuitively obvious. And the more complex our models become, the greater is the premium on being explicit and rendering the models amenable to mathematical analysis.

This is particularly true in the field of economic growth and development. Here we are grappling with *dynamic* phenomena; with continuous processes of change; and with discrete changes, the consequences of which are felt in subsequent years.

The mathematics of economic growth and development can be found on the frontiers of applied mathematical analysis. But fortunately, one can obtain useful insights into growth mechanisms with more modest tools: elementary calculus and the theory of simple differential and difference equations.

Differential equations are emphasized in the chapters that follow. In this chapter, difference equation is employed to introduce the idea of a dynamic model.

Suppose that the *change* in an economic variable is related to its *value*. For example, suppose that the increase (or decrease) of net national product during a year $[\Delta X(1969) = X(1970) - X(1969)]$ depends on the value of the product during the year $[X(1969)]$. Then we can write

$$X(1970) - X(1969) \quad \text{depends on} \quad X(1969)$$
$$\Delta X(1969) \quad \text{depends on} \quad X(1969)$$

In general,

$$\Delta X \quad \text{depends on} \quad X$$

To say the same thing symbolically,

$$\Delta X = F(X)$$

This is *functional* notation, and it denotes in a general way that there is a relation between X and ΔX. A theory of economic growth would specify that relation precisely. Only the first difference of $X(\Delta X)$ appears in this equation. It is therefore called a *first order* difference equation. Higher order difference equations contain higher order terms ($\Delta^2 X, \Delta^3 X, \ldots, \Delta^n X$), but we shall not be concerned with them here.

A THEORY OF GROWTH[1]

An economy grows by passing from one stage to the next. A stage is defined by the values of crucial economic variables associated with it. A theory of economic growth explains how each stage generates self-destructive forces that inevitably propel the economy forward to the next stage. The theory must show how each stage is related to its predecessor and how it, in turn, is related to its successor. We want to understand how each stage produces conditions such that the next stage is completely determined.

Even simple theories of economic growth meet these requirements. Consider an economy where output is produced with capital and labor. Available capital is always fully utilized, but there is a "reserve army" of unemployed labor. Assume that technology imposes a strict one machine-one man combination of inputs. If one more machine were made available,

---

[1] The growth model in this chapter is suggested by the models of Sir Roy Harrod, *Towards a Dynamic Economics* (London: Macmillan, 1948) and Evsey Domar, *Essays in the Theory of Economic Growth* (New York: Oxford, 1957). It is employed here for illustrative purposes and does not pretend to do justice to their theories.

4 Economic Growth, Economic Development, and Economic Models

another worker would be absorbed to man it. To keep matters simple, suppose that output is simply "potatoes" or "putty," which serves equally well as a consumption good and as a capital good (machine). Thus, the total output (X) of the economy consists of a product that can be eaten (C) or invested to increase the stock of capital ($I = \Delta K$).

$$X = C + I = C + \Delta K \tag{1.1}$$

If there are constant returns to scale in production, it always takes a certain stock of machines to produce a given flow of output during the year (stage).

$$X = \frac{1}{\kappa} K \tag{1.2}$$

The letter κ is the capital-output ratio. If it takes two machines in production during the year (stage) to produce one unit of output, then[2]

$$\kappa = \frac{K}{X} = \frac{2}{1}$$

Another way to think about (1.2) is to realize that K must increase by κ units to make possible a one-unit increase in output.

$$\Delta X = \frac{1}{\kappa} \Delta K \tag{1.3}$$

But what is the source of new capital? In this case, we can imagine that new capital is saved up (not consumed) during the year (stage) and invested at the end of the year (stage). Suppose that a constant proportion (s) of output is not consumed, but put aside to augment the capital stock (ΔK).

$$\Delta K = sX \tag{1.4}$$

The next year is the next stage. It is significantly different from its predecessor because it begins the production year with more capital and more employment. How does the economy move from stage to stage through time? Substitute (1.4) into (1.3).

$$\Delta X = \frac{s}{\kappa} X \tag{1.5}$$

---

[2] Since the labor-capital ratio is one, it follows that the labor-output ratio is equal to the capital-output ratio.

The *change* in output in each equally spaced stage is proportional to the *level* of output. That proportion is greater: the greater is s and the less is κ (the greater is the proportion of output which is invested and the less capital that is required to produce a unit of output).

Stated another way, the *proportional growth rate* is

$$\frac{\Delta X}{X} = \frac{s}{\kappa} \qquad (1.5')$$

For example, if one tenth of output is invested, and two machines are required to produce a unit of output, then $s = 0.10$ and $\kappa = 2$ so that

$$\frac{\Delta X}{X} = \frac{0.10}{2} = 0.05 = 5\%$$

Output grows at the rate of 5 percent per year.

THE TIME-PATH SOLUTION

Equation 1.5, $\Delta X = (s/\kappa)X$, is a simple first-order difference equation. We seek its *solution*, which shows the *time path* of X, a general expression for the sequence

$$X(0), X(1), X(2), X(3), \ldots, X(n)$$

The numbers in parentheses refer to the years since the initial year.

Perhaps we can infer what the time path looks like by calculating the values of X for the first few periods. Let the initial value of X be 100 and s/κ be 0.05. Then the initial X, $X(0)$ is

$$X(0) = 100$$

and

$$X(1) \text{ is } X(0) \text{ plus } 5\% \text{ of } X(0)$$
$$X(1) = 100 + 0.05(100) = (1 + 0.05)100$$

and

$$X(2) \text{ is } X(1) \text{ plus } 5\% \text{ of } X(1)$$
$$X(2) = [(1 + 0.05)100] + 0.05[(1 + 0.05)100]$$

or

$$X(2) = (1 + 0.05)(1 + 0.05)100 = (1 + 0.05)^2 100$$

6 Economic Growth, Economic Development, and Economic Models

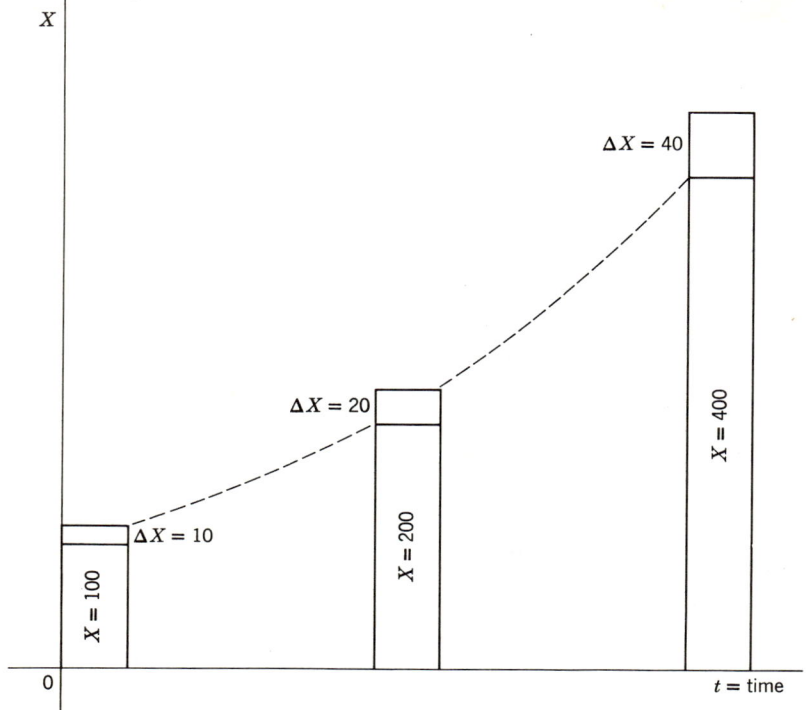

Figure 1.1 The time path of output.

The pattern is now clear for subsequent values of X.

$$X(3) = (1 + 0.05)^3 100$$
$$X(4) = (1 + 0.05)^4 100$$

In general, for any value of $t = 1, 2, 3, \ldots$, etc.,

$$X(t) = 100(1 + 0.05)^t$$

or

$$X(t) = X(0)\left(1 + \frac{s}{\kappa}\right)^t \tag{1.6}$$

This is the *solution* of

$$\Delta X = \frac{s}{\kappa} X \tag{1.5}$$

The *difference equation* (1.5) shows how the *change* in a variable is related to its *value*. From this we infer its *solution* (1.6), which shows how the *value* of the variable depends upon its initial value and the passage of *time*. The *theory* of economic change is embodied in the *structural equations* $\Delta X = (1/\kappa) \Delta K$ and $\Delta K = sX$. It describes how changes are related to values. From this we infer the ever-rising *time path* for X illustrated in Figure 1.1.[3] The time-path equation (1.6) may be called the *reduced-form* equation for X. It rises with ever greater "jumps," some of which have been omitted in the figure.

STATICS AND DYNAMICS

Compare the preceding *dynamic* model to an example of a *static* model of supply and demand for a factor of production (a). The quantity of the factor is fixed to society as a whole ($a = \bar{a}$), but it must be allocated between two alternative uses ($a_1 + a_2 = \bar{a}$). The available quantity of $a = \bar{a}$ is plotted along the horizontal axis in Figure 1.2. The quantity absorbed in the first

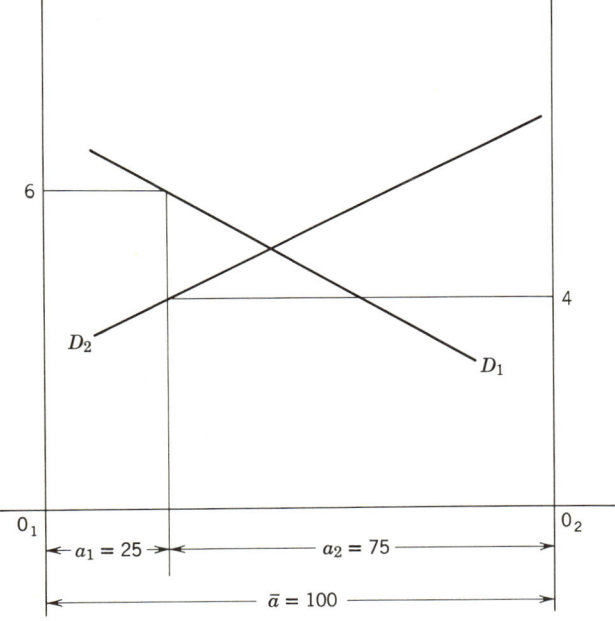

Figure 1.2 Allocation of a resource.

[3] We can also infer a time path for K. Since $K = \kappa X$, $K(t) = \kappa \cdot X(0)(1 + s/\kappa)^t$. But $X(0) = (1/\kappa)K(0)$, so $K(t) = K(0)(1 + s/\kappa)^t$.

use is measured from left to right; the remaining quantity, absorbed in the second use, is measured from right to left. Social-demand curves are drawn for each use and labeled D_1 and D_2. These curves show the *addition* to social product that results when alternative quantities of a are employed in each use. In the figure, suppose there are 100 units of a, divided between $a_1 = 25$ units of a_1 and $a_2 = 75$ units of a_2. Then the figure shows that adding the twenty-fifth unit of a in the first use adds six units of social product, and that adding the seventy-fifth unit of a in the second use adds four units of social product.

The resource is clearly misallocated. If one unit of a were transferred from the second to the first use, the loss of 4 units in the second use is more than compensated for by the gain of 6 units of product in the first use. Only where D_1 and D_2 intersect is social product the greatest. All other allocations of a are misallocations.

Many problems in development economics can be reduced to misallocation problems in one form or another, and the development economist is concerned with devising feasible programs for improving allocation. It is usually difficult, and it takes time to do so. Human resources are misallocated within a caste system, but rigid social structures are not quickly broken down. Underdeveloped financial markets misallocate capital, but banks and stock exchanges are not created overnight. A weak government fails to make "profitable" investments in education and social overhead capital, but adequate revenue systems and a competent civil service are not quickly built up.

Development occurs when misallocations are eliminated. But this is a *comparative-statics* phenomenon. The economy "grows" as resources are shifted toward their more highly valued uses. This is a once-and-for-all effect, a temporary source of "growth," but it may have *dynamic* implications.

For example, if resources are better allocated, more output is possible for any given level of inputs. This may affect the subsequent growth rate of the economy. For example, the capital-output ratio may fall as a consequence of better allocation. Less capital may be required per unit of output. The dynamic model in this chapter would then predict a higher sustainable rate of growth (κ is smaller). The once-and-for-all development phenomenon (a comparative statics problem) has a permanent growth effect (a dynamic problem).

A comparative statics problem from the analytical point of view may refer to a process that takes many years to work itself out in historical time. For example, the capital-output ratio may fall slowly as misallocation disappears. The long-run growth mechanism undergoes change during this period as κ declines. This suggests that we should look for dynamic theories of resource reallocation. But these seem beyond our grasp at the present time.

Whether a model is static or dynamic, it should be as explicit as possible. There should be no question about the nature of the theory and what is being assumed. This reduces the chances of misunderstanding, and the models can be judged on their merits. Thus, one might attack the growth model by questioning the assumption that the capital-output ratio is a constant. But the model cannot be attacked on the grounds that it makes no provision for capital capacity as a constraint on output. It is also clear from the specification of the model that labor-force growth is assumed to place no constraint on output growth. One could question that assumption too.

It is in its favor that the model is presented in *symbolic* form, so that the tools of symbolic logic (simple mathematics in this case) can be brought to bear to deduce the reduced forms from the structural equations. The chance of logical error is thus reduced in working out the implications of the theory.

The model is simple. But hopefully, it features fundamental economic relations and yields valid insights, which we would not have had without the model. But it is possible that important variables have been left out, or that included variables are not properly related to one another. The model may represent a bad theory in the sense that its explanatory power is low. It may not yield valid insights.

For example, the growth model predicts that, other things being equal, larger saving ratios are associated with more rapid growth. This is a conceptually testable hypothesis. Moreover, it is actually testable if data on a number of countries and for some years are available, and if one can contrive to take into account the fact that other things are not equal, when comparing the growth experience of observed economies. If credible econometric studies conclude that the saving ratio does not go very far in explaining growth experience, one would tend to reject the theory of economic growth embodied in the model. Econometric studies are never completely conclusive, however, so one might still believe that saving is somehow related to economic growth. That belief should then stimulate the search for alternative theories that incorporate saving as a central explanatory variable.

The growth model and the allocation model in this chapter are both quite simple. More complex models may be required to give us the desired level of explanatory power. But less austere theories employ more variables and structural equations. The problem of deducing the reduced-form equations, dynamic or static, becomes more formidable as a consequence. Mathematical aids become more valuable as complexity increases.

This is particularly true in growth and development theory. Most of us are trained to think in terms of statics and comparative statics, and our intuitions are unreliable in thinking through the consequences of even primitive dynamic theories. For this reason, the mathematics of economic dynamics is particularly useful to the growth-and-development theorist.

10 Economic Growth, Economic Development, and Economic Models

EXERCISES

1. Using the growth model in this chapter, assume that the saving ratio is 0.08 and the capital coefficient ($\kappa = K/X$) is 2.
   (a) What is the growth rate of the economy?
   (b) Find the equation that shows the time path of output. Draw a rough graph of it.
   (c) Using this equation, suppose that output is 100 at $t = 0$. What is output when $t = 3$?

2. Draw rough graphs of the time path of output that are qualitative representations of these situations:
   (a) Between the years 0 and T, the economy grows steadily with $s = 0.10$ and $\kappa = 4$. Then suddenly the capital coefficient falls to $\kappa = 2$ at T, and remains at 2 thereafter.
   (b) Between the years 0 and T, the economy grows steadily with $s = 0.08$ and $\kappa = 4$. Then suddenly the saving ratio rises to $s = 0.12$ and remains at 0.12 thereafter.

REFERENCES AND SUGGESTIONS FOR FURTHER READING

1. Archibald, G. C., and R. G. Lipsey, *A Mathematical Treatment of Economics*. London: Weidenfeld and Nicolson, 1967, pp. 3–11.
2. Baumol, W. J., *Economic Dynamics*. New York: Macmillan, 1959, pp. 3–55.
3. Domar, E. D., *Essays in the Theory of Economic Growth*. New York: Oxford, 1957.
4. Harrod, R., *Towards a Dynamic Economics*. London: Macmillan, 1948.

Chapter Two

PROPORTIONAL GROWTH

The Constant Proportional Rate of Growth
The Derivatives of the Growth Path
The Equation of Constant Proportional Growth
Proportional Growth and Natural Logarithms
A Recapitulation
Exercises
References and Suggestions for Further Reading

THE CONSTANT PROPORTIONAL RATE OF GROWTH

Economic growth (or decline) occurs when key economic variables become larger (or smaller) from one period of time to the next in a systematic way. Population growth is a commonplace example. The current stock of women in their child-bearing years give birth to new members of society. Deaths are occurring at the same time. The population grows if births exceed deaths.

The process of capital accumulation is another example. To the extent that society does not consume all its gross income, resources are released for production of capital equipment to replace worn-out equipment and to add to the existing capital stock. There is net investment (the capital stock has grown) if the output of new capital equipment exceeds the depreciation of old equipment.

How should we describe these growth processes? As a first approximation, we might assume that an economic or demographic variable grows in a linear way (along a straight line) between observations. Population censuses,

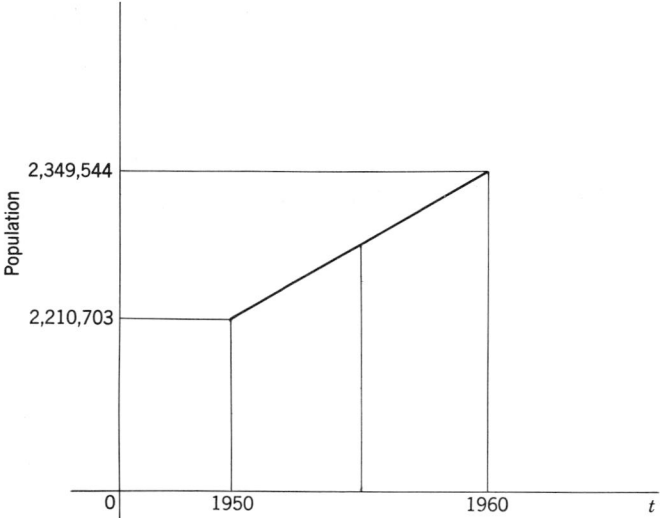

Figure 2.1 A linear approximation of Intercensual population growth: Puerto Rico, 1950–1961 (*Source. United States Census of Population, 1960: Puerto Rico*, PC(1), 53A, P.R. [Washington: U.S. Government Printing Office, 1961]).

for example, are often taken every ten years. A linear approximation of intercensual population growth would be a straight line drawn between census observations. This is illustrated in Figure 2.1 for the Puerto Rican population, 1950–1960. The straight line represents our guesses of the population size for the (unobserved) intercensual years. In the absence of other information, we might guess, for example, that the 1955 population was the simple average of the 1950 and 1960 populations.

$$P(1955) = \frac{P(1950) + P(1960)}{2}$$

$$= \frac{2,210,703 + 2,349,544}{2} = 2,280,124$$

What can be said about the proportional (or percentage) rate of growth? Proportional growth rates are often more revealing because they take into account the absolute size of an economic unit and focus on underlying behavioral and technical relations.

Examples

1. Two different bank accounts each pay 5 percent on deposited funds per annum. One contains $100 and earns $5 in the course of the year. The other contains $200 and earns $10. The absolute increase is twice as great as in the second account—a fact of little interest in itself. It is the percentage of return (5 percent), or the proportional growth (0.05), that counts to the investor.

2. We shall see that many economic models make sense only when underlying *proportional* growth rates are constant. Constant *absolute* rates of growth imply that an economy grows slower and slower in proportional terms.

3. Two populations each grow by one million persons in the same period of time. One population began the period with a population only one half the size of the other. Fertility and mortality rates were quite different in the two populations and it is these rates, expressed as proportions, that are of interest to economists and demographers.

To obtain a proportional growth rate for the Puerto Rican population, an obvious first try is to relate the intercensual increase to the base-year (1950) population. But why not use 1960 as a base year? Or perhaps 1955 would be more appropriate. One gets a different figure for the proportional growth during the period, corresponding to the choice of different base years. Which is correct (in some sense)? Can we do better, perhaps, than the linear approximation of intercensual growth?

A little reflection suggests that we probably can. Since the population grew during the period, it is reasonable to think that the number of women capable of bearing children also increased. Let us assume that this group of women increased in proportion to the rest of the population, and that deaths were proportional to population size. Then the appropriate base population at any time is the population at that time. The base population *itself* is growing throughout the ten-year period.

As a second approximation, therefore, we might try to apportion the ten-year increment in population in such a way that the *proportionate* increase is the same in *each* year of the ten years. The greater the population at the beginning of each year, the greater should be the absolute increment during the year. The absolute increase in population (ΔP) is proportional to the population (P) at the beginning of the year, and the proportion is the same each year.

$$\frac{\Delta P(t)}{P(t)} = g \qquad \text{for each and every year } (t)$$

14 Proportional Growth

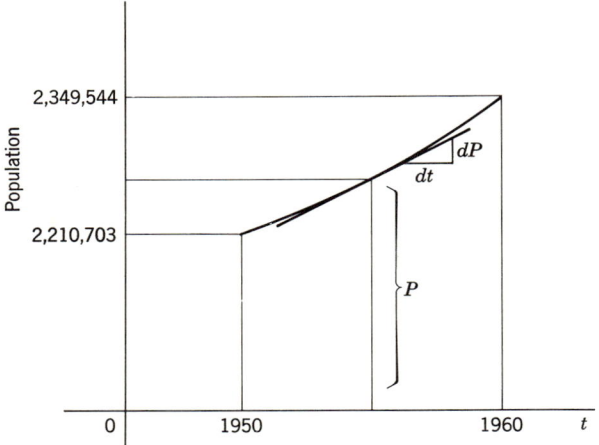

Figure 2.2 A proportional growth approximation of intercensual population growth: Puerto Rico, 1950–1960 (*Source: United States Census of Population, 1960: Puerto Rico*, PC(1), 53A, P.R. [Washington: U.S. Government Printing Office, 1961]).

Or simply

$$\frac{\Delta P}{P} = g$$

We observed in Chapter One that this implies a time path of proportional growth given by

$$P(t) = P(0)(1 + g)^t$$

The growth rate (g) is like an annual rate of interest paid on borrowed money, with the interest compounded every year. The resulting growth path of the money (or population) is the result of *discontinuous compounding* at the given annual rate of interest (rate of growth).

But there is no reason why a year should be the only appropriate interval. Why not six months, or 6 days, or six hours, or six seconds? Or, since many growth processes are virtually continuous, why not make the appropriate interval infinitesimally small? In that case, the instantaneous rate of absolute increase is always proportional to the instantaneous value of the population itself. We replace the ΔP with the time derivative of differential calculus, dP/dt. Thus

$$\frac{dP}{dt} \cdot \frac{1}{P} = g \qquad \text{for each and every instant}$$

We now have the smooth curve illustrated in Figure 2.2 (and also in Figure 1.1). This is sometimes called an organic growth curve, because natural organisms often grow at a rate that is roughly proportional to their magnitudes.

Now the *slope* of the growth curve (dP/dt) is everywhere proportional to the *population* (P) at that point. In terms of stock-flow concepts, indispensable in economic analysis, the *flow* of population increments (dP/dt) is proportional to the *stock* of the population (P)

$$\frac{dP}{dt} = gP$$

where g is the (constant) proportional rate of growth.

Growth curves of this kind have a number of remarkable and useful properties, some of which will be explored in the rest of this chapter.

THE DERIVATIVES OF THE GROWTH PATH

Net investment is defined as the net increase in the capital stock during a period of time. If we choose that period of time to be infinitesimally small, then net investment is simply the first time derivative of the capital stock.

$$I = \frac{dK}{dt}$$

For notational convenience, let us denote the first time derivative of a variable by putting a dot over it:

$$\dot{K} = \frac{dK}{dt}$$

Now

$$I = \dot{K}$$

Suppose that the capital stock of a country is growing at a constant proportional rate, g. This means that the first time derivative of the capital stock (investment) is a constant proportion of the capital stock, so that

$$I = \dot{K} = gK; \quad \frac{I}{K} = \frac{\dot{K}}{K} = g \quad (2.1)$$

For example, if the capital stock (K) equals 100 and the proportional rate of growth (g) is 0.05 or 5 percent, then net investment $(I = \dot{K})$ is 5.

Proportional Growth

An obvious and very important property of (2.1) is that *investment is growing at the same proportional rate as the capital stock*. This can be proved by differentiating (2.1) with respect to time.

$$\dot{I} = \ddot{K} = g\dot{K}; \qquad \frac{\dot{I}}{I} = \frac{\ddot{K}}{\dot{K}} = g \qquad (2.2)$$

The proportional growth of investment ($\dot{I}/I$) equals g, just as the proportional growth of capital ($\dot{K}/K$) equals g.

We can go further. How fast is the rate of growth of investment changing? Differentiate (2.2) with respect to time.

$$\ddot{I} = \dddot{K} = g\ddot{K}; \qquad \frac{\ddot{I}}{\dot{I}} = \frac{\dddot{K}}{\ddot{K}} = g \qquad (2.3)$$

Considering (2.1), (2.2), and (2.3) together, we can infer that along a proportional growth path:

1. Each time derivative of successively higher order is a constant number, g, of its predecessor. For example,

$$\dot{K} = gK; \qquad \dot{I} = g\dot{K}$$

2. Stated another way, each time derivative, when expressed as a proportion, has the same constant value, g. For example,

$$\frac{\dot{K}}{K} = g; \qquad \frac{\dot{I}}{I} = g$$

THE EQUATION OF CONSTANT PROPORTIONAL GROWTH

Thus far we have assumed that a growth curve can be fitted between two observations, as was done in Figure 2.2, without suggesting how we can actually go about doing it. Using population growth as an example, we need a *function* that (1) relates the population to time, (2) has the properties of constant proportional growth, and (3) passes through the two observations. We want to find the *continuous* compounding counterpart of the *discontinuous* compounding expression

$$P(t) = P(0)(1 + g)^t$$

where the *annual* compound rate of growth is g. Suppose we compound every six months at the same annual rate. Then we have twice as many compounding periods ($2t$) as before (t), and the six month rate ($g/2$) is half the yearly rate (g).

$$P(t) = P(0)\left(1 + \frac{g}{2}\right)^{2t}$$

If g is 1 percent and t is one,

$$P(1) = P(0)(1 + 0.005)^2 = P(1)(1.010025)$$

Compounding quarterly, there are four times as many compounding periods ($4t$) and the quarterly rate ($g/4$) is one-fourth the annual rate (g).

$$P(t) = P(0)\left(1 + \frac{g}{4}\right)^{4t}$$

If g is 1 percent and t is one,

$$P(1) = P(0)(1 + 0.0025)^4 = P(0)(1.011773) \quad \text{(approximately)}$$

Compounding for as many periods (n) as we like,

$$P(t) = P(0)\left(1 + \frac{g}{n}\right)^{nt}$$

which can be written as

$$P(t) = P(0)\left[\left(1 + \frac{g}{n}\right)^{n/g}\right]^{gt} \tag{2.4}$$

We want an expression for continuous compounding. In terms of (2.4), we want to know what happens when n becomes indefinitely large. Looking at the expression in the square brackets

$$\left(1 + \frac{g}{n}\right)^{n/g}$$

we notice two effects on its value as n gets larger and larger (assuming that g exceeds zero):

1. The expression tends to get larger because n appears in the numerator of the exponent.
2. The expression tends to get smaller because n appears in the denominator within brackets.

18 Proportional Growth

It can be shown that the expression converges toward a pure number as the number of compoundings during the year becomes indefinitely large (the interval between the compoundings becomes indefinitely small):

$$\lim_{n \to \infty} \left(1 + \frac{g}{n}\right)^{n/g} = 2.71828$$

correct to five decimal places. This is a fundamental number in mathematics and it is labeled "e."

By increasing the number of compoundings indefinitely, we have converted the *discontinuous* compounding operation

$$P(t) = P(0)(1 + g)^t$$

into a *continuous* compounding operation.

$$P(t) = P(0)e^{gt} \qquad (2.5)$$

Given g and t, continuous compounding will yield a greater value for P than discrete compounding. But for small values of g encountered in growth economics, the difference is not great. For example, if a population of 1000 grew at the discontinuous compounding rate of five percent for one year, it would have grown to 1050 by the end of the year. If the compounding were done continuously at the same five percent rate, it would have grown to about 1051 by the end of the year.[1]

Our task of curve-fitting is nearly complete. It remains only to find the value of g that corresponds to $t = 10$ and ensures that the curve will pass through the desired points. When $t = 10$, $P = P(1960)$, so that we wish to find g in the equation

$$P(1960) = P(1950)e^{g \cdot 10}$$

Whenever one wishes to solve for an unknown that appears in an exponent, as does g in this case, one takes logarithms. Since g is a power of e, it would seem natural to use base e, or natural (sometimes called Napierian) logarithms.

$$\log_e P(1960) = \log_e P(1950) + g \cdot 10 \log_e e$$

$\log_e e$ equals one, so that

$$\log P(1960) = \log P(1950) + g \cdot 10$$

---

[1] Taking natural logs, $\log P(1) = \log 1000 + g = 6.90776 + 0.05 = 6.95776$. Taking the antilog, $P(1) = 1051$, approximately.

on the understanding that "log" means "log to the base e." Solving for g,

$$g = \frac{\log P(1960)/P(1950)}{10}$$

$$= \frac{\log 1.0624}{10} = 0.0059 = 0.59\%$$

Finally, the sought-after equation is

$$L(t) = 2{,}210{,}703 e^{0.0059t}$$

PROPORTIONAL GROWTH AND NATURAL LOGARITHMS

If the capital stock of a country grows at a constant proportional rate, we now know that it can be expressed as

$$K = K(0)e^{gt} \tag{2.6}$$

With a little manipulation, we can also find the time path of investment. Recall that

$$I = \dot{K} = gK \tag{2.7}$$

along a growth path. Substituting (2.6) into (2.7),

$$I = \dot{K} = gK(0)e^{gt} \tag{2.8}$$

This result can be generalized. *The derivative of an organic growth function of the form*

$$x = ae^{gt} \tag{2.9}$$

is the proportional growth rate (g) times the original function.

$$\frac{dx}{dt} = \dot{x} = g \cdot ae^{gt} \tag{2.10}$$

As an example, when plotted on a graph in the usual way, the capital *stock* will be a gently rising curve, and its derivative, the *flow* of investment, will also be a gently rising curve that is everywhere proportional to the capital stock. This is illustrated in Figure 2.3, where g is taken to be 0.10 or 10 percent.

20   Proportional Growth

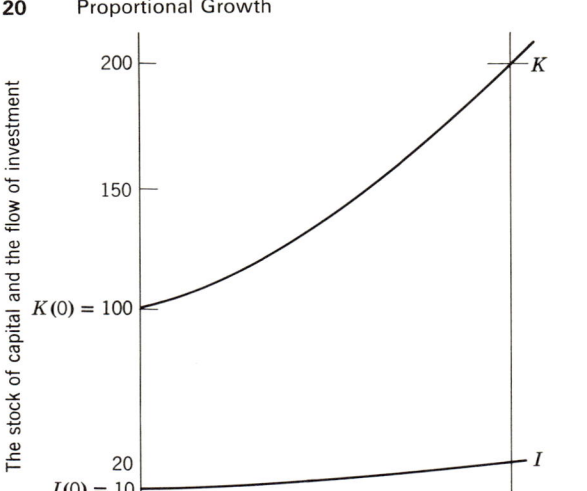

Figure 2.3   Proportional growth of the capital stock and investment (natural scale).

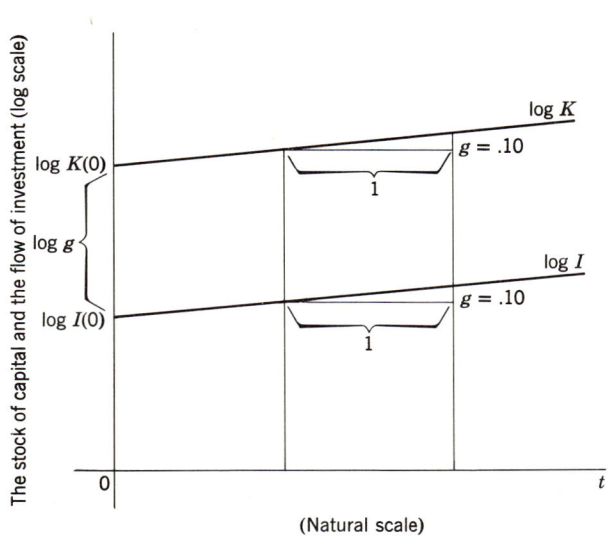

Figure 2.4   Proportional growth of the capital stock and investment (semilog scale).

There is another way to graph these relations, which is often more convenient. Suppose we plot the natural logarithms of capital and investment on the vertical axis, while time is plotted in ordinary units on the horizontal axis. Taking logs of (2.6) and (2.8), we have:

$$\log K = \log K(0) + gt \tag{2.6'}$$

$$\log I = \log K(0) + gt + \log g \tag{2.8'}$$

These equations are plotted in Figure 2.4. Clearly, the slope of each line is a constant and equal to the growth rate, g. Put another way, the derivative of the logarithm is the organic rate of growth:

$$\frac{d}{dt}\log K = \frac{\dot{K}}{K} = g \tag{2.6''}$$

$$\frac{d}{dt}\log I = \frac{\dot{I}}{I} = g \tag{2.8''}$$

A RECAPITULATION

To sum up our discussion of constant proportional growth with continuous compounding (organic growth), some of the more important results are set out here in general terms.

Proportional growth is described by an equation of the form

$$x(t) = ae^{gt} \tag{2.11}$$

or, simply $x = ae^{gt}$, where g is the rate of growth and a is a constant. The first derivative of the curve is the growth rate multiplied by the original equation:

$$\frac{dx}{dt} = \dot{x} = g \cdot ae^{gt} \tag{2.12}$$

By dividing (2.12) by (2.11), we confirm the proportional growth property.

$$\frac{1}{x} \cdot \frac{dx}{dt} = \frac{\dot{x}}{x} = g \tag{2.13}$$

The natural logarithm of (2.11) is

$$\log x = \log a + gt$$

Finally, the first derivative of the natural logarithm is the constant proportional (organic) rate of growth.

$$\frac{d}{dt}\log x = \frac{1}{x}\cdot\frac{dx}{dt} = \frac{\dot{x}}{x} = g \tag{2.14}$$

EXERCISES

1. Using a table of natural logarithms, compute how long it would take the capital stock of a country to double if it grows at a constant proportional rate of three percent.

2. Suppose the net national product of one country is initially smaller than that of another, but growing more rapidly. How long will it take for the product of the initially smaller economy to become larger than the product of the initially larger economy? Illustrate your answer, using both natural and semilogarithmic scales.

3. Hla Myint has made the following assertion: "... the widening gap [of incomes per capita in developed and underdeveloped countries] depends not only on the difference in rates of growth but also on the initial width of the gap. We cannot say that the gap will not widen even for those underdeveloped countries whose per capita incomes are growing at a faster rate than those of the developed countries."[2] Is this always true? The problem can be set up in the following way: Let x be per capita income in a developed but slower-growing country; let y be per capita income in the underdeveloped but faster-growing country; and let each grow at a constant proportional rate:

$$x = x(0)e^{gt}$$
$$y = y(0)e^{ht}$$
$$x(0) > y(0), \quad h > g$$

The gap widens when $dx/dt > dy/dt$. For what values of t is this true?

REFERENCES AND SUGGESTIONS FOR FURTHER READING

1. Allen, R. D. G., *Mathematical Analysis for Economists*. London: Macmillan, 1960, chaps. IX, X.
2. Baumol, W. J., *Economic Dynamics*. New York: Macmillan, 1963, pp. 283–286.

[2] Hla Myint, *The Economics of the Developing Countries* (New York, Praeger, 1965), p. 18.

3. Dinwiddy, Caroline, *Elementary Mathematics for Economists*. Nairobi: Oxford, 1967, chap. XII.
4. Lewis, J. Perry, *Mathematics for Students of Economics*. London: Macmillan, 1959, chaps. XIII, XIV.
5. Yamane, Taro, *Mathematics for Economists*. Englewood Cliffs: Prentice-Hall, 1968, pp. 96–103.

Chapter Three

AN INTRODUCTION TO GROWTH IN AN ADVANCED ECONOMY

Introduction
The Production Function
The Saving and Investment Function
The Population-Growth Function
The Equilibrium Rate of Growth
Net National Product and its Distribution
A Single Technological Improvement
Continuous Technological Improvement
Increases in the Saving Ratio
Decreases in the Rate of Population Growth
The Sources of Growth
The Case of Fixed Proportions
Exercises
References and Suggestions for Further Reading

INTRODUCTION

What are the sources of economic growth? Why do some economies grow faster than others? How is national income divided between labor income and the returns to capital? How is this division related to growth rates? To levels of per capita income? There are no clear-cut answers to these questions, and none are proposed here. But a fruitful investigation of economic growth requires that we have models of growing economies that show how the relevant variables interact with one another through time. We need theoretical pegs to hang our hats on—analytical frameworks, based on economic theory, that reduce the complex real world to manageable proportions, and thus assist in finding answers to questions such as those raised above.

Although one can imagine a wide variety of social and economic forces that might impinge on the process of economic growth, many of them can be accounted for (if not explained) in a simple model of economic growth that can be constructed with the most elementary and familiar tools of economic analysis. The purpose of this chapter is to construct such a model, while more complex models are reserved for subsequent chapters.

There are but three fundamental relationships that underlie the model:[1]

1. A production function, which shows the relation of the inputs (resources) employed by society and the output (national product) that they produce.

2. A saving and investment function, which shows the proportion of output that society decides not to consume, but rather to save and invest.

3. A population growth function, which shows how the population and work force grows over time.

These relationships will be taken up in turn and then combined in a model of economic growth.

THE PRODUCTION FUNCTION

A familiar notion in everyday life, as well as in economic analysis, is that inputs can be combined to yield an output. A relation between inputs and output is called a production function. Thus, if a and b are inputs and x is output, the production relation can be set out symbolically as

$$x = F(a, b)$$

This is read, "The output flow of x *depends* upon the input flow of a and b; how x is related to a and b is given by the *function* $F(\ )$." It is a technological relationship showing the *maximum* amount of x that can be obtained for given amounts of a and b. The *level of technology* is given for the circumstances

---

[1] The seminal articles that presented the model are T. W. Swan, "Economic Growth and Capital Accumulation," *Economic Record* (November 1956), and R. M. Solow, "A Contribution to the Theory of Economic Growth," *Quarterly Journal of Economics* (February 1956).

at any point in time. But as time goes on, and as circumstances change, it may be possible to obtain more x for the same amount of a and b. There may be *technological improvement* (a positive change in the level of technology). Technological improvement has dynamic implications, and we shall consider it later. We are concerned for now with the form of the function $F(\ )$ corresponding to a specified level of technology.

The form of the function is not known *a priori*, but casual observation and more careful empirical investigations suggest that the *law of diminishing returns* governs its form. Loosely put, this means that as more b is added per unit of a, a becomes more "productive" and b becomes less "productive." For example, if b is machines and a is labor, it is reasonable to think that more machines per man will render labor more "productive." The *more* machines that each man works with, the *more* "productive" is each worker. But more machines per man also means that each machine has *fewer* men to work with, and thus the *less* "productive" is each machine.

Figure 3.1 illustrates the law of diminishing returns. The total physical product (x on the vertical axis) increases as more of an input (b on the horizontal axis) is added while the other input (a in parentheses) is held constant. The TPP_b (total physical product of b) curve shows this relation. The curve *slopes* upward, showing a positive relation between b and x (a held constant). More b is associated with more x. But the curve *bends* downward. Adding more and more b adds less and less x.

Now the *law of diminishing returns* can be defined more precisely. First, the curve shows diminishing average returns, where average returns are

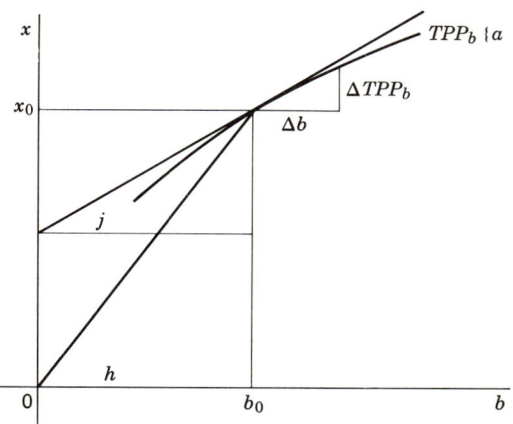

Figure 3.1   **The total physical product of x curve.**

27

defined as output per unit of input. That is:

$$APP_b = \frac{TPP_b}{b} = \frac{0x_0}{0b_0}$$

APP_b = average physical product of b

Recall that the tangent of an angle is its opposite side divided by its adjacent side. Thus APP_b is nothing but tan h in the figure. It is clear that as more b is added per unit of a, tan h declines; the average physical product of $b(APP_b)$ falls. The greater b is, given a, the less x is produced per unit of b. In short, there are *diminishing average returns* to b when more b is added per unit of a.

Second, the curve also shows *diminishing marginal returns*, where marginal returns to b are defined as the *addition* to total product when b is increased by a small amount and a is held constant. That is:

$$MPP_b = \frac{\Delta TPP_b}{\Delta b} \quad \text{when } a \text{ is held constant}$$

MPP_b = marginal physical product of b

In Figure 3.1, when b is increased a little from b_0 by Δb, x rises from x_0 by ΔTPP_b. The smaller Δb is, the more similar the triangle with the sides Δb and ΔTPP_b becomes to the larger triangle whose tangent is j. This means that MPP_b is nothing but tan j when Δb is very small.

Tan j measures the *slope* of the TPP_b curve. It is clear that tan j declines as more b is added per unit of a. The more b that a unit of a is *already* working with, the less *additional* x is obtained if another unit of b is *added*. For example, the more capital-intensive a process *already* is, the less *additional* output is obtained when another machine is added, holding the work force constant. In short, there are also *diminishing marginal* returns to b, when more b is added per unit of a.[2]

It is convenient to show how these average and marginal products of b depend on the amount of b used per unit of a.

As b was added to a constant amount of a in Figure 3.1, the *ratio* of b to a rose, and both the APP_a and the MPP_a fell.[3] But note that APP_a(tan h) is always greater than MPP_a(tan j). These relations are shown in Figure 3.2.

---

[2] In intermediate price-theory textbooks, diminishing average *and* marginal returns are sometimes said to be characteristic of the "second stage of production." See, for example, R. H. Leftwich, *The Price System and Resource Allocation*, Third Edition (New York: Holt, Rinehart and Winston, 1966), pp. 114–115, or G. H. Stigler, *The Theory of Price*, Third Edition (New York: Macmillan, 1966), p. 126.

[3] Constant returns to scale (*CRTS*) are assumed. For example, doubling both a and b doubles x. This means that production relations depend only on the ratio of inputs and not at all on the scale of operations. The assumption permits us to relate APP_b and MPP_b to b/a in Figure 3.2. These matters are discussed in Chapter Five.

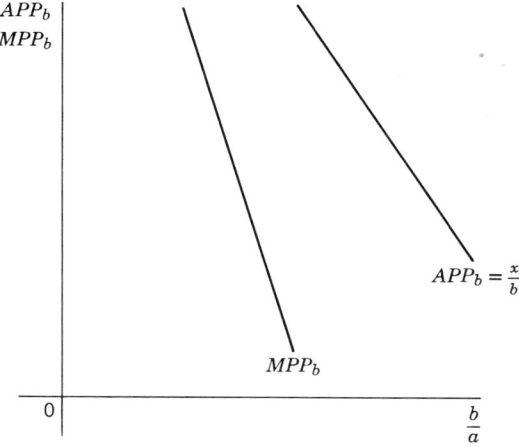

Figure 3.2 The average and marginal products of b.

These are familiar concepts associated with the theory of the firm in microeconomic analysis, and they are important building blocks in the theory of economic growth. One can imagine an entire economy made up of identical production units, competitive firms, each operating at the low point of its "U"-shaped long-run average-product curve, and producing a homogeneous product called national product. Each firm is of optimal size and the economy expands or contracts through the addition or subtraction of (identical) firms. Although *each firm* may individually encounter diminishing returns and rising costs, the *economy* as a whole can escape them through uniform expansion. Proportional increases of labor, capital, *and* firms yield equal proportional increases in national product. Let us assume that these labor (L) and capital (K) inputs are also homogeneous. Then we can write the production function for the entire economy as

$$X = F(K, L) \tag{3.1}$$

where X is *net* national product—product left over after replacing worn out capital equipment.

Equation 3.1 is an *aggregate production function.* Is it a useful concept, considering the homogeneity assumptions which underly it? If there is any input more heterogeneous than labor, it is capital. And who ever heard of an economy that produces but one good? Realism aside, (3.1) is a useful fiction, if real economies behave *as if* they produce according to (3.1): more capital and more labor produce more output, and there are diminishing marginal and average returns to capital (labor) as more capital (labor) is

30   An Introduction to Growth in an Advanced Economy

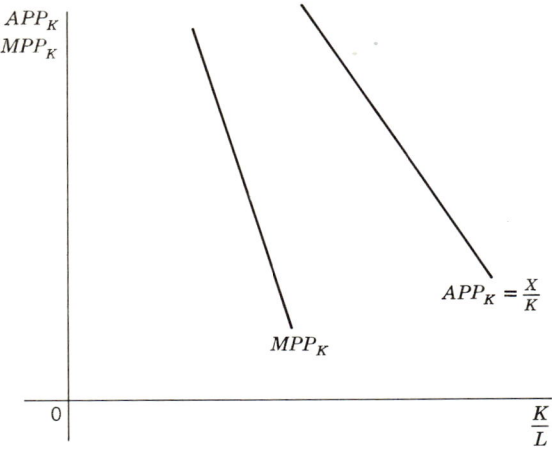

Figure 3.3   The average and marginal products of capital.

added per unit of labor (capital). Diminishing returns to capital are illustrated in Figure 3.3.[4]

Since X is *net* of capital depreciation, MPP_K is the *net* product of capital. If capital yields an annual gross return of 10 percent, and 4 percent of it depreciates during the year, then the net marginal return on capital is 6 percent. The APP_K and MPP_K functions are drawn as straight lines for convenience. Their exact shape will depend upon more detailed characteristics of the production function than have been specified so far. In any event, the straight lines can be taken as linear approximations of the true lines in the neighborhood that we are investigating.

THE SAVING AND INVESTMENT FUNCTION

Net national product is the product remaining after capital depreciation has been made up. It is the material income of society, providing that capital used to produce that income has been kept intact.

If there are no forms of wealth other than real capital, all net income that is not consumed must be invested in increasing the capital stock. Not to

---

[4] The aggregation problem has not been solved to everyone's satisfaction. Two discussions of the problem should be mentioned: P. A. Samuelson, "Parable and Realism in Capital Theory: The Surrogate Production Function," *Review of Economic Studies*, (June 1962), and F. M. Fisher, "The Existence of Aggregate Production Functions," *Econometrica* (October 1969).

do so would be sheer waste.[5] Since net product equals net income, this means that output is divided into consumption goods and investment goods. Recall that output is assumed to be homogeneous. Thus the one-good net national product is an all-purpose good that serves equally well as a consumption or an investment good.

If it is assumed that a constant proportion of net income is saved, then the saving and investment relation appears as

> NET INVESTMENT
>
> = THE CHANGE IN THE CAPITAL STOCK
>
> = SAVING OUT OF NET NATIONAL PRODUCT

Net investment could be thought of as the net annual increment to the country's capital stock. In that case, we could write

$$I = \Delta K = sX$$

using annual values for net investment ($I = \Delta K$) and net national product (X), where s is the proportion of income or product that is saved and invested. But by using annual values, we imply that economic processes take place "by the year" when, in fact, they are going on continuously. For our purposes, it is more convenient to think of investment as the instantaneous rate of increase of the capital stock with respect to time. This is analogous to thinking of an instantaneous rate of increase in the population with respect to time, as suggested in Chapter Two. Thus, we can write

$$I = \frac{dK}{dt} = sX$$

It is often useful to express this investment or capital growth equation in proportional terms. We use the relation

> THE ABSOLUTE CHANGE IN THE CAPITAL STOCK
> ――――――――――――――――――――――――――――――
> THE CURRENT VALUE OF THE CAPITAL STOCK
>
> = THE PROPORTIONAL CHANGE IN THE CAPITAL STOCK

---

[5] Money and government bonds are alternative forms of wealth in real-world economics. Net accumulation of these assets may cause a deficiency in aggregate demand, so that desired levels of investment may fall short of saving. For simple growth models that incorporate money, see J. Tobin "Money and Economic Growth," *Econometrica* (October 1965), and H. Johnson, "Money in a Neo-Classical One-Sector Growth Model," *Essays in Monetary Economics* (London: George Allen and Unwin, 1967), Chap. IV.

An Introduction to Growth in an Advanced Economy

Symbolically

$$\frac{I}{K} = \frac{dK}{dt} \cdot \frac{1}{K} = s\frac{X}{K}$$

We have simply divided both sides of the capital growth relation by the current value of the capital stock, K. For example, if

$$K = 200$$
$$s = 0.20 = 20\%$$
$$X = 100$$

then the proportional growth of the capital stock is

$$\frac{dK}{dt} \cdot \frac{1}{K} = (0.20)\frac{100}{200} = 10\%$$

For notational convenience, denote the *proportional* change in a variable by an asterisk. Thus

$$\frac{dK}{dt} \cdot \frac{1}{K} = K^* = s\frac{X}{K} \qquad (3.2)$$

Recall that Figure 3.3 showed how $X/K (APP_K)$ depends upon the ratio of capital to labor. Now it is possible to show how the growth of capital also depends upon the ratio of capital to labor. Using Figure 3.3, plot the capital growth relation by taking a proportion, s, of the X/K line in Figure 3.3 at every value of K/L. The resulting line in Figure 3.4 shows the growth of capital relative to the capital-labor ratio. The growth of capital is a declining function of the capital-labor ratio, given a constant saving ratio. As capital increases relative to labor (capital deepening), the output per unit of capital declines. Since a proportion of output is reinvested, the *proportional* growth of capital falls as a consequence of capital deepening. For any given saving ratio, a higher level of capital intensity (K/L higher) is associated with a lower growth rate of capital (K^* lower). Note that this effect depends crucially on technology, since it is technology that determines how quickly diminishing returns set in as capital grows relative to labor. If capital is a relatively poor substitute for labor, capital deepening will be associated with more powerfully diminishing average returns to capital, and the X/K relation will fall more steeply. For any given saving ratio (s), this means that the proportional rate of capital accumulation (K^*) will fall more rapidly as K/L increases, if capital is a relatively poor substitute for labor.

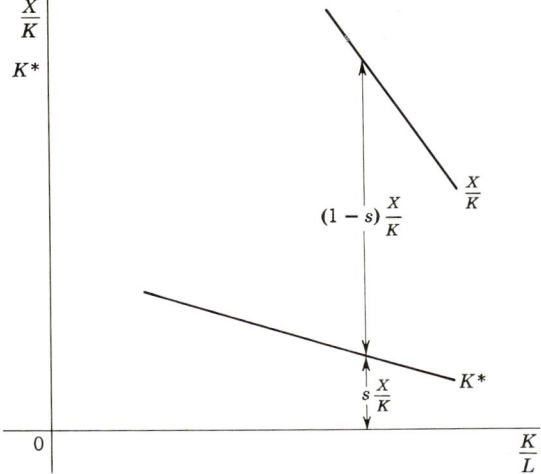

Figure 3.4 The growth of capital. The average product of capital (X/K) falls with capital deepening (higher $K/L = k$) because of diminishing average returns to capital. Since saving and investment are equal, and a constant proportion of output, the growth of capital (K^*) also falls with capital deepening.

Notice that if capital were a perfect substitute for labor, then capital and labor would be identical from the production point of view. In that case, "capital deepening" merely increases the scale of the economy (adding more capital is like adding more labor), and the average return to capital is a technological constant. The X/K line in Figure 3.4 would be a horizontal straight line, and so would the K^* line.

THE POPULATION-GROWTH FUNCTION

The population and employed labor are assumed to be proportional to one another, and to grow at a constant proportional rate that is determined by demographic forces. As we saw in Chapter Two, this means that the absolute change in the labor force is proportional to the current size of the labor force.

$$\frac{dL}{dt} = gL$$

or

$$\frac{dL}{dt} \cdot \frac{1}{L} = g$$

34 An Introduction to Growth in an Advanced Economy

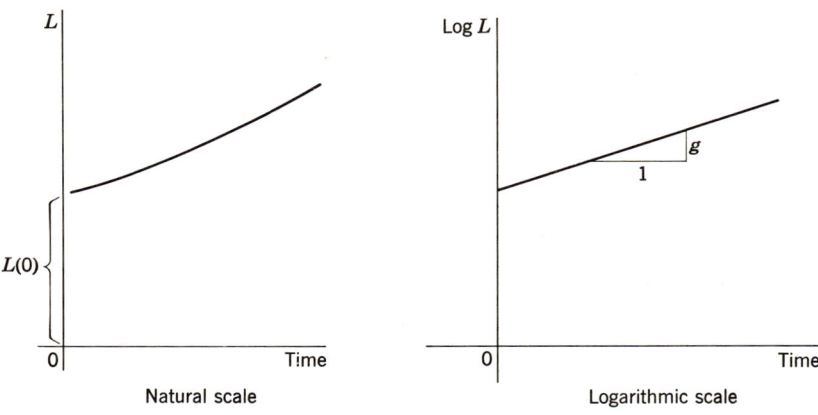

Figure 3.5 The growth of labor through time.

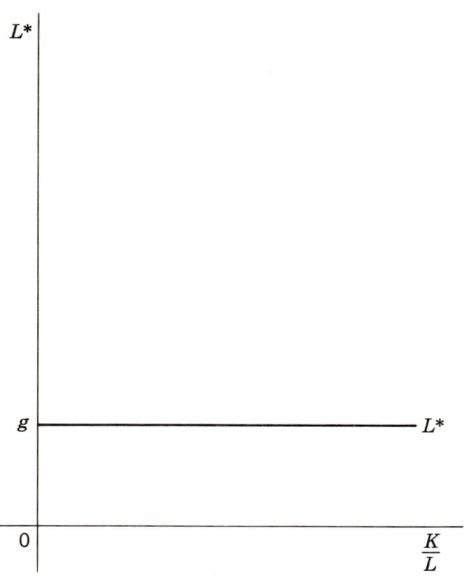

Figure 3.6 The growth of labor and the ratio of capital to labor. The labor force grows at a constant proportional rate (g) that is independent of the capital-labor ratio.

Again, using the asterisk to denote *proportional* changes,

$$L^* = g \tag{3.3}$$

Here, g is some figure like 2 percent or 0.02. The growth of the labor force can be illustrated on either natural or logarithmic scales, as in Figure 3.5. Unlike the growth of capital, however, labor-force growth does not depend upon the capital-labor ratio. The growth of labor is *given* as a constant. Since it is determined outside the model, we say that it is *exogenously determined*, or simply *exogenous*. The exogenous labor growth rate, g, is shown in Figure 3.6.

THE EQUILIBRIUM RATE OF GROWTH

It is now time to draw together the relations which constitute a model of economic growth. The growth of capital (Figure 3.4) depends upon technology and the savings ratio. It falls as capital accumulates relative to labor. The growth of labor is, however, given by the constant g (Figure 3.6). These relations are shown in Figure 3.7, where Figures 3.4 and 3.6 are superimposed on one another. An equilibrium capital-labor ratio is at $\bar{k}$, where the growth lines of K and L intersect, and both grow at the rate g. This growth rate is sometimes called the "natural" rate of growth.

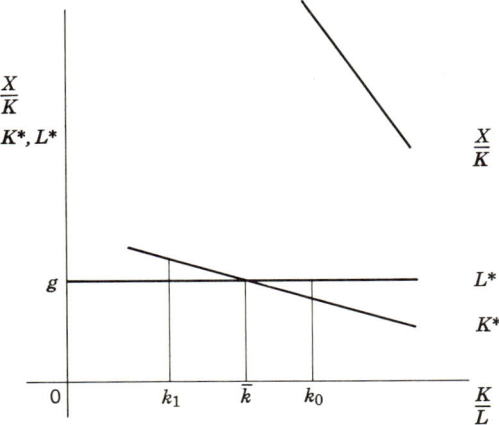

Figure 3.7   The equilibrium rate of growth. The growth of capital (K^*) slows down with capital deepening (higher $K/L = k$) because of diminishing average returns to capital (X/K falls as $K/L = k$ rises) and a constant saving ratio (s). Labor grows at a constant proportional rate (g). A stable long-run equilibrium is at $\bar{k}$ where K^* and L^* are equal.

That $\bar{k}$ is the long-run equilibrium capital-labor ratio can be established by the following reasoning: suppose we observe an economy with a capital-labor ratio equal to k_0, greater than $\bar{k}$. The economy is in *momentary* equilibrium (saving = investment, and the like), but it is not in *long-run* equilibrium because labor is growing faster than capital. The capital-labor ratio is receding toward $\bar{k}$, its long-run equilibrium value. For example, at k_0, labor may be growing at 2 percent and capital at 1 percent. Thus, $k = K/L$ is falling at the momentary rate of 1 percent.

Conversely, an actual k may be at k_1, where there is more labor per unit of capital than in equilibrium. As a consequence, capital grows more rapidly than labor, and k rises towards its equilibrium value.

Once equilibrium is reached, all variables grow at the exogenous rate of labor force growth (g). This rate does not depend upon the saving ratio (s) or anything else.

$$X^* = K^* = L^* = g$$

Such a balanced growth configuration is called a "Golden Age," and it has the very interesting property that *the output-capital ratio depends upon the saving ratio and the growth rate and not at all upon the efficiency of production methods.* Since $K^* = sX/K = g$ in equilibrium,

$$\frac{X}{K} = \frac{g}{s}$$

and this has been derived without reference to the technical condition of production.

Figure 3.7 is useful for analyzing the effects of forces widely held to be associated with growth. These are improvements in technology, changes in the saving ratio, and changes in the population growth rate. But, first, we should interpret Figure 3.7 in terms of net national product and its distribution.

NET NATIONAL PRODUCT AND ITS DISTRIBUTION

Since capital and labor are the only inputs in production, the entire net national product must be imputed or "paid" to these two factors. If there are constant returns to scale in production, it is well known that the product can be exactly "divided up" if each factor is imputed or "paid" its marginal product.[6] In terms of the production function (Equation 3.1) this means that

$$X = MPP_K \cdot K + MPP_L \cdot L$$

[6] This is proved in Chapter Five. See G. Stigler, *op. cit.*, pp. 136–137, for an elementary exposition.

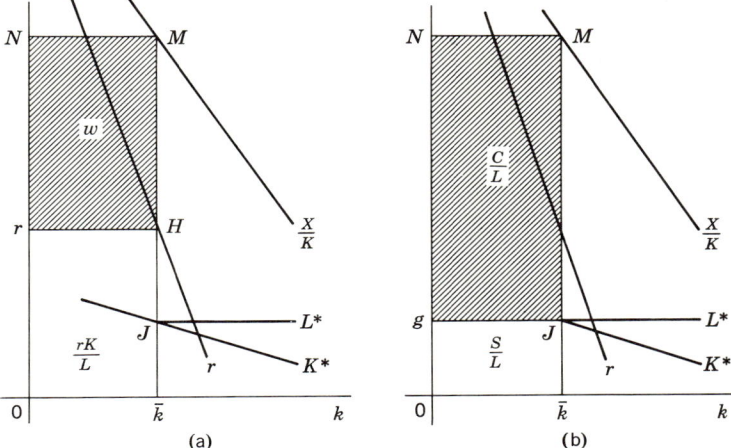

Figure 3.8 Sources of income and its uses. (*a*) Sources of income. (*b*) Uses of income.

For notational convenience, one can identify MPP_K with the rate of return on capital (the interest rate) and MPP_L with the wage rate of labor. Letting $r = MPP_K$ and $w = MPP_L$,

$$X = rK + wL$$

It is now possible to identify the shares of output imputed or "paid" to capital and labor, as well as the value of net national product itself. Figure 3.8 is identical with Figure 3.7, except that the $MPP_K = r$ curve has been added from Figure 3.3. In terms of units of product per worker, net national product is $X/L = X/K \cdot K/L = X/K \cdot k$. In the diagram, per worker income is seen to be the rectangle $0\bar{k}MN$. Again, in per worker terms, the product imputed to capital is $r \cdot K/L = rk$. This is simply the rectangle $0\bar{k}Hr$. The rest of the product must be imputed to labor. Thus, the wage is $rHMN$. The ratio of wage income (wL/L) to capital income (rK/L) is $rHMN$ divided by $0\bar{k}HR$, or simply rN divided by $0r$.

The division of net national product between saving and consumption can also be seen in Figure 3.8. Recall that saving and investment equals sX and that the growth of capital, K^*, equals $s(X/K)$; or, sX equals gK. Thus, saving per worker, $s(X/L)$, equals $g(K/L) = gk$. This is the rectangle $0\bar{k}Jg$ in the diagram.

The product that is not saved is consumed. If the rectangle representing saving per worker is subtracted from the rectangle representing income per worker, the remainder is consumption per worker. This is the rectangle

38 An Introduction to Growth in an Advanced Economy

$gJMN$. The ratio of consumption to investment is simply gN divided by $0g$.

To sum up, expressing all magnitudes in per worker terms:

1. Net national product $= 0\bar{k}MN = \dfrac{X}{L}$

2. Product imputed to capital $= 0\bar{k}Hr = \dfrac{rK}{L}$

3. Product imputed to labor $= rHMN = \dfrac{wL}{L} = w$

4. Net saving and investment $= 0\bar{k}Jg = \dfrac{I}{L}$

5. Consumption $= gJMN = \dfrac{C}{L}$

The ratio of product imputed to labor and capital is (3) divided by (2).

6. $\dfrac{wL}{rK} = \dfrac{rN}{0r}$

The ratio of consumption to investment is (5) divided by (4).

7. $\dfrac{C}{I} = \dfrac{gN}{0g}$

We might note here that consumption equals labor income and investment equals capital income if conditions are such that r equals g.

Once an equilibrium is established, all these magnitudes are stable rectangles in the diagram. Since labor is growing at a constant proportional rate, g (the "natural" rate of growth), net national product, the product imputed to capital, and so on, are also growing at the proportional rate, g. If the population grows at the rate g, along with the labor force, then per capita income is constant through time. Since many countries have a long history of rising per capita incomes, the sources of economic growth that can improve the human material condition will be taken up next.

A SINGLE TECHNOLOGICAL IMPROVEMENT

Changes may occur from time to time that permit more output to be produced for given quantities of inputs. If they occur, we say there has been technological improvement (or change). An improvement may result because better production methods have been devised as a consequence of an advance in knowledge, or because resources have become better allocated among competing uses. The invention of the steam engine is a good example of the former kind of improvement; the breakdown of rigid social structure is a good example of the latter.

Technological change may be of the *embodied* variety; it must be embodied in newly produced capital equipment and/or in new generations of workers. Here, we assume that technological change is *disembodied*, affecting all generations of machines and men in the same way.[7] This is consistent with our assumption that these inputs are homogeneous.

The impact of a single technological change is felt (1) *initially* as more output is made possible from the resource base existing at the time the improvement occurs and (2) *ultimately* as the initial impact is absorbed through a long-run adjustment process. These impacts are discussed in turn.

Initially, a technological improvement always raises the *average* products of *both* capital and labor. Given the quantities of these inputs, when the improvement occurs, output rises, and therefore both average products rise. Otherwise, the change would not be an improvement.

On the other hand, a technological improvement need not increase the marginal product of both inputs, although one must clearly rise. A technological change can be *biased* in the sense of raising the marginal product of one input more than another, or even lowering the marginal product of one.[8]

The *ultimate* impact of a technological change is most clearly illustrated if we assume that the economy is in initial growth equilibrium when the change occurs. Glancing back to Figure 3.7 or 3.8, assume for simplicity that the change occurs when the capital-labor ratio has stabilized at $\bar{k}$. The change will raise the average product of capital (X/K) and, with the saving ratio constant, it must therefore raise the rate of capital accumulation ($K^* = sX/K$) while labor growth is steady ($L^* = g$). The ultimate effect of the change is not fully realized until diminishing returns to capital deepening ($k = K/L$ rising) has lowered the output-capital (X/K) ratio to its original level so that capital once again grows at the same proportional rate as labor.

A technological improvement that increases the marginal and average products of capital for all values of the capital-labor ratio is illustrated in Figure 3.9. The average product of labor will also rise, but let us assume that

---

[7] Technological change is seldom of one kind without a concomitant dose of the other. See R. M. Solow, *Capital Theory and the Rate of Return* (Amsterdam: North Holland, 1963), Chap. II.

[8] A more detailed analysis of the bias of the technological change is undertaken in Chapter Six of the present volume.

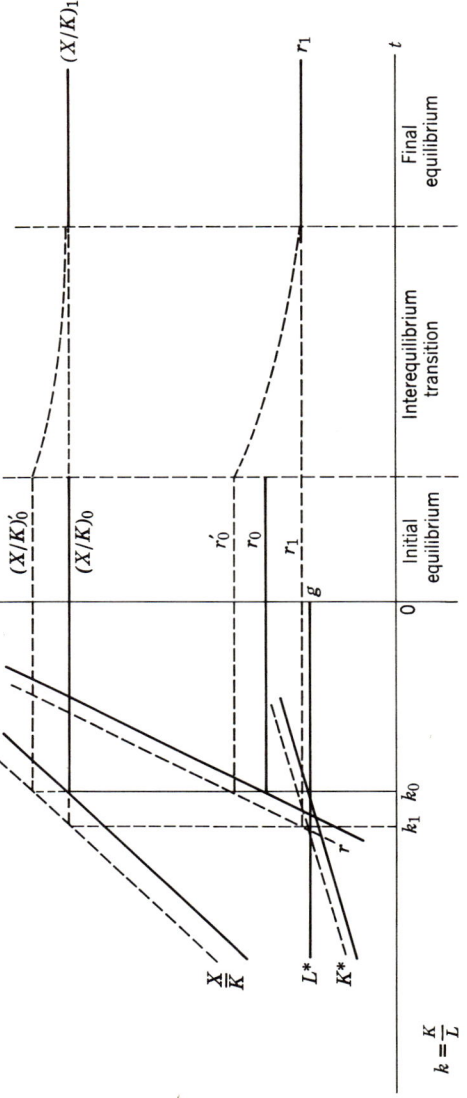

Figure 3.9 A single technological improvement.

A Single Technological Improvement

the change itself does not affect wages at the initial capital-labor ratio. This is but one of many conceivable kinds of technological change. It is used to illustrate that we must distinguish between the *initial* impacts on average and marginal products and the *ultimate* impacts on these products that gradually emerge as the economy approaches its new equilibrium.

The initial equilibrium is shown by the solid lines in Figure 3.9. The initial capital-labor ratio is k_0, with $(X/K)_0$ and r_0 the corresponding initial values of the output-capital ratio and the marginal product of capital. The technological improvement raises the average product of capital curve to the dotted position. At k_0, (X/K) rises from $(X/K)_0$ to $(X/K)'_0$ and the marginal product of capital rises from r_0 to r'_0. Note that the rise in r is precisely equal to the rise in X/K. This is because we assume the technological change to leave wages unaffected. To see this, recall that output can be imputed to labor and capital according to their marginal productivities.

$$X = rK + wL$$

or

$$\frac{X}{K} = r + w\frac{L}{K}$$

Any change in the output-capital ratio due to the improvement must be attributable to a change in r or a change in wL/K

$$\Delta \frac{X}{K} = \Delta r + \Delta \frac{wL}{K}$$

We assume that w is unchanged by the improvement. The value of L/K is what it is when the improvement occurs. Thus, $\Delta(wL/K)$ is zero and Δr equals $\Delta(X/K)$.

If the saving ratio is unaffected by the improvement, the K^* line rises proportionately to the X/K curve. This is shown by the dotted capital accumulation line. Capital is now growing faster than labor; the capital-labor ratio begins to rise from its initial value, k_0, toward its ultimate equilibrium value, k_1. The output-capital ratio begins to fall after its initial rise from $(X/K)_0$ to $(X/K)_1$. How far will it fall as k approaches k_1? We already know the answer. We know that $X/K = g/s$ in any long-run growth equilibrium (in any Golden Age). The values of g and s have not changed by assumption. Therefore, X/K must recover its original value $(X/K)_0$ once it reaches its final equilibrium value $(X/K)_1$. This is illustrated in the right-hand panel of Figure 3.9, which shows the time path of adjustment. Comparing the initial and final Golden Ages, the output-capital ratio is unchanged. After rising at first, it gradually recovers during the interequilibrium transition.

42 An Introduction to Growth in an Advanced Economy

The marginal product of capital (r) experiences a rise from r_0 to r'_0 when the improvement occurs. Subsequent capital deepening reverses its movement, and it falls from r'_0 to r_1 during the transition to the new Golden Age.

The marginal product of labor (the wage) is the rectangle inscribed between the X/K and r lines. Although unaffected by the improvement itself, the wage rises subsequently with capital deepening.

The average product of labor is the rectangle inscribed under the X/K line. It rises under the direct impact of the change and is further increased by capital deepening. Initially, the wage was $(X/K)_0$ minus r_0, multiplied by k_0. It is initially unaffected by the improvement, but eventually rises to $(X/K)_0$ minus r_1, multiplied by k_1.

CONTINUOUS TECHNOLOGICAL IMPROVEMENT

Although great technological epochs (the age of steam, and the like) might be identified with single technological improvements, other readings of history suggest that technological change has been more persistent and pervasive, propelled by the gradual advance of abstract and applied knowledge. Keeping in mind that technological "breakthroughs" occur from time to time, it might still be useful to investigate the consequence of continuous improvement.

Let us assume that technological change has the effect of improving worker efficiency. This suggests the concept of an "efficiency worker," or workers measured in "efficiency units." Designate an index of worker efficiency, Q. Then the effective or efficiency work force is $Q \cdot L$. If, for example, workers in 1970 are twice as effective as workers in 1900, then Q has risen from 1 to 2, and 100 workers in 1970 would have the same productive power as 200 workers in 1900. Now rewrite the production function so that output is related to capital and efficiency labor:

$$X = F(K, Q \cdot L)$$

If technological progress proceeds at a constant proportional rate, n, then the effective labor force grows at the rate of labor-force growth (g) plus the rate of technological improvement (n).

This new consideration is easily incorporated into the foregoing analysis by simply:

1. Redefining the production function so that output depends on capital and labor measured in efficiency units:

$$X = F(K, Q \cdot L)$$

Continuous Technological Improvement

2. Redefining the horizontal axes of Figures 3.3, 3.4, 3.6, and 3.7 to be the ratio of capital to efficiency labor:

$$k = \frac{K}{Q \cdot L}$$

3. Increasing the growth rate by the proportional growth in labor efficiency. The new "natural" rate of growth is

$$g = \begin{matrix}\text{THE GROWTH OF}\\ \text{POPULATION}\\ \text{(AND THE}\\ \text{LABOR FORCE)}\end{matrix} + \begin{matrix}\text{THE GROWTH OF}\\ \text{LABOR EFFICIENCY}\end{matrix}$$

For example:

$$0.05 = 0.02 \quad +0.03$$
$$5\% = 2\% \quad +3\%$$

Now, in the long-run equilibrium (Golden Age), all variables, including income, grow at the same proportional "natural" rate as efficiency labor, g. But per capita income is growing at the rate at which labor efficiency improves:

$$\begin{matrix}\text{THE GROWTH OF PER}\\ \text{CAPITA INCOME}\end{matrix} = \begin{matrix}\text{THE GROWTH}\\ \text{OF INCOME}\end{matrix} - \begin{matrix}\text{THE GROWTH}\\ \text{OF POPULATION}\end{matrix}$$

For example:

$$0.03 = 0.05 - 0.02$$
$$3\% = 5\% - 2\%$$

It is evident in Figures 3.7 and 3.8 that it is only technical improvement that can account for material progress (in per capita terms) in long-run equilibrium. This must be true, for all the rectangles in Figure 3.8 are unchanging through time, including the one representing the ratio of income to "efficiency" labor, $0\bar{k}MN$. In terms of "efficiency" labor, per capita income is constant. In terms of "natural" labor, per capita income can rise only if there is technical improvement that makes "efficiency" labor grow faster than "natural" labor.

But this is only part of the story. Increases in the saving ratio and declines in population growth can have a temporary impact on the growth of per capita income. These considerations are taken up next.

INCREASES IN THE SAVING RATIO

Suppose society decides to save and invest a greater proportion of its income. What will be the impact of this decision on per capita income and its rate of growth? Figure 3.10 can be used to suggest an answer.

If the saving ratio rises, the effect is to shift up the growth of capital line (the K^* line). At every capital-labor ratio, more is saved and invested. As a consequence, there is capital deepening that takes place over time. The capital-labor ratio rises to a new and higher equilibrium value, and the interest rate falls. The dynamics of the transition to a new equilibrium are traced out in Figure 3.11, based on information contained in Figure 3.10.

When the saving ratio rises, the capital growth line in Figure 3.10 shifts up to the position indicated by the dotted line, K_1^*. For the moment, the capital-labor ratio is unchanged. Although the *flow* of new capital is increased, the capital *stock* is momentarily unaffected. (By analogy, when the floodgates of a dam are opened, the *flow* from the reservoir is increased, but the *stock* of water it contains is momentarily unaffected.) However, the growth of capital now exceeds the growth of labor. Capital is now growing at a new and higher rate, indicated by the point J_0'. But labor is still growing at the same old rate, g. As a consequence, the capital-labor ratio, k, is rising. Capital is accumulating faster than the labor force grows. There is capital deepening, which must go on until k rises to $\hat{k}_1$ and a new equilibrium is

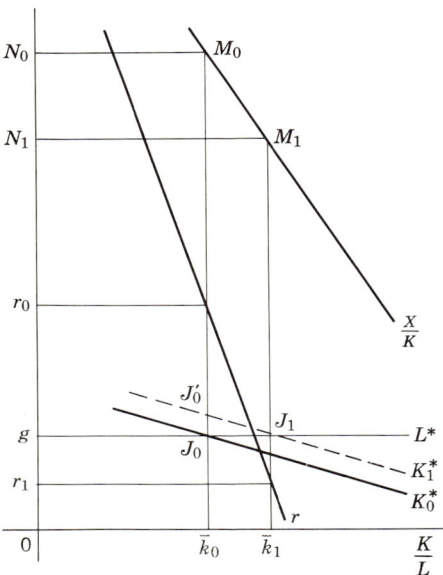

Figure 3.10 A rise in the saving ratio.

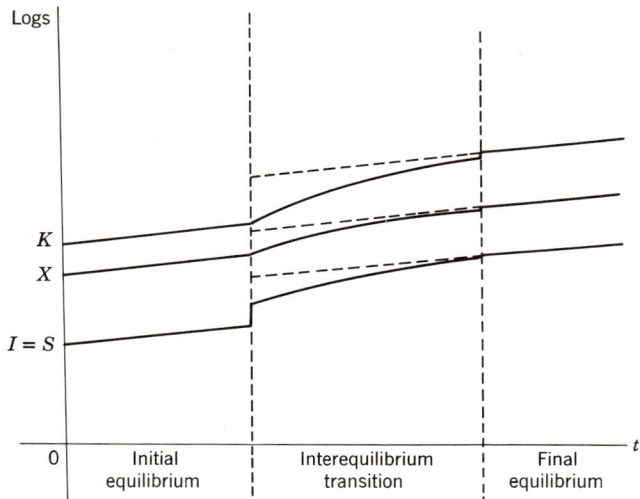

Figure 3.11 An interequilibrium transition.

established at J_1, where the interest rate has fallen from r_0 to r_1, the ratio of output to capital has fallen from $0N_0$ to $0N_1$, and the capital-labor ratio has risen from $0\bar{k}_0$ to $0\bar{k}_1$.

At any time during the transition to the new equilibrium, we can see what is happening to the system. Pick any k between $\bar{k}_0$ and $\bar{k}_1$, then move the eye vertically up the graph. The first relevant fact is revealed when the eye crosses the L^* line. Labor is still growing at the rate g, say 2 percent. Moving further up the graph, we note that capital is growing even faster than labor, say 3 percent. Since capital growth exceeds labor growth, the capital-labor ratio must be rising until the new equilibrium is established. Meanwhile, the *disequilibrium* values of net national product, the product imputed to capital and labor, net saving and consumption, can be read off the diagram in the usual way. But remember that during the transition to the new equilibrium, the rectangles representing these values (in per worker terms) are not stable. They are always changing until the new equilibrium is attained.

An interequilibrium transition is illustrated in Figure 3.11, which is based on Figure 3.10, but shows the time path of certain selected variables. The natural logarithms of these variables are plotted on the vertical axis, and time on the horizontal axis. As explained in Chapter Two, this means that a variable that grows at a constant proportional rate has a constant slope. Thus, during the initial equilibrium, capital, output, and investment all grow apace with labor; all growth lines have the common slope, g. Moreover,

46 An Introduction to Growth in an Advanced Economy

Figure 3.10 tells us that the final equilibrium must be marked by all these variables once more growing apace at the same old rate, g. What happens in between?

Since the ratio of output to capital falls from $0N_0$ to $0N_1$, we know that capital must grow faster than output. Note that while these variables rise steadily toward their new equilibrium growth paths, saving and investment experience a discrete rise when the saving ratio rises.

What will be the effect on per-worker and per capita income as a result of capital deepening? Recall that per-worker income is the rectangle inscribed under the average product of capital line. Thus, in Figure 3.10, per-worker income changes from $0\bar{k}_0 M_0 N_0$ to $0\bar{k}_1 M_1 N_1$ as the economy moves from initial to final equilibrium. Which rectangle is larger? By analogy with the theory of consumer demand, per-worker income will rise if the elasticity of the average product of capital line is greater than one. Note that the *marginal* product of capital (r) bears the same formal relation to the *average* product of capital (X/K) that *marginal* revenue bears to *average* revenue (demand). Thus, the elasticity of the average product of capital curve is greater than one so long as the marginal product of capital is greater than zero. A rise in the saving ratio increases per-worker income so long as the interest rate is positive. Since the labor force is assumed to be proportional to the population, a rise in the saving ratio also increases per capita income if the interest rate is positive.

DECREASES IN THE RATE OF POPULATION GROWTH

Decreases in the population growth rate change the equilibrium level of per capita income in the same direction as *increases* in the saving ratio. This can be seen in Figure 3.8 or 3.10 by imagining that the population growth component of the "natural" rate of growth (g) declines rapidly, then stabilizes at a lower level.

At the initial capital-labor ratio, $\bar{k}$ (Figure 3.8) or $\bar{k}_0$ (Figure 3.10), capital is growing faster than labor, so the capital-labor ratio rises. As before, per capita income will rise so long as the elasticity of the average product of capital curve is greater than one (or the marginal product of capital is positive).

THE SOURCES OF GROWTH

A model of economic growth has just been outlined. Although a crude approximation of reality, it is a useful tool when employed with discretion.

It is clear that higher saving ratios and lower population growth rates are associated with higher equilibrium per capita incomes, but that sustained improvement in the human material condition seems linked, in the long run, to continuous improvement in the technical conditions of production. This variable has been taken as determined outside the model. The sources of rising per capita income in the long run have been identified, but not explained. Later on, in Chapter Eight, we will consider a model in which technological change is regarded as an economic activity that competes for resources in other uses. If technological change must be "produced," can it be a source of sustained economic growth?

THE CASE OF FIXED PROPORTIONS

The growth model we have been working with in this chapter assumes that it is technically possible to select different levels of capital intensity. The capital-labor ratio (k) is assumed to be adjustable, and the average product of capital (X/K) declines as more capital intensive techniques are used. We found for any Golden Age (balanced growth path), that $X/K = g/s$. More rapidly growing economies with lower saving ratios will use less capital-intensive techniques (k will be smaller), and the average product of capital will be higher (X/K higher).

Contrast this model with the one suggested in Chapter One. There we assumed that X/K was a *technologically determined parameter* and equal to a constant $1/\kappa$.

$$X = \frac{1}{\kappa} K \qquad (1.2)$$

We also assumed that labor must be combined with machines in one-to-one proportions; that is,

$$k = \frac{K}{L} = 1$$

and that the supply of labor is no constraint. With a constant proportion of output being saved and invested,

$$\Delta K = sX \qquad (1.4)$$

so that

$$\frac{\Delta K}{K} = s \frac{X}{K}$$

An Introduction to Growth in an Advanced Economy

Combining this with (1.2) yields

$$\frac{\Delta K}{K} = K^* = \frac{s}{\kappa}$$

and with a fixed output-capital ratio

$$\frac{\Delta X}{X} = X^* = \frac{s}{\kappa}$$

and with a fixed capital-labor ratio,

$$\frac{\Delta L}{L} = L^* = \frac{s}{\kappa}$$

Employment growth is seen to be linked to the growth of capital capacity in this fixed-proportions model. Nevertheless, the equilibrium (Golden Age) growth path superficially resembles the one that emerges from the variable-proportions, full-employment model. There, X/K is an *endogenous* variable (determined within the model).

$$\frac{X}{K} = \frac{s}{g}$$

The values of X, K, and L grow at an *exogenously* determined rate (g) in any Golden Age.

$$X^* = K^* = L^* = g$$

The fixed-proportions model regards X/K as a *technologically determined parameter* ($1/\kappa$) and X, K, and L grow at the rate s/κ. If we let g denote this rate, we can write

$$g = \frac{s}{\kappa}$$

or

$$g = \frac{K}{X} = \frac{s}{g}$$

And

$$X^* = K^* = L^* = g = \frac{s}{\kappa}$$

But here, the capital-output ratio is *exogenous* and the growth rate, g, is *endogenous*.

What happens if the growth of employment ($g = s/\kappa$) exceeds the growth of population and the labor force (the "natural" rate of growth)? Will not the army of unemployed be absorbed eventually and capital become redundant? What if the population and labor force grow faster than employment? Will not unemployment continue to grow and impose intolerable burdens on the economy? Only if labor-force growth *just happens* to equal s/κ and only if there *just happens* to be full employment at the outset, will the economy grow with full employment of capital and labor. Full-employment growth hinges on a parametric coincidence and historical accident in the fixed-proportions model.

How does one choose between the models? Factor proportions are undoubtedly more rigid in the short run than in the long run. Once in place, machinery must be worked according to design specifications. But machines wear out and new machines are put in their place. The design specifications of new equipment can be altered to reflect current conditions of factor supply. Higher wages and lower interest rates can induce more capital-intensive techniques on new equipment.

This observation suggests a compromise model in which capital-labor ratios are variable before investments are made but are fixed thereafter. These models are more complicated and cannot be explored here.[9]

EXERCISES

1. Draw a diagram similar to Figure 3.10, which shows the time path of per capita income and the rate of interest subsequent to a rise in the saving ratio.

2. The following data pertain to a model economy in balanced growth equilibrium:

Growth of population	0.02
Growth of labor efficiency	0.03
Net saving ratio	0.10

    (a) Find the ratio of output to capital.
    (b) Find the rate of growth of per capita income.

[9] The model in this chapter could be called a "putty-putty" model, since capital is malleable to permit any capital-labor ratio both before and after investment. The fixed-proportions model could be called a "clay-clay," model since capital-labor substitution is never possible. "Putty-clay" models are in R. M. Solow, "Substitution and Fixed Proportions in the Theory of Capital," *Review of Economic Studies* (June 1962) and L. Johansen, "Substitution Versus Fixed Production Coefficients in The Theory of Economic Growth: A Synthesis," *Econometrica* (April 1959). In these models, capital is like putty before investment, and like clay afterwards.

(c) Assuming that capital is "paid" its marginal product (r) (this means that the total payment to capital equals rK) and further assuming that capital's share of output is $\frac{1}{4}$, find the marginal product of capital (r).

3. Draw a diagram similar to 3.9, which shows the consequences of a technological change that leaves the marginal product of capital unaffected as a consequence of the change itself.

REFERENCES AND SUGGESTIONS FOR FURTHER READING

1. Allen, R. D. G., *Macro-Economic Theory*. London: Macmillan 1967, pp. 260–274.
2. Denison, E. F., "The Unimportance of the Embodied Question." *American Economic Review*, March 1964.
3. Fisher, F. M., "The Existence of Aggregate Production Functions." *Econometrica*, October 1969.
4. Johansen, L., "Substitution Versus Fixed Production Coefficients in the Theory of Economic Growth: A Synthesis." *Econometrica*, April 1959.
5. Johnson, H. G., "Money in a Neo-Classical One-Sector Growth Model." Chapter IV of Harry G. Johnson, *Essays in Monetary Economics*. London: George Allen and Unwin, 1967.
6. Kogiku, K. C., *An Introduction to Macroeconomic Models*. New York: McGraw-Hill, 1968, chaps. 7–8.
7. Leftwich, R. H., *The Price System and Resource Allocation*, Third Ed. New York: Holt, Rinehart and Winston, 1966, pp. 114–115.
8. Meade, J. E., *A Neo-Classical Theory of Economic Growth*, Second Ed. New York: Oxford, 1961, chaps. 1–4.
9. Samuelson, P. A., "Parable and Realism in Capital Theory: The Surrogate Production Function." *Review of Economic Studies*, June 1962.
10. Sirkin, G., *An Introduction to Macroeconomic Theory*. Homewood: Irwin, 1965, chap. 10.
11. Solow, R. M., *Capital Theory and the Rate of Return*. Amsterdam: North Holland, 1963.
12. Solow, R. M., "Substitution and Fixed Proportions in the Theory of Capital." *Review of Economic Studies*, June 1963.
13. Solow, R. M., "A Contribution to the Theory of Economic Growth." *Quarterly Journal of Economics*, February 1956.
14. Stigler, G. H., *The Theory of Price, Third Edition*. New York: Macmillan, 1966, p. 126.
15. Swan, T. W., "Economic Growth and Capital Accumulation." *Economic Record*, November 1956.
16. Tobin, J., "Money and Economic Growth." *Econometrica*, October 1965.

Chapter Four

AN INTRODUCTION TO GROWTH IN A PRIMITIVE ECONOMY

Introduction
The Production Function
The Population-Growth Function
The Equilibrium Rate of Growth and the Distribution of National Income
Improvements in Technology
A Decline in the Propensity to Proliferate
A Fall in the Death Rate
Exercises
References and Suggestions for Further Reading

INTRODUCTION

While many economies have achieved rising average incomes over long periods of time, others have remained "underdeveloped" by comparison. In these economies, per capita incomes have been relatively constant, but often their populations have grown.

If these characteristics are roughly in accord with the stylized facts of preindustrial societies, how should we account for them? This chapter suggests a simple model of growth that is based on two primary relationships:[1]

1. A production function that shows the relation of the inputs (resources) employed by a basically agricultural society to the output that these resources produce.

2. A population growth function that relates population increase to the level of per capita income.

These relationships will be taken up in turn and then combined in a model of economic growth.

THE PRODUCTION FUNCTION

The production function in this chapter relates the output of a primarily agricultural society to inputs of labor and land. Symbolically

$$X = F(L, N) \tag{4.1}$$

The output (X) is thought of as a homogeneous agricultural commodity. The inputs, labor (L) and land (N), are also assumed to be homogeneous. Note that capital is not formally included in the function. This reflects the (perhaps mistaken) view that capital plays a minor role in more primitive agriculture. Alternatively, one can imagine that capital is combined in fixed proportions with land. In that case, N is simply a composite input embodying fixed proportions of land and capital.

The function itself, $F(\ )$, is assumed to have the familiar properties outlined in the preceding chapter: constant returns to scale, and diminishing average and marginal returns to labor as more labor is added per unit of land. These relations are plotted in Figure 4.1. Again, these functions are drawn as straight lines for convenience, and can be thought of as linear approximations of the true functions in the neighborhood of investigation.

Notice that, compared with our discussion of the advanced economy, the roles of capital and labor have simply been reversed. In the preceding chapter, we thought of diminishing returns to capital as more capital was applied per unit of labor. Here, diminishing returns to labor set in as more labor is applied per unit of land. However, for the advanced economy, the

---

[1] Key ideas that underlie the model can be traced back to the classical economists, notably, T. R. Malthus and D. Ricardo. Modern versions have appeared in several places. See, for example, D. W. Jorgenson, "The Development of a Dual Economy," *Economic Journal* (June 1961) and R. R. Nelson, "A Theory of the Low Level Equilibrium Trap," *American Economic Review* (December 1956).

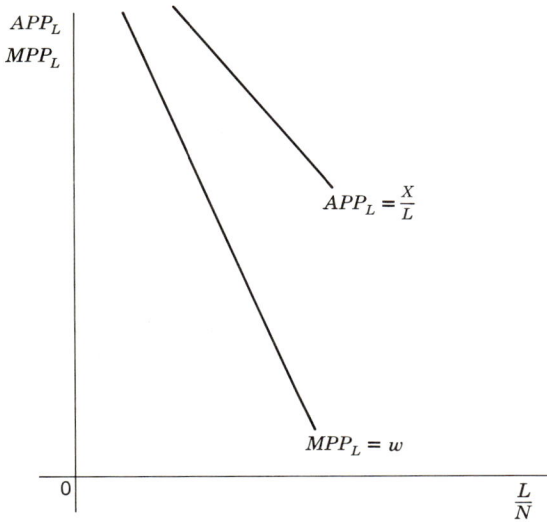

Figure 4.1 The average and marginal physical products of labor. These fall as more labor is added to the land.

resource other than labor (capital) was augmentable through saving, and grew through time. Here, the resource other than labor (land) is assumed to be nonaugmentable. We assume that virtually all suitable agricultural land has already been brought under cultivation, and consequently the supply of land cannot grow. Thus, when we think of adding more labor per unit of land, we are really adding more labor to a constant amount of land. Diminishing returns to labor are, of course, experienced in either case.

THE POPULATION-GROWTH FUNCTION

Fertility, mortality, and the dynamics of population growth are complex subjects indeed, and it is perhaps fortunate for economists that demographers study them in detail. Yet economists must often take demographic factors into account when constructing growth models, for three important reasons. First, labor is an important input in production, and a larger population can usually be counted on to furnish a larger work force. Second, income or product is often measured most meaningfully in per capita terms. A larger population is likely to have lower per capita income, if other resources are not proportionately greater. Finally, economic forces are sometimes thought to bear on the growth of population and the work force.

54 An Introduction to Growth in a Primitive Economy

In this model, we employ a simple population growth function that seems reasonable for many "underdeveloped" countries. Simplicity, however, is gained by making a number of heroic assumptions that deny us certain insights afforded by more elaborate demographic models.

We begin with a definition of population growth for a closed economy that cannot experience migration. Then any change in population (ΔP) recorded over a period of time is attributed to the births and deaths during that period.

$$\Delta P \equiv \text{BIRTHS} - \text{DEATHS} \qquad (4.2)$$

Demographers find it convenient to express births and deaths as proportions of the population. Dividing (4.2) by an estimate of the population that itself produced the births and deaths, we have

$$\frac{\Delta P}{P} = \frac{\text{BIRTHS}}{P} - \frac{\text{DEATHS}}{P} \qquad (4.3)$$

These birth-and-death ratios are called the crude birth rate (CBR) and crude death rate (CDR) respectively.[2] For example, the natural rate of increase in Venezuela from 1950 to 1954 can be attributed to the average annual CBR and the average annual CDR as follows:[3]

$$\frac{\Delta P}{P} \equiv CBR - CDR$$
$$0.0341 = 0.0447 - 0.0106 \qquad (4.4)$$
$$3.41\% = 4.47\% - 1.06\%$$

The next step is to link the CBR to per capita income. We assume that the birth rate depends in a positive and, for convenience, in a linear way upon per capita income up to some limit imposed by physiological or other considerations. The function is illustrated in Figure 4.2. The CBR is shown on the vertical axis. Product *per worker* is plotted on the horizontal axis, instead of product *per unit of population*. We allow ourselves this simplification by assuming that the working population is always proportional to the population as a whole.

---

[2] Demographers usually express these rates in terms of vital events per thousand population. The rates are termed "crude" because they refer to the population as a whole rather than specific age groups.

[3] Computed from United Nations, *Demographic Yearbook*, 1956.

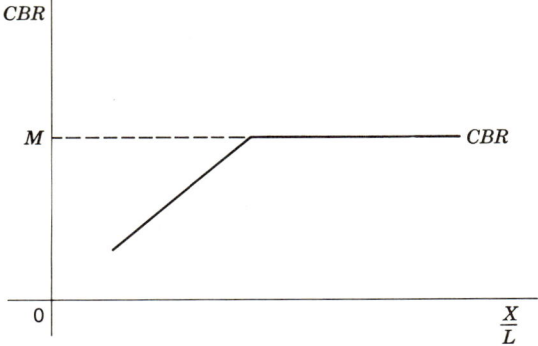

Figure 4.2 The crude birth rate. This rises as per capita income increases, up to a maximum rate determined by physiological considerations or by custom.

The function has two distinct portions in the relevant range of per-worker income. For lower levels of income, we have the rising portion, where higher levels of per-worker income are associated with higher birth rates. The function can be expressed as

$$CBR = B\left(\frac{X}{L}\right) \qquad (4.5a)$$

where B might be called the "propensity to proliferate." It is a positive number. As income rises, people feel they can "afford" more children. Moreover, we can think of a "birth" as occurring after the child has survived his first year or eighteen months. Higher per capita income and associated higher nutritional levels, enjoyed by both child and his mother, would seem to ensure a higher rate of "births," even if the number of conceptions remains the same.[4]

We should recognize that there is a biological upper limit on the birth rate, which seems to be on the order of 4 percent. A lower maximum may be

---

[4] Define: "Births" ≡ Conceptions − Infant Deaths. Then

$$\frac{\text{"}B\text{"}}{P} \equiv \frac{C}{P} - IMR \cdot \frac{C}{P}$$

where IMR is the "infant mortality rate" defined as infant deaths per conception, C is conceptions and P is population. If the conception rate is constant and the IMR falls as per capita income rises, then the "birth" rate rises as per capita income rises.

56 An Introduction to Growth in a Primitive Economy

imposed by custom or by the state of medical knowledge. However determined, the maximum is denoted by M in Figure 4.2, which refers to the horizontal position of the line.

$$CBR = M \qquad (4.5b)$$

Turning next to the crude death rate, we assume that the number of deaths is proportional to the numbers in the population and the work force, so the CDR is a constant.

$$CDR = D \qquad (4.6)$$

By making this assumption we overlook the obvious fact that a rapidly growing, younger population will have a lower death rate than a slowly growing population with relatively more people in the older age groups.[5] This will occur even if the death rate for people in each age group is the same in both populations.

By combining Equations 4.4, 4.5a, 4.5b, and 4.6, we have an expression that shows the dependence of population and labor force growth upon per capita income and upon the constant force of mortality, if the biological limit on reproduction has not been reached:

$$\frac{\Delta L}{L} = B \cdot \frac{X}{L} - D$$

If this limit has been reached,

$$\frac{\Delta L}{L} = M - D$$

Presumably, for viable populations

$$M > D$$

As before, it is convenient to think of the time interval of analysis as being infinitely small, so that ΔL is replaced by $dL/dt = \dot{L}$. Thus

$$\frac{1}{L} \cdot \frac{dL}{dt} = \frac{\dot{L}}{L} = L^*$$

---

[5] The assumption that the CDR is a constant also ignores the effect of higher per capita income on lowering adult mortality.

is the proportional rate of growth of the labor force, so that

$$L^* = B \cdot \frac{X}{L} - D \qquad (4.7a)$$

or

$$L^* = M - D \qquad (4.7b)$$

To facilitate a solution of the model, which will be undertaken in the next section, we want to plot these relationships on the same axes that were used for the production function in the preceding section. That is, we want to show how labor-force growth depends on the ratio of labor to land.

This is easily done. The production relation showed that the average product of labor declined as labor increased relative to land. Equation 4.7a links labor growth, in turn, to the average product of labor. We can accomplish our purpose by simple construction.

The average product-of-labor curve from Figure 4.1 is repeated here in Figure 4.3. Taking first the impact of births on labor growth, we plot from 4.7a the $CBR = B \cdot X/L$ proportional to the X/L line.[6] This *would* be labor growth rate if no one died. But in a society of mortals, we must subtract

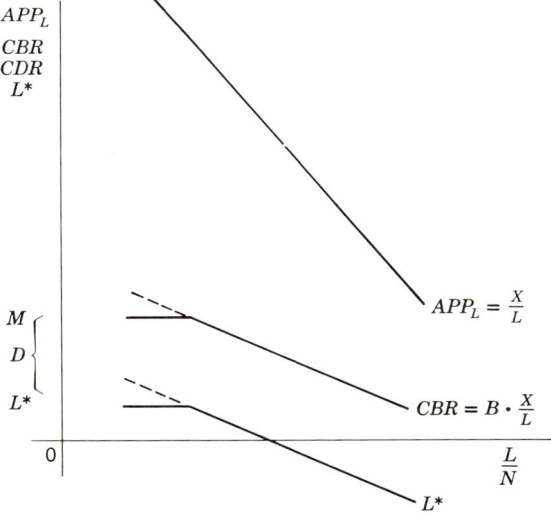

Figure 4.3 The growth of labor and the ratio of labor to land. The growth of labor declines as population increases, because larger populations have lower per capita incomes and lower birth rates. The death rate is a constant.

[6] Units have been chosen so that B lies between zero and one.

58 An Introduction to Growth in a Primitive Economy

the constant death rate, $CDR = D$, from everywhere along the CBR line. The result is the desired growth of labor (L^*) line, which combines the impact of births and deaths.

The downward slope of the L^* line indicates that labor-force growth declines as more labor is combined with the available land. According to our argument, a larger labor force has a lower average product. A lower average product is associated with a lower birth rate. With a constant death rate, a lower birth rate means that the population and the labor force grow more slowly in larger populations.

The next step is to plot Equation 4.7b, which puts a limit on the growth of labor by imposing a maximum possible rate of births. We know that this limit applies to the high per capita incomes associated with low labor-land ratios on the left-hand side of Figure 4.3. This is done by plotting the components of Equation 4.7b as horizontal straight lines in Figure 4.3. The final labor-force growth relation is the solid line with two straight segments.

Although this line consists of two linear segments, the true relation, if it exists, would probably show a horizontal portion to the left, but a smooth transition to the downward slope. Such a curve would be represented by a very complex algebraic expression. What we have done is to construct a *piecewise* linear approximation of the "true" curve.

THE EQUILIBRIUM RATE OF GROWTH AND THE DISTRIBUTION OF NATIONAL INCOME

We can now bring together the production function and the labor-growth relations, and, adding one more condition, complete the model. This last condition has already been mentioned: the supply of land is constant; it does not grow; $N^* = 0$. Symbolically, the model now stands as:

$$X = F(L, N) \tag{4.1}$$

$$L^* = B \cdot \frac{X}{L} - D \tag{4.7a}$$

or

$$L^* = M - D \tag{4.7b}$$

$$N^* = 0 \tag{4.8}$$

Graphically, the model is contained in Figures 4.1 and 4.3, which are superimposed on Figure 4.4, with the additional condition that land does not grow ($N^* = 0$).

An equilibrium ratio of labor to land is at $\bar{n}$, where labor-force growth is zero. Since population is assumed to be proportional to workers, the population as a whole is also stationary.

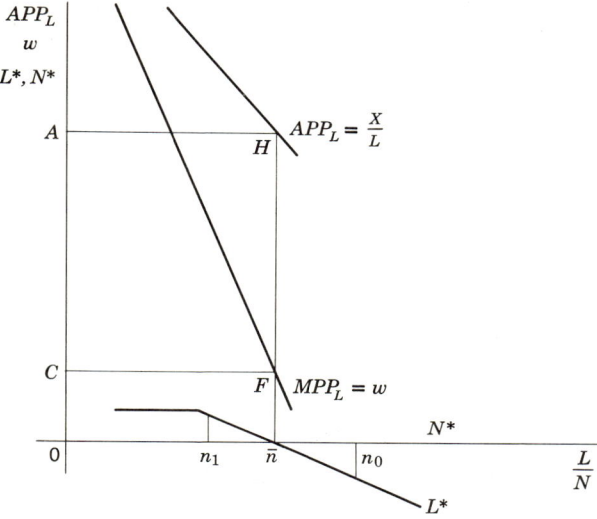

Figure 4.4 The equilibrium rate of growth and the distribution of national income. With the supply of land fixed, the equilibrium ratio of labor to land is $\bar{n}$. More labor on the land reduces the birth rate and the labor force declines. Less labor on the land raises the birth rate and the labor force grows.

That $\bar{n}$ is an equilibrium labor-land ratio can be established in the usual way: suppose an actual labor-land ratio were at n_0, greater than $\bar{n}$. Then the L^* line shows negative growth for labor, while the amount of land is unchanging. The labor-land ratio must then be falling. For example, at n_0, labor may be growing at minus one percent and land at zero percent. Thus, $n = L/N$ is falling.

Conversely, at n_1, less than $\bar{n}$, labor is growing at a positive rate, while land is stationary. As a consequence, $n = L/N$ is rising.

Thus, $\bar{n}$ is an equilibrium that corresponds to a stationary state in which nothing grows. National product and its components stabilize in terms of both labor and land.

Output per unit of labor can be read directly from Figure 4.4: $0A = \bar{n}H$. In terms of land, output is the average product of labor multiplied by the equilibrium ratio of labor to land.

$$\frac{X}{N} \equiv \frac{X}{L} \cdot \frac{L}{N} = \frac{X}{L} \cdot \bar{n}$$

This is the rectangle $0\bar{n}HA$.

The quantity of output that can be attributed to the two inputs is also constant in equilibrium. If labor is paid its marginal product, then the equilibrium wage (w) is $0C = \bar{n}F$. In terms of land, the output attributed to labor is

$$\frac{wL}{N} = w \cdot \bar{n}$$

This is the rectangle $0\bar{n}FC$. With total product equal to $0\bar{n}HA$, the remainder, $CFHA$, is simply the rental per unit of land (r).

To sum up, expressing all magnitudes in terms of land:

National product $= 0\bar{n}HA$

Product imputed to land $= CFHA$

Product imputed to labor $= 0\bar{n}FC$

IMPROVEMENTS IN TECHNOLOGY

Technical improvement occurs from time to time, even in economies that are "primitive" by modern standards. Such inventions as the calendar, plant and animal husbandry, and the deep-furrow plow, were pre-industrial revolution inventions. These came, nevertheless, rather late in the history of improving technique, which must be as old as mankind. In addition, contemporary "underdeveloped" economies can often improve the efficiency of their technology by importing techniques from the rest of the world. Internally generated improvements may occur as well.

What will be the impact of a technical improvement on the material welfare of these societies? Our model offers an answer which, however consistent with the historical record, is not encouraging for the prospects of the "underdeveloped" world. We will find that population growth has a persistent tendency to eat up the gains in per capita income that would otherwise occur as a consequence of a technical change.

A once-and-for-all technical improvement is illustrated in Figure 4.5. With better technology, a greater amount of output is obtainable from a given endowment of land and labor. The improvement is illustrated by a *uniform* upward shift in the APP_L function, although *any* change in technology that improves labor's average product at the existing ratio of labor to land could be called an improvement. The old technology was associated with the solid $APP_L = X/L$ line; the new technology gives rise to the dotted line just above it. Assuming the economy is in equilibrium when the improvement occurs, the initial ratio of labor to land is $\bar{n}$ and per capita income is $0A$.

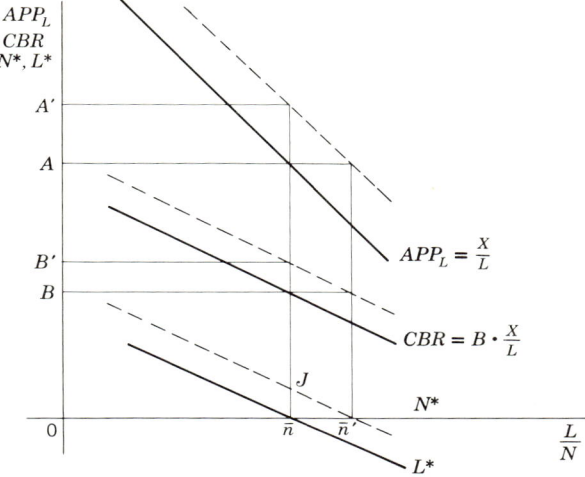

Figure 4.5 An improvement in technology.

Births, $0B$, are just offset by deaths. But as a consequence of the improvement, which raises average income to $0A'$, the birth rate will rise, but by how much? We know that

$$CBR = B \cdot \frac{X}{L} \qquad (4.5a)$$

Therefore, it must be true that

$$\triangle CBR = B \cdot \Delta \frac{X}{L}$$

Graphically, $\triangle CBR$ is BB' and $\Delta(X/L)$ is AA'. Thus

$$BB' = B \cdot (AA')$$

is the initial rise in the birth rate due to the improvement. The *flow* of new members of society has increased but, for the moment, the *stock* of population has not increased. The death rate, however, is constant, so the new L^* line shifts up the same absolute amount as the CBR line. Now births exceed deaths, so the population and labor force are growing. At point J, just after the improvement occurred, the population might be growing at 1 percent, while land is growing at 0 percent. Thus, n must be rising, and it will continue to do so until a new equilibrium is established at $\bar{n}'$.

During the transition, per capita income is falling slowly, as increased numbers experience diminishing average returns on the available land and the birth rate is falling concomitantly.

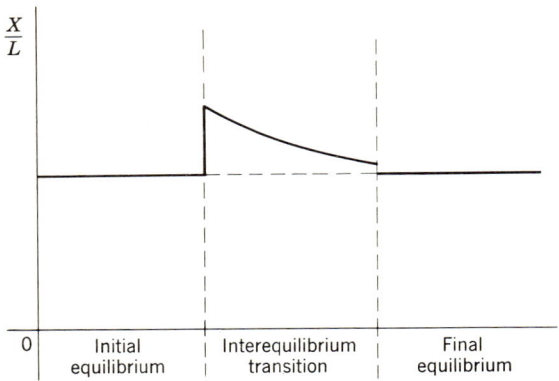

Figure 4.6 An interequilibrium transition.

Finally, per capita income is driven down to the point where the birth rate no longer exceeds the death rate, and the new equilibrium is established.

It can be proved geometrically that the new and the old equilibrium are associated with the same per capita income. But an intuitive proof is perhaps more revealing. We can tell from the diagram that equilibrium is marked by a stationary population ($L^* = 0$). But, from (4.7a),

$$L^* = B \cdot \frac{X}{L} - D \qquad (4.7a)$$

Thus

$$\frac{X}{L} = \frac{D}{B} \qquad (4.9)$$

when

$$L^* = 0$$

Two constants of the system, D and B, are sufficient to determine per capita income in equilibrium. We need no production information—the equilibrium level of per capita income is independent of the technical efficiency of production.

Incomes have, of course, risen above their equilibrium levels during the transition. This is illustrated in Figure 4.6, where X/L is plotted on the vertical axis and time on the horizontal axis. Per capita income is greatest just after the improvement occurs. Then "labor deepening" gradually wipes out the initial gains. The new and better technology ultimately supports a larger population, but at the same average income.

Another way to introduce technical change is to assume that it occurs at a continuous proportional rate. Unfortunately, this assumption is not easily incorporated into our simple graphical analysis in this chapter. It will be dealt with later on in Chapter Seven, when more powerful analytical tools can be brought to bear. The outcome there is that a sufficiently high rate of continuous technical improvement can overcome the effects of population growth, and per capita income can rise continuously.

A DECLINE IN THE PROPENSITY TO PROLIFERATE

It is already clear from Equation 4.9 that a decline in the "propensity to proliferate" (B) will raise the equilibrium level of per capita income. But as with an improvement in technique, the transition to a new equilibrium will take some time. This is illustrated in Figure 4.7.

If a birth control campaign or some other force results in a lower B for the society, this means that the birth rate falls for every level of per capita income. If the solid CBR line represents the original birth function, the dotted CBR line, corresponding to a smaller B, must lie below the original one and in addition have a more shallow slope. This is because we take a smaller fraction, B, of the per capita income line when drawing the new CBR function. The new L^* line results when the constant $CDR = D$ is subtracted from the new CBR line just obtained.

The initial consequence of the lower B is that births fall short of deaths at the original equilibrium $\bar{n}$. The population now declines, and will continue to do so until $\bar{n}'$ is reached. Average income has risen gradually from A to A', where it stabilizes at the new and higher level. The population is again

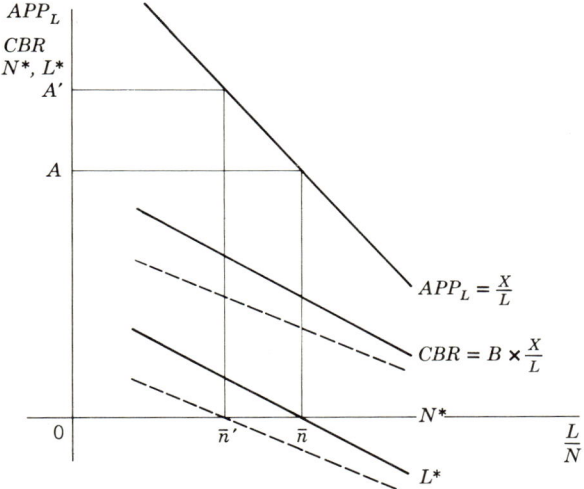

Figure 4.7 A decline in the propensity to proliferate.

stationary but smaller, and material welfare is higher. Fewer workers on the available land have a higher average product.

By how much has per capita income increased? Again, we can turn to Equation 4.9:

$$\frac{X}{L} = \frac{D}{B} = D \cdot \frac{1}{B} \qquad (4.9)$$

We wish to know how much X/L changes when B changes.

The simplest method is to take logarithms and then differentiate. Recall from Chapter Two,

$$\frac{d}{dt} \log x = \frac{1}{x} \cdot \frac{dx}{dt} \qquad (2.17)$$

Here we are considering a "timeless" comparison of two equilibrium positions. In this case we should think of a change in the logarithm of the variable without respect to time. Thus

$$d \log x = \frac{1}{x} \cdot dx$$

Now, taking logarithms of (4.9),

$$\log \frac{X}{L} = \log D - \log B$$

Differentiating, and recalling that D does not change,

$$d\frac{X}{L} \cdot \frac{L}{X} = -\frac{dB}{B}$$

The proportional *rise* in per capita income is equal to the proportional *fall* in the "propensity to proliferate."

A FALL IN THE DEATH RATE

A decline in the death rate, which affects all ages equally, and leaves the ratio of the labor force to the population unaffected, lowers per capita income.[7] This will happen even if there is a concomitant rise in worker efficiency. Consider Figure 4.8.

Suppose for the moment that the elimination of an endemic disease such as malaria reduces the crude death rate, but does *not* enhance worker efficiency. The economy is in initial equilibrium at $\bar{n}$, corresponding to the solid L^* line. A fall in the death rate means that a smaller CDR must be subtracted from the CBR line to get the L^* line. The new L^* line is the dotted

---

[7] If "births" are interpreted as survival past 12 to 18 months of age, then a change in the death rate should be thought of as affecting those who are older.

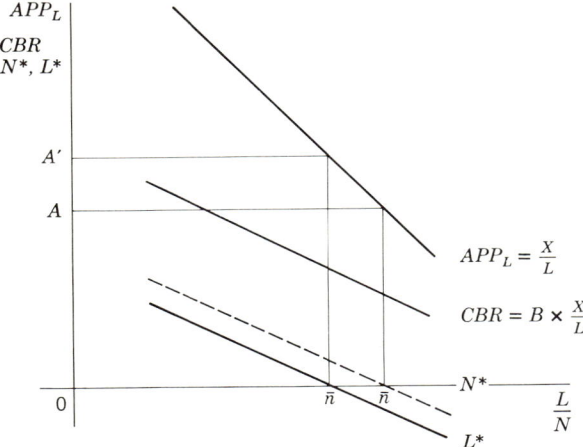

Figure 4.8 A fall in the death rate.

one, above the original solid line. Births now exceed deaths, and the population rises against the fixed land resources. Diminishing returns to labor reduce average income as the population grows. Eventually, per capita income falls enough to bring the birth rate into line with the lower death rate, and a new equilibrium is established at $\bar{n}'$ with a greater population but with an average income that has fallen from A to A'.

If the same event that reduced the CDR also increases labor efficiency, we must add in this second effect to get the final outcome on per capita income. Increased labor efficiency means that more output can be produced by each worker, given the available land. Higher labor efficiency is a kind of technological change which, as we have seen, can be represented by shifting up the APP_L curve at each ratio of labor to land in the relevant range. We also know the long-run consequences of such a shift: a greater population, but the same per capita income. Thus, if the effect of malaria eradication on the *death rate* is to lower per capita income and increase the population, the additional impact on *labor efficiency* is to increase the population even more, leaving per capita incomes unchanged at the new and lower level.

The argument can be put another way. The antimalaria campaign has a *partial* impact on per capita income through the death rate alone.

We can calculate this effect from Equation 4.9 by differentiating with respect to the death rate, holding B constant. Taking logarithms in (4.9),

$$\frac{X}{L} = \frac{D}{B} = \frac{1}{B} \cdot D$$

$$\log \frac{X}{L} = \log \frac{1}{B} + \log D$$

(4.9)

Differentiating

$$d\frac{X}{L}\cdot\frac{L}{X}=\frac{dD}{D}$$

The proportional *fall* in per capita income is equal to the proportional *fall* in the death rate.

EXERCISES

1. In Figure 4.4, find two line segments, the ratio of which is the proportion of total product imputed to labor.
2. Prepare a diagram similar to Figure 4.6, which shows the time path of per capita income when
   (a) There is a sudden fall in the "propensity to proliferate," (B).
   (b) There is a sudden fall in the death rate, (D).
3. Using natural logarithms, show that Equation 4.9 implies that

$$d\frac{X}{L}\cdot\frac{L}{X}=\frac{dD}{D}$$

   when D alone is allowed to change.
4. If the death rate (D) is reduced:
   (a) What must be the change in the "propensity to proliferate" (B) to leave equilibrium per capita income unaffected?
   (b) What is the ultimate impact on the size of the population if the effect of a fall in D on average income is offset by a change in B?

REFERENCES AND SUGGESTIONS FOR FURTHER READING

1. Nelson, R. R., "A Theory of the Low Level Equilibrium Trap." *American Economic Review*, December 1956.
2. Jorgenson, D. W., "The Development of the Dual Economy." *Economic Journal*, June, 1961.
3. Baumol, W. J., *Economic Dynamics*. New York: Macmillan, 1959, pp. 18–21.

Chapter Five

THE CONSTANT RETURNS TO SCALE PRODUCTION FUNCTION

The Function
The Marginal Products of Capital and Labor
The Elasticities of the Wage and the Interest Rate
With Respect to the Capital-Labor Ratio
The Elasticity of Substitution and the Elasticity of Factor Rewards
The Average Products of Labor and Capital
The Shares of Output Imputed to Labor and Capital
A Recapitulation
Dynamic Production Relations
Exercises
References and Suggestions for Further Reading

THE FUNCTION

A central relation in the two growth models that we have just discussed was the constant returns to scale-production function. It is now time to explore in more detail this concept as a foundation for the more demanding analysis of growth and development in subsequent chapters. In the present chapter we shall assume that the production relation is unchanging through time.

Technical progress will be allowed for in the next chapter, before we return to growth and development models.

Consider the following production function:

$$X = F(K, L) \tag{5.1}$$

As it is written, the function asserts only that the flow of output (X) *depends upon* the flow of capital services (K) and the flow of labor services (L). For short, we can say that output depends upon capital and labor. This is a very general assertion, and generality is a desirable quality, other things being equal. But the function is *too* general for our purposes. We must give up some generality to endow it with properties that are either analytically convenient or economically compelling. The first property we shall impose on the function is more convenient than compelling: we assume *constant returns to scale*. This means that if the two inputs are increased in the same proportion, then output will increase in precisely the same proportion. For example, if both capital and labor are doubled, then output will exactly double. Symbolically, let q be any positive number; then, given the constant returns to scale assumption,

$$q \cdot X = F(q \cdot K, q \cdot L)$$

is a true statement. Sometimes we say that such a function is *homogeneous of degree one*, or *homogeneous of the first degree*. This is because the constant returns to scale function is a special case of a more general class of homogeneous functions that have the property

$$q^n \cdot X = F(q \cdot K, q \cdot L)$$

where n is the *degree of homogeneity*.

For example, the quadratic function with constants A and B

$$X = A \cdot K + B \cdot \frac{K^2}{L}$$

is homogeneous of the first degree in K and L. To see this, multiply both inputs by q and output by q^n.

$$q^n \cdot X = A \cdot (q \cdot K) + B \cdot \frac{(q \cdot K)^2}{q \cdot L}$$

$$= q(A \cdot K) + q\left(B \cdot \frac{K^2}{L}\right)$$

$$= q\left(A \cdot K + B \cdot \frac{K^2}{L}\right)$$

$$q^n = q$$

$$\therefore n = 1$$

The function is homogeneous because we can solve for n. It is homogeneous of the first degree because $n = 1$. If inputs are doubled, the output is doubled; there are constant returns to scale.

The function
$$X = K^2 + L^2$$
is homogeneous of the second degree. We can prove this by multiplying both inputs by q and output by q^n.

$$q^n \cdot X = (q \cdot K)^2 + (q \cdot L)^2$$
$$q^n \cdot X = q^2(K^2 + L^2)$$
$$q^n = q^2$$
$$\therefore n = 2$$

The function is homogeneous because we can solve for n. Homogeneity is of the second degree because $n = 2$. If inputs are doubled, output is quadrupled; there are increasing returns to scale.

There could be decreasing returns to scale. The reader can show that

$$X = \frac{K^{2.5} + L^{2.5}}{K \cdot L}$$

is homogeneous of degree one half. If inputs are doubled, output increases by the square root of two; there are diminishing returns to scale.

A common production relation in economics is the Cobb-Douglas production function
$$X = AK^b L^a$$

This function is homogeneous to the degree $n = b + a$. There are constant returns if $n = 1$, diminishing returns if $n < 1$ and increasing returns if $n > 1$. But if

$$X = AK^b L^a + a \text{ constant}, \qquad a + b > 0$$

the function is not homogeneous of any degree, because we could not solve for n.

The general constant returns to scale production function has a number of remarkable and very useful properties that we shall develop in this chapter. Recall that if $F(\ )$ is homogeneous of the first degree

$$q \cdot X = F(q \cdot K, q \cdot L)$$

is true for any positive q. Suppose we let $q \equiv 1/L$.

$$\frac{X}{L} = F\left(\frac{K}{L}, 1\right)$$

Now we can define a new function, $f(\ )$, which absorbs the constant, 1. The average product of labor is homogeneous of degree zero in capital and labor. If K and L increase in the same proportion, X/L is unchanged.

$$\frac{X}{L} = f\left(\frac{K}{L}\right) \tag{5.2}$$

Or, defining $x \equiv K/L$ and $k \equiv K/L$,

$$x = f(k) \tag{5.2'}$$

This is the basic formulation that will be used to derive the properties of the constant returns to scale-production function. It states that the average product of labor depends only upon the *ratio* of capital to labor, but *not at all upon the scale of operations.*

Of course, this statement holds for the average product of capital as well. Dividing both sides of (5.2) by $k \equiv K/L$,

$$\frac{X}{K} \equiv \frac{X}{L} \cdot \frac{L}{K} = \frac{f(k)}{k} \tag{5.3}$$

So far we have not specified how product per worker (x) depends on the amount of capital per worker (k), but economic considerations suggest that more capital per worker is associated with more output per worker. Capital deepening (k greater) increases the average product of labor (x greater). This is the second important property of the production function: x is positively related to k.

The third property is that production is subject to diminishing marginal returns to proportions. Adding more capital per worker increases output per worker *but* at a decreasing rate. The *more* capital each laborer is already working with, the *less* his average product will rise if he is provided with another unit of capital.

These three properties are illustrated in Figure 5.1.

1. The constant returns to scale assumption permits us to show the average product of labor (x) depending on the capital-labor ratio (k) *alone*, and independent of the scale of operations.

2. The average product of labor (x) increases as the capital-labor ratio (k) increases. The curve *slopes upward*.

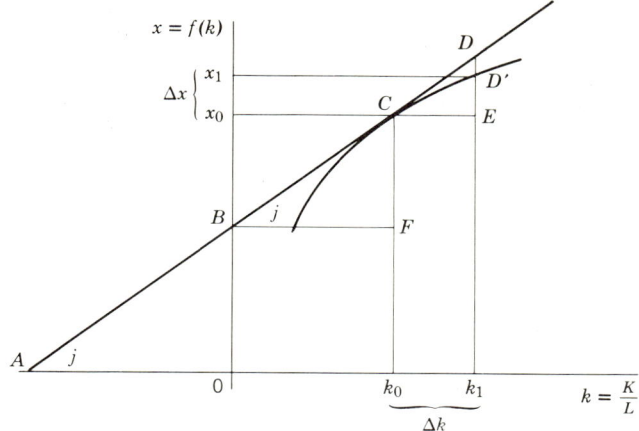

Figure 5.1a The average product of labor.

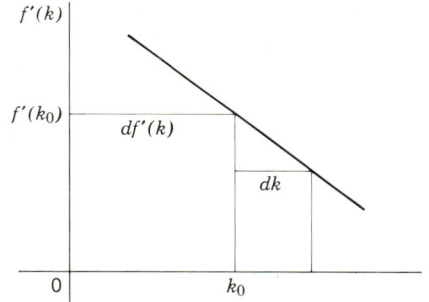

Figure 5.1b The first derivative of the average product of labor.

3. The average product of labor (x) increases at a decreasing rate with increases in the capital-labor ratio (k). The average product-of-labor curve bends downward.

In short, x depends on k alone. There are positive but diminishing returns to proportions.

We should restate these production relations in terms of the calculus for analytical purposes. The *slope* of function is its *first derivative*. We measure the slope at any point on the curve by drawing a line like $ABCD$ in Figure 5.1a, so that it *just touches* the curve at the desired point. The line $ABCD$ is just *tangent* to the production function at k_0 and the corresponding x_0. This line forms the angle j with the horizontal axis. When $k = k_0$, the slope of the

The Constant Returns to Scale Production Function

function is measured by the tangent of the angle j, the opposite side divided by the adjacent side. Tan j is positive in accord with our assumption that a greater k gives rise to a greater x.

Now suppose that k is increased from k_0 to k_1. We could *approximate* the corresponding rise in x from x_0 to x_1 by using what we know about tan j at k_0. Looking at the smallest of the three (similar) triangles,

$$\tan j = \frac{ED}{EC} = \frac{x_1 - x_0}{k_1 - k_0} \quad \text{approximately}$$

so that the corresponding increase in x is

$$x_1 - x_0 = \tan j \times (k_1 - k_0) \quad \text{approximately}$$

or simply

$$\Delta x = \tan j \times \Delta k \quad \text{approximately}$$

But we are not being as precise as we could be. Our approximation has it that x rises by ED when it really rises by only ED'. Our approximation overestimates the rise in x by DD' (the error). But we could talk about indefinitely small increases in k and the associated rise in x. For smaller and smaller Δk, the error DD' gets smaller and smaller and tan j becomes an increasingly better approximator. The *derivative* of the function is the *ratio* of Δx to Δk as Δk becomes indefinitely smaller (as $\Delta k \to 0$).

$$\frac{dx}{dk} = \lim_{\Delta k \to 0} \frac{\Delta x}{\Delta k}$$

and $\tan j = dx/dk$

It is convenient to denote the derivative of a function with a "prime." Thus

$$\frac{dx}{dk} \equiv f'(k)$$

Or simply

$$\frac{dx}{dk} \equiv f'$$

In the case of the production function, we specify that the first derivative is positive. The curve *slopes* upward in Figure 5.1a.

$$\frac{dx}{dk} \equiv f'(k) \equiv f' > 0 \tag{5.4}$$

We now introduce the concept of a *differential*. We saw before that we could *estimate* the increment in x (Δx) associated with an increment in k (Δk) if we knew the slope of the curve at the appropriate point. The slope was measured by tan j.

$$\Delta x = \tan j \times \Delta k \quad \text{approximately}$$

But now we have identified the slope of the curve (tan j) with the derivative of the function.

$$\Delta x = f'(k) \cdot \Delta k \quad \text{approximately}$$

It can be seen in Figure 5.1a that the approximation gets better and better if we allow Δk and the associated Δx to be ever-smaller increments. If we denote a small increment in k as dk, and a small increment in x and dx, then

$$dk \equiv \text{the } differential \text{ of } k$$

and

$$dx \equiv \text{the } differential \text{ of } x$$

The *differentials* are related to one another by the *derivative*:

$$dx = f'(k)\, dk \quad \text{approximately}$$

But the smaller is dk and the associated dx, the better the approximation.

The equation states that a (small) change (dk) in the capital-labor ratio (k) gives rise to a (small) change (dx) in the output-labor ratio (x), which is determined by the function $f'(k)$. We have not specified the function $f'(k)$, except to say that it is positive. Thus, a (small) change (dk) in the capital-labor ratio (k) gives rise to a (small) change (dx) in the output-labor ratio *in the same direction*.

Finally, we assume, as the third property of the function, that the *more* capital each laborer is already working with, the *less* his average product will rise when he is provided another unit of capital. That is, the slope of the average product-of-labor curve, while positive, is declining as k is increased. Algebraically, this means that the first derivative of the average product-of-labor curve, $f'(k)$, while positive, is declining as k rises. In symbols

$$\frac{d}{dk} f'(k) = f''(k) < 0 \tag{5.5}$$

or simply $f'' < 0$. The double prime is used to indicate the second derivative of the function, $f(k)$, or the slope of its first derivative, $f'(k)$. We assume that $f''(k)$ exists and is negative in the relevant range.

Other notations for the second derivative are sometimes used. Recalling that

$$f'(k) = \frac{d}{dk} \cdot \frac{X}{L} = \frac{d}{dk} x$$

it follows that

$$\frac{d}{dk} f'(k)$$

can be written

$$\frac{d}{dk} \cdot \frac{d}{dk} x$$

which is usually abbreviated to the equivalent expressions

$$\frac{d^2}{dk^2} x$$

or

$$\frac{d^2 x}{dk^2}$$

Thus, the following expressions are equivalent:

$$\frac{d}{dk} f'(k) = \frac{d^2 x}{dk^2} = f''(k) = f''$$

All refer to the second derivative of the function (the first derivative of the function's first derivative).

The first derivative of the production function is illustrated in Figure 5.1b. It is derived from the average product-of-labor function in Figure 5.1a. There, we observe that tan j (the derivative) is positive throughout the relevant range of the function. The average product of labor rises when more capital is added per unit of labor. Thus, when we draw a picture of the first derivative, $f'(k)$ in Figure 5.1b, we know that it must appear in the positive quadrant. But how should *it* slope?

Tan j (the derivative) is smaller for larger values of k. Since tan j is $f'(k)$, we know that $f'(k)$ must be smaller for larger values of k. Thus the slope $df'(k)/dk$ must be negative. For example, when k rises from k_0 by dk, $f'(k)$ falls from $f'(k_0)$ by $df'(k)$. Thus, $f''(k) < 0$. The greater the capital-labor ratio is, the less the average product of labor rises when an additional unit of capital is added per unit of labor. The $f'(k)$ function is drawn as a straight line for convenience. It could *curve* up or down, so long as its *slope* is everywhere negative.

To sum up, we assume that the production function

$$X = F(K, L) \tag{5.1}$$

is homogeneous of the first degree (has constant returns to scale), so that we can define a new function for the average product of labor:

$$\frac{X}{L} = f(k), \qquad k \equiv \frac{K}{L} \tag{5.2}$$

and one for the average product of capital:

$$\frac{X}{K} = \frac{f(k)}{k} \tag{5.3}$$

These we endow with the additional properties that

$$f' > 0 \tag{5.4}$$

and

$$f'' < 0 \tag{5.5}$$

It will be found later on that the constant returns to scale assumption will allow us to express all marginal as well as average products in terms of the capital-labor ratio alone. The restrictions on the algebraic sign of the first derivatives will ensure that the marginal products of labor and capital are always positive. The restriction on the algebraic sign of the second derivative will ensure that the marginal product of labor (capital) rises (falls) when the capital-labor ratio rises.

THE MARGINAL PRODUCTS OF CAPITAL AND LABOR

The marginal products of capital and labor are the first partial derivatives of the production function with respect to the two inputs. If we have reason to believe that competitive institutions dominate production and the distribution of income among resource owners, we can identify the marginal physical product of capital with the real rental or interest rate on capital, and the marginal physical product of labor with the real wage. In both cases, the factor reward is expressed in terms of the product that it produces. If

76 The Constant Returns to Scale Production Function

the product is taken to be net of capital depreciation, the real rental rate is a net rate. If the product is taken to be gross, the real rental rate is a gross rate.

For a centrally planned economy, the marginal physical products can be thought of as shadow rentals (prices). They show the addition to social product that would be produced if another unit of a resource were added. The shadow rental (price) is the marginal social "value" of the resource and has nothing to do with whether or how the resource is "paid."

The marginal physical product of a factor is defined as the change in total product when all other inputs are held constant. Consider our two-input production function,

$$x = f(k); \quad x \equiv \frac{X}{L}, \quad k \equiv \frac{K}{L}$$

or

$$X = L \cdot f\left(\frac{K}{L}\right)$$

The marginal product of capital is the change in total product when capital is increased and the labor input is held constant. That is, we want the *partial derivative* of output with respect to capital. We obtain the partial derivative by employing the usual rules of differentiation, but remembering to treat the other input as if it were a constant. To remind ourselves that we are taking a partial derivative, we use the "∂" instead of "d."

As it stands, the production function shows that output is equal to the *product* of two terms, L and $f(K/L) \equiv f(k)$. Since we want the partial derivative with respect to capital, we treat L as if it were a *constant*.

To differentiate, we begin by employing the *product rule* and then the rule for differentiating a constant.[1] First we use the product rule.

IN GENERAL

If

$$x = f(z) \cdot g(z)$$

then

$$\frac{dx}{dz} = f(z) \cdot \frac{d}{dz} g(z) + g(z) \frac{d}{dz} f(z)$$

or

$$\frac{dx}{dz} = f(z) \cdot g'(z) + g(z) \cdot f'(z)$$

---

[1] The derivation of differentiation rules is succinctly presented in Taro Yamane, *Mathematics for Economists*. (Englewood Cliffs: Prentice-Hall, 1968), Chap. 3. An alternative is R. D. G. Allen, *Mathematical Analysis for Economists* (London: Macmillan, 1960), Chaps. VI and VII.

SPECIFICALLY

If

$$X = L \cdot f(k)$$

then

$$\frac{\partial X}{\partial K} = L \cdot \frac{\partial}{\partial K} f(k) + f(k) \frac{\partial}{\partial K} L$$

The second term on the right-hand side calls for differentiating L with respect to K. We treat L as a constant, and the derivative of a constant is zero.

IN GENERAL

If

$$x = a, \quad a = a \text{ constant}$$

then

$$\frac{dx}{dz} = 0$$

where z is any variable whatever

SPECIFICALLY

If

$$L = L$$

then

$$\frac{\partial L}{\partial K} = 0$$

The second term on the right-hand side disappears, and we are left with

$$\frac{\partial X}{\partial K} = L \cdot \frac{\partial}{\partial K} f(k)$$

Now we are faced with having to take the partial derivative of a function $f(\ )$, whose *argument*, k, is itself a function of the variable of conern, K. It is as if we had

$$\frac{\partial}{\partial K} f\{g(K)\}$$

where

$$g(K) = k$$

The Constant Returns to Scale Production Function

We have to differentiate an expression that is a *function of a function*. In more general terms, the problem may be expressed like this: suppose x is a function of y.

$$x = f(y)$$

But, in addition, y is a function of z.

$$y = g(z)$$

We want to know how x varies when z varies. That is, we want to know how dx is related to dz.

$$x = f(y), \qquad y = g(z)$$

or

$$x = f\{g(z)\}$$

To find a solution, we begin by finding out how x varies with y.

$$\frac{dx}{dy} = f'(y)$$

In terms of differentials,

$$dx = f'(y)\, dy$$

This tells us that the variation in x is equal to the way $f(\ )$ varies with y, multiplied by the variation in y.

In the same way, we can find out how y varies with z.

$$\frac{dy}{dz} = g'(z)$$

In terms of differentials,

$$dy = g'(z)\, dz$$

This states that the variation in z is equal to the way $g(\ )$ varies with z, multiplied by the variation in z.

Now we can substitute the expression for dy into the expression for dx to obtain

$$dx = f'(y) \cdot g'(z)\, dz$$

The Marginal Products of Capital and Labor

This is the case of a function of just one other function. Clearly, the same techniques could be used to differentiate a function of a function of a function, and so on. For this reason, the rule is sometimes called the *chain rule*.

Let us apply the rule to a specific problem. Suppose that

$$x = y^3 \quad \text{and} \quad y = 1 + z^2$$

Then we have

IN GENERAL	SPECIFICALLY
$x = f(y)$	$x = y^3$
and	and
$y = g(z)$	$y = 1 + z^2$

Finding the differentials,

$dx = f'(y)\, dy$	$dx = 3y^2\, dy$
and	and
$dy = g'(z)\, dz$	$dy = 2z\, dz$

Substituting

$dx = f'(y) \cdot g'(z)\, dz$	$dx = 3y^2 \cdot 2z\, dz$
or	or
$\dfrac{dx}{dz} = f'(y) \cdot g'(z)$	$\dfrac{dx}{dz} = 6y^2 z$

Of course, one could have substituted $y = 1 + z^2$ into $x = y^3$ and gotten the same answer, but usually this is not the best strategy. Note that dx and dz are differentials, so the ratio dx/dz is simply a ratio of differentials. But from the practical point of view, the *ratio of differentials is a derivative*, *if the variables are functionally related*. In this problem, x and z are functionally related by $x = f\{g(z)\}$. Thus the *derivatives* are

$$\frac{dx}{dy} = f'(x) \cdot g'(z) \qquad \frac{dx}{dz} = 3y^2 \cdot 2z$$

The Constant Returns to Scale Production Function

Returning now to the marginal product of capital function, we can employ the chain rule (the function of a function rule) to evaluate

$$\frac{\partial}{\partial K} f(k)$$

IN GENERAL

$$x = f(y)$$

$$y = g(z)$$

SPECIFICALLY

$$f(k) = f(k)$$

$$k = \frac{1}{L} \cdot K$$

Using the chain rule,

$$\frac{dx}{dz} = f'(y) \cdot g'(z)$$

$$\frac{\partial f(k)}{\partial K} = f'(k) \cdot \frac{\partial}{\partial K} k$$

Remembering that L is regarded as a constant

$$\frac{\partial}{\partial K} k = \frac{\partial}{\partial K}\left(\frac{K}{L}\right) = \frac{1}{L} \frac{\partial K}{\partial K} = \frac{1}{L}$$

Thus

$$f'(k) \frac{\partial}{\partial K} k = f'(k) \cdot \frac{1}{L}$$

Recall that we had

$$\frac{\partial X}{\partial K} = L \cdot \frac{\partial}{\partial K} f(k)$$

Now we can write

$$\frac{\partial X}{\partial K} = L \cdot f'(k) \cdot \frac{1}{L}$$

$$\frac{\partial X}{\partial K} = f'(k) \tag{5.6}$$

Figures 5.1a and 5.1b can now be reinterpreted. They reappear here as Figures 5.2a and 5.2b. We now know that $\tan j = f'(k)$ in Figure 5.2a is the interest rate (r), the real rental rate on capital.

$$r = \tan j = \frac{\text{opposite side}}{k}$$

The Marginal Products of Capital and Labor   81

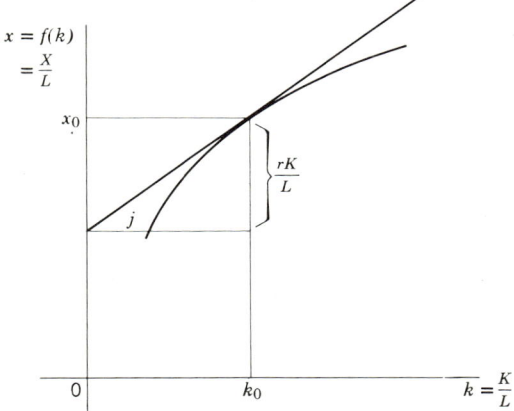

Figure 5.2a   The average product of labor and capital rental per worker.

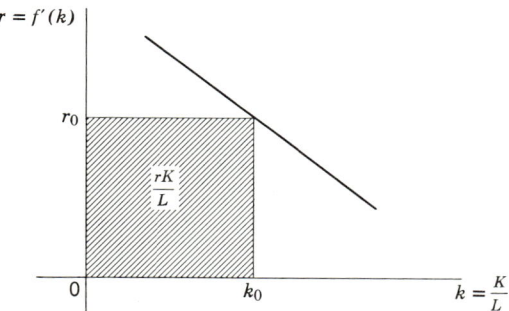

Figure 5.2b   The interest rate and capital rental per worker.

Solving for the opposite side of the triangle

$$\text{opposite side} = rk = \frac{rK}{L}$$

This line segment is labeled in the figure. It is the total return to capital in the economy, divided by the number of workers. If each worker owned an equal share of a competitive economy's capital stock, then rK divided by L would be each worker's "dividend and interest" income.

This magnitude also appears in Figure 5.2b. It is the rectangle inscribed under the $f'(k) = r$ function. For example, at k_0 the base of the rectangle is $0k_0$ and its altitude is $0r_0$. The shaded rectangle is $0k_0 \times 0r_0$ and equals rK/L.

82 The Constant Returns to Scale Production Function

Finding the marginal product of labor is more difficult than finding that of capital, but no new principles are involved. This time, we want to find how output changes when labor alone is varied. We want the partial derivative of the production function with respect to L. The rules of ordinary differentiation apply, but this time we must remember to treat K as a constant. Writing the production function as

$$X = L \cdot f(k)$$

output equals the product of L and $f(k)$. This time, L cannot be regarded as a constant, as it was before. The *product rule* must be employed again.

IN GENERAL

If

$$x = f(z) \cdot g(z)$$

then

$$\frac{dx}{dz} = f(z) \cdot \frac{d}{dz} g(z) + g(z) \cdot \frac{d}{dz} g(z)$$

or

$$\frac{dx}{dz} = f(z) \cdot g'(z) + g(z) f'(z)$$

SPECIFICALLY

If

$$x = L \cdot f(k)$$

then

$$\frac{\partial X}{\partial L} = L \cdot \frac{\partial}{\partial L} f(k) + f(k) \frac{\partial}{\partial L} L$$

Now $\partial/\partial L [f(k)]$ must be evaluated. The function-of-a-function rule must be employed, for we see that $k = K/L$ is a function of L. Proceeding as before:

$$\frac{\partial}{\partial L} f(k) = f'(k) \cdot \frac{\partial k}{\partial L}$$

$$\frac{\partial}{\partial L} f(k) = f'(k) \cdot \frac{\partial}{\partial L} \frac{K}{L}$$

Since we are taking the partial derivative with respect to L, K is treated as a constant. Thus

$$\frac{\partial}{\partial L} \cdot \frac{K}{L} = K \cdot \frac{\partial}{\partial L} \cdot \frac{1}{L}$$

which might as well be written

$$\frac{\partial}{\partial L} \frac{K}{L} = K \cdot \frac{d}{dL} \frac{1}{L}$$

since it is not necessary to indicate partial differentiation when there is only one variable. This variable appears in the denominator, so we apply the rule for differentiating a quotient.

IN GENERAL

If

$$x = \frac{f(z)}{g(z)}$$

then

$$\frac{dx}{dz} = \frac{g(z) \cdot d/dz[f(z)] - f(z) \cdot d/dz[g(z)]}{[g(z)]^2}$$

or

$$\frac{dx}{dz} = \frac{g(z) \cdot f'(z) - f(z)g'(z)}{[g(z)]^2}$$

SPECIFICALLY

If we want to differentiate $1/L$ with respect to L, then

$$\frac{d}{dL}\left(\frac{1}{L}\right) = \frac{L \cdot d/dL \cdot 1 - 1 \cdot d/dL(L)}{L^2}$$

or

$$\frac{d}{dL}\left(\frac{1}{L}\right) = -\frac{1}{L^2}$$

Substituting this back again,

$$\frac{\partial}{\partial L} f(k) = -f'(k) \cdot \frac{K}{L^2}$$

Recalling that

$$\frac{\partial X}{\partial L} = L \cdot \frac{\partial}{\partial L} f(k) + f(k)$$

we have by a second substitution,

$$\frac{\partial X}{\partial L} = -L \cdot f'(k) \cdot \frac{K}{L^2} + f(k)$$

Cancelling out the L, rearranging terms, and letting $k = K/L$,

$$\frac{\partial X}{\partial L} = f(k) - k \cdot f'(k)$$

For convenience, identify the marginal product of labor with the real wage (w).

$$w = f(k) - k \cdot f'(k) \tag{5.7}$$

Note that, as in the case of the interest rate, the wage depends on nothing but the capital-labor ratio.

A very important statement can now be made. *With the factors of production "paid" according to their marginal products, the total product is precisely exhausted by factor "payments."*

To prove this, recall that we have found for the constant returns to scale production function,

$$X = L \cdot f(k), \qquad k \equiv \frac{K}{L}$$

that

$$\frac{\partial X}{\partial K} = f'(k)$$

and

$$\frac{\partial X}{\partial L} = f(k) - k \cdot f'(k)$$

If we substitute $f'(k) = \partial X/\partial K$ into the last equation, we have

$$\frac{\partial X}{\partial L} = f(k) - k \cdot \frac{\partial X}{\partial K}$$

or
$$f(k) = \frac{\partial X}{\partial L} + k\frac{\partial X}{\partial K}$$

or
$$\frac{X}{L} = \frac{\partial X}{\partial L} + \frac{K}{L} \cdot \frac{\partial X}{\partial K}$$

or
$$X = \frac{\partial X}{\partial L} \cdot L + \frac{\partial X}{\partial K} \cdot K$$

Note that this result holds true for any values of K and L whatever. The statement is an *identity*, and it follows directly from the constant returns to scale assumption.[2]

If factors are paid their marginal products, the wage equals $\partial X/\partial L$ and the interest rate equals $\partial X/\partial K$.

$$X = wL + rK \tag{5.8}$$

Factor payments exhaust the product.[3] This property is illustrated in Figures 5.3a and 5.3b. Output per worker must be accounted for by rental payments per worker or wages.

$$\frac{X}{L} = w + \frac{rK}{L}$$

We already know that rental payments per worker (rK/L) are indicated by the upper segment of the line rising from k_0 in Figure 5.3a. The lower segment of the line must be wages (w). It could be shown by construction that w rises when k rises, but it is more instructive to prove this in Figure 5.3b.

The most elementary (and fundamental) principle of the integral calculus is that integration reverses the process of differentiation. Thus if

$$y = f(x)$$

---

[2] See R. D. G. Allen, *Mathematical Analysis for Economists* (London: Macmillan, 1960), pp. 317–320. The result that $X = (\partial X/\partial L) \cdot L + (\partial X/\partial K) \cdot K$ is known as *Euler's Theorem*.

[3] There are no "excess profits" in competitive equilibrium, so the factors of production are paid their marginal products. Constant returns to scale for the economy as a whole does not mean that *each firm* produces with constant returns to scale. It is more reasonable to suppose that individual firms encounter diminishing returns to scale at some point and operate at lowest average cost. The economy expands in scale through equal proportion increases in K, L, *and firms*.

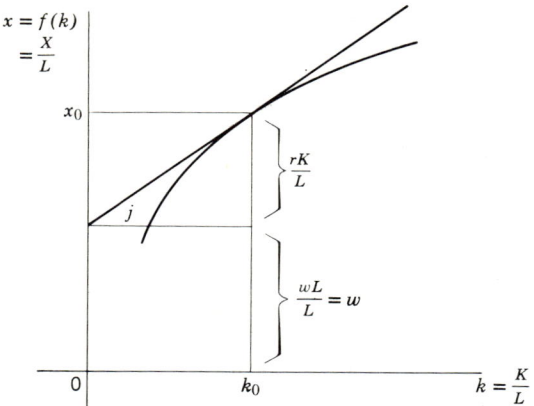

Figure 5.3a The average product of labor, capital rental, and wages per worker.

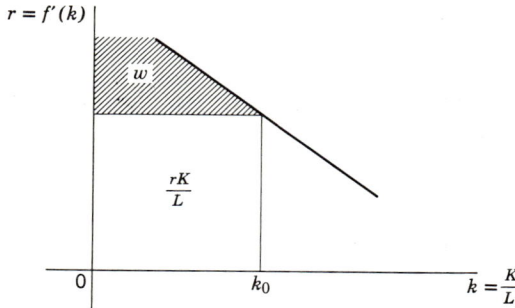

Figure 5.3b The interest rate, capital rental, and wages per worker.

then

$$dy = f'(x)\, dx$$

and

$$\int dy = \int f'(x)\, dx$$

or

$$y = f(x) + \text{constant of integration}$$

In Figure 5.3b, the rate of interest, r, is drawn as a function of the capital-labor ratio. By integration, we can prove that the *area* under the curve up to, say, k_0 is the average product of labor corresponding to, say, k_0. If

$$\frac{X}{L} = f(k)$$

then

$$d\frac{X}{L} = f'(k)\,dk$$

and

$$\int d\frac{X}{L} = \int f'(k)\,dk$$

or

$$\frac{X}{L} = \int f'(k)\,dk + \text{constant of integration}$$

or

$$\frac{X}{L} = \int r\,dk + \text{constant of integration}$$

The constant of integration must be evaluated. Let us assume that capital is *indispensable* in production. If K is zero, X is zero. Then if $k = K/L$ is zero, X/L is zero. Also, if k is zero, the "summing up" indicated by $\int r\,dk$ is zero as well. Thus the Constant of Integration is zero and

$$\frac{X}{L} = \int r\,dk$$

It was discovered before that the *rectangle* inscribed under the curve in Figure 5.3b corresponds to rental payments per worker. Now we know that the *entire area* under the curve is total product per worker. Consequently the (shaded) *triangle* lying above the inscribed rectangle must be wages.

So long as the condition holds that $f''(k)$ is negative, the $f'(k)$ curve must slope downward, and the triangle representing wages must increase in area as k rises. Wages, the marginal product of labor, must be a positive function of the capital-labor ratio. The greater the amount of capital employed with each worker, the greater will be the increase in total product when another unit of labor is added.

Now we can combine the functions that relate wages and the interest rate to the capital-labor ratio in one diagram, Figure 5.4. The wage increases and the interest rate decreases as the capital-labor ratio rises. The next step is

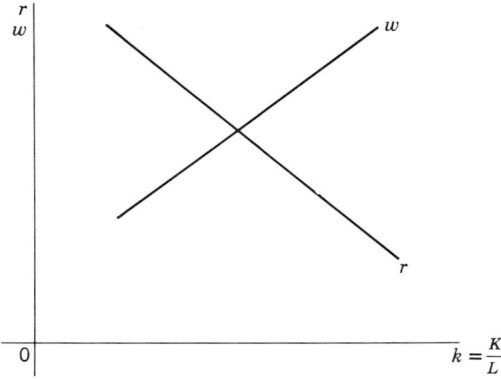

Figure 5.4 The interest rate and wages.

to derive expressions for *how much* these variables change in response to a change in capital per worker.

THE ELASTICITIES OF THE WAGE AND THE INTEREST RATE WITH RESPECT TO THE CAPITAL-LABOR RATIO

To find out how the interest rate changes in response to a change in the capital-labor ratio, we need only differentiate

$$r = f'(k) \tag{5.6}$$

with respect to k.

$$\frac{dr}{dk} = f''(k) \tag{5.9}$$

Recall we had assumed that $f''(k)$ is negative.

The variation of the wage rate when the capital-labor ratio varies is found by differentiating

$$w = f(k) - k \cdot f'(k)$$

with respect to k.

$$\frac{dw}{dk} = f'(k) - k \cdot f''(k) - f'(k)$$

The first and last terms on the right hand side cancel, so that

$$\frac{dw}{dk} = -k \cdot f''(k) \tag{5.10}$$

This confirms that the wage is an increasing function of the capital-labor ratio, since $f''(k)$ is assumed to be negative.

It is convenient to express these derivatives as elasticities, so that they show *proportional* rather than *absolute* changes. For example, the slope of the interest rate curve is dr/dk, a ratio of absolute changes. The elasticity of the curve at any point is the slope expressed in proportional terms. The proportional change in k is dk/k and the proportional change in r is dr/r.

Define the elasticity (u) of the interest rate (r) with respect to the capital-labor ratio (k) as the ratio of the proportional changes.

$$u \equiv -\frac{dr/r}{dk/k} = -\frac{dr}{dk} \cdot \frac{k}{r}$$

Elasticities are positive by convention, so we insert the negative sign because the slope is negative.

We know from (5.6) that dr/dk is $f''(k)$. Therefore

$$u \equiv \text{THE ELASTICITY OF THE INTEREST RATE WITH RESPECT TO THE CAPITAL-LABOR RATIO}$$

and

$$u = -f''(k) \cdot \frac{k}{r}$$

which is positive, since $f''(k)$ is negative by assumption. Thus

$$\frac{dr}{r} = -u \cdot \frac{dk}{k}, \qquad u = -f''(k) \cdot \frac{k}{r} \tag{5.11}$$

The same procedure can be used to convert (5.10) to show a proportional relationship.

$$\frac{dw}{w} \cdot \frac{k}{dk} = -k \cdot f''(k) \cdot \frac{k}{w}$$

The Constant Returns to Scale Production Function

But (5.11) shows that $f''(k) \cdot k$ equals (minus) $u \cdot r$. Thus

$$\frac{dw}{w} \cdot \frac{k}{dk} = k \cdot u \cdot \frac{r}{w}$$

$$= u \cdot \frac{rK}{wL}$$

or

$$\frac{dw}{w} = u \cdot \frac{rK}{wL} \cdot \frac{dk}{k}$$

It is convenient to define:

$$a \equiv \frac{w}{X/L} \equiv \frac{wL}{X} \equiv \begin{array}{c}\text{THE RATIO OF THE} \\ \text{MARGINAL TO THE} \\ \text{AVERAGE PRODUCT} \\ \text{OF LABOR}\end{array} \equiv \begin{array}{c}\text{THE PROPORTION} \\ \text{OF OUTPUT} \\ \text{IMPUTED TO} \\ \text{LABOR}\end{array}$$

and, therefore,

$$1 - a \equiv \frac{r}{X/K} \equiv \frac{rK}{X} \equiv \begin{array}{c}\text{THE RATIO OF THE} \\ \text{MARGINAL TO THE} \\ \text{AVERAGE PRODUCT} \\ \text{OF CAPITAL}\end{array} \equiv \begin{array}{c}\text{THE PROPORTION} \\ \text{OF OUTPUT} \\ \text{IMPUTED TO} \\ \text{CAPITAL}\end{array}$$

The two proportions must total one because of assumed constant returns to scale in production.[4] Now

$$\frac{rK}{wL} = \frac{1-a}{a}$$

so that

$$\frac{dw}{w} = u \cdot \frac{1-a}{a} \cdot \frac{dk}{k}$$

The expression $u \cdot (1-a)/a$ links a proportional change in k to a proportional change in the wage. Hence, if we define

$$v \equiv \begin{array}{c}\text{THE ELASTICITY OF THE} \\ \text{WAGE WITH RESPECT TO} \\ \text{THE CAPITAL-LABOR RATIO}\end{array}$$

---

[4] It was shown above that $X = wL + rK$. Dividing by X, $1 = wL/X + rK/X$. If $a \equiv wL/X$, $rK/L \equiv 1 - a$.

then

$$v \equiv u \cdot \frac{1-a}{a} = -k \cdot f''(k) \cdot \frac{k}{w}$$

which is positive, since $f''(k)$ is negative by assumption. Thus

$$\frac{dw}{w} = v \cdot \frac{dk}{k}, \qquad v \equiv -k \cdot f''(k) \cdot \frac{k}{w} \qquad (5.12)$$

Equations 5.11 and 5.12 link proportional changes in k to proportional changes in r and w respectively. If (5.11) is divided by (5.12),

$$\frac{dr}{r} \equiv -\frac{u}{v} \cdot \frac{dw}{w}$$

But u and v are related to one another by the ratio of proportions of output imputed to the two factors. From above,

$$\frac{u}{v} \equiv \frac{a}{1-a} \qquad (5.13)$$

Substituting

$$\frac{dr}{r} \equiv -\frac{a}{1-a} \cdot \frac{dw}{w} \quad {}^5 \qquad (5.14)$$

If we know the ratio of distributive shares based on marginal productivity in an economy, we know how wages would change relative to interest rates if there were a change in the capital-labor ratio.

Suppose we observe an actual economy in which wages and salaries account for two thirds of national income, and there is reason to believe that the assumption about the production function and income distribution correspond somewhat with reality. Then

$$\frac{dr}{r} = -2 \cdot \frac{dw}{w}$$

A rise in the capital-labor ratio would cause the interest rate to fall, in proportion, about twice as much relative to the proportionate rise in the wage. For example, the interest rate might fall 4 percent and the wage rise 2 percent.

[5] This is the elasticity of what Samuelson has called the "factor-price frontier." See P. A. Samuelson, "Parable and Realism in Capital Theory: The Surrogate Production Function," *Review of Economic Studies* (June 1962).

THE ELASTICITY OF SUBSTITUTION AND THE ELASTICITY OF FACTOR REWARDS

So far, we have simply *defined* the elasticities of the interest rate and the wage, with respect to the capital-labor ratio, as u and v respectively. It is revealing to think of u and v in terms of the *elasticity of substitution* between capital and labor in production. This elasticity is a measure of the ease with which capital and labor can be substituted for one another.

Suppose that an economy experiences capital deepening (an increase in capital relative to labor). If substitution is comparatively easy (the elasticity of substitution is comparatively high), then (competitive) firms can be induced to absorb the increased capital (relative to labor) by a comparatively small rise in wages and fall in the interest rate. On the other hand, if substitution is comparatively difficult (the elasticity of substitution is comparatively low), then (competitive) firms will absorb the increased capital (relative to labor) only after they have bid down the interest rate and bid up wages by comparatively greater amounts.

More precisely, the elasticity of substitution is defined as

$$\sigma \equiv \frac{dk/k}{d(w/r) \cdot r/w}; \quad k \equiv \frac{K}{L}, \quad w = \frac{\partial X}{\partial L}, \quad r = \frac{\partial X}{\partial K} \quad (5.15)$$

or

$$\sigma \equiv \frac{a}{1-a} \cdot \frac{dk}{d(w/r)}$$

It relates the proportional change in the ratio of the wage to the interest rate, to the proportional change in the capital-labor ratio. Recall from Chapter Two that for any variable, x,

$$d \log x = \frac{dx}{x}$$

Thus, another way to write the elasticity of substitution is

$$\sigma \equiv \frac{d \log k}{d \log (w/r)} \quad (5.15a)$$

This relation is illustrated in Figure 5.5 using a double-log scale. The natural logarithm of the capital-labor ratio is plotted on the vertical axis, with the natural logarithm of the wage-interest rate ratio plotted on the horizontal axis. According to (5.15a), the *slope* of the function relating log k and log w/r is the elasticity of substitution. The possible values of σ are ≥ 0 and $\leq \infty$,

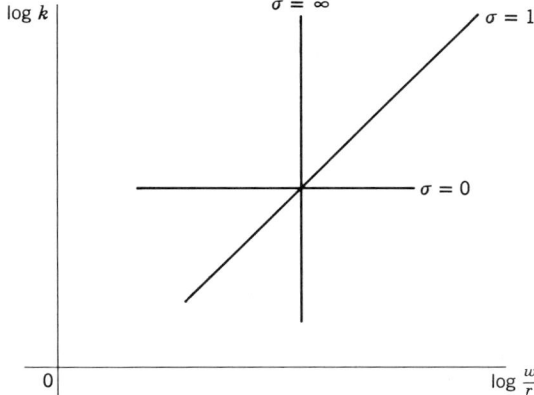

Figure 5.5 The elasticity of substitution.

and it is not generally constant. If no substitution is possible ($\sigma = 0$), production must occur with fixed proportions, and w/r is undefined. If the inputs are perfect substitutes ($\sigma = \infty$), the wage-interest rate ratio is the same for all capital-labor ratios. For values of the elasticity of substitution greater than zero and less than infinity, a finite variation in w/r is associated with some finite variation in k. The *degree* of variation is given by the elasticity of substitution.

By plotting $\log k$ on the vertical axis, the inference is made that k is the dependent variable, and that variations in w/r *cause* variations in k. Algebraically

$$\frac{dk}{k} \equiv \sigma \cdot d\left(\frac{w}{r}\right) \cdot \frac{r}{w}$$

This is an appropriate notion for the case of the individual firm that responds to a change in the relative price of inputs by hiring relatively more of the cheaper input. The larger the elasticity of substitution is, the more capital deepening will occur in response to a rise in wages relative to the interest rate as the firm seeks to maximize profits.

On the other hand, if we write

$$d\left(\frac{w}{r}\right) \cdot \frac{r}{w} \equiv \frac{1}{\sigma} \cdot \frac{dk}{k}$$

the inference is that the wage-interest rate ratio responds to a change in the capital-labor ratio. This is the more appropriate concept for a closed economy, taken as a whole, where the capital-labor ratio is given by the country's

94   The Constant Returns to Scale Production Function

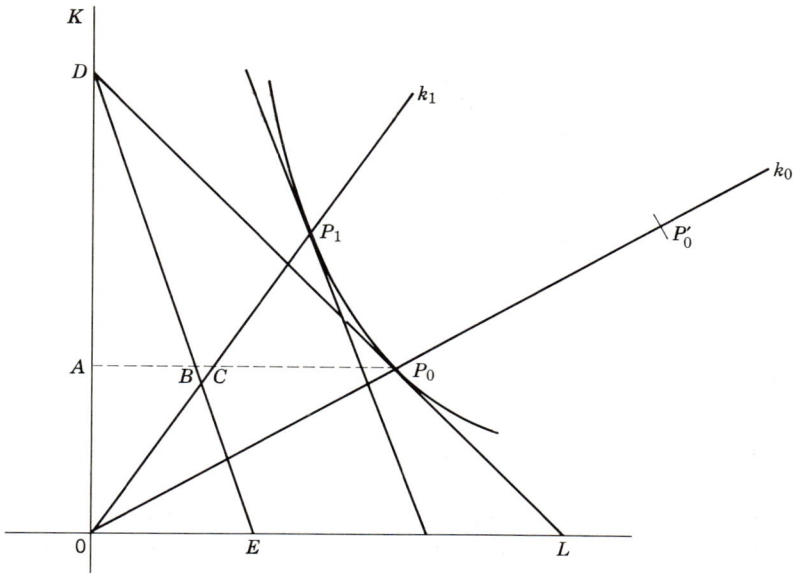

Figure 5.6   The unit isoquant and the elasticity of substitution.

resource base at a point in time. The ratio of wages to the interest rate then adjusts to the resource endowment. The greater the elasticity of substitution is, the less wages will rise relative to the interest rate as a consequence of capital deepening.

The elasticity of substitution is illustrated again in Figure 5.6, which portrays the production function by means of the familiar isoquant map. Only one isoquant is shown, but only one is necessary. Since we are concerned with a constant returns to scale-production function, it is easy to show that everything we wish to know about the entire production surface can be represented by a single isoquant. Recall that the marginal products of the two inputs depend only upon the capital-labor ratio and not at all upon the scale of production. Thus, the ratio of wages to the interest rate depends only on the capital-labor ratio. Dividing (5.7) by (5.6),

$$\frac{w}{r} = \frac{f(k)}{f'(k)} - k$$

This is the *marginal rate of substitution* in production, which is the slope of the isoquant. Note that as the capital-labor ratio rises from k_0 to k_1, the slope of the isoquant becomes greater—wages rise relative to the interest rate.

The Elasticity of Substitution and the Elasticity of Factor Rewards

A given capital-labor ratio is denoted by a ray out of the origin, like $0k_0$. Let the *point* P_0 lie on the *ray* $0k_0$, corresponding to a capital-labor ratio of k_0. The *slope* of the isoquant at that point is given by (5.15).

$$\left(\frac{w}{r}\right)_0 = \frac{f(k_0)}{f'(k_0)} - k_0$$

Now we know everything about the isoquant at the point P_0 except the quantity of output to which it corresponds. Since the isoquant was drawn arbitrarily in the first place, let us arbitrarily say that P_0 corresponds to a single unit of output. Now the illustrated isoquant can be called the *unit isoquant*.

The next step is to show that we now have sufficient information to move to any other point on the isoquant map and specify it completely. With some loss of generality to the argument, suppose that both inputs were doubled. The new production point would then be P_0' on the ray k_0 at a distance from the origin $0P_0'$, precisely twice the original distance $0P_0$. Since the capital-labor ratio has not changed, we know that the slope of the new isoquant must be precisely the same at P_0' as the slope of the old isoquant at P_0. We also know, from the given constant returns to scale, that P_0' must correspond to precisely two units of output. More generally, *any proportional change in inputs will move the production point the same proportional distance along a ray to an isoquant corresponding to the same proportional change in output with no change in the ratio of wages to the interest rate.*

It follows that we could perform the same move to another production point in the same way, starting from any other position on the unit isoquant. Thus, all statements made about the elasticity of substitution along the unit isoquant apply precisely to any other isoquant (that is, to the production surface as a whole).

Suppose capital deepening were to occur, increasing the capital-labor ratio (k) in Figure 5.6 from k_0 to k_1.[6] Holding output constant, the production point moves from P_0 to P_1. There is a concomitant rise in the ratio of wages to the interest rate (w/r), as indicated by the increase in the slope of the isoquant. The elasticity of substitution defines, in proportional terms, the change in (w/r) associated with the change in k.

In the figure, the absolute change in k is measured by P_0C, and the proportional change is P_0C/P_0A. The change in w/r is measured with the aid of the line DBE, which is drawn parallel to the line tangent to the isoquant at P_1. Using this line, the absolute change in (w/r) is seen to be P_0B, and the

---

[6] The following geometrical treatment is adapted from R. W. Jones, "'Neutral' Technological Change and the Isoquant Map," *American Economic Review* (September 1965).

proportional change is P_0B/AP_0. Thus

$$\sigma = \frac{P_0C/P_0A}{P_0B/P_0A} = \frac{P_0C}{P_0B}$$

In this case, the elasticity of substitution is less than one.

It is clear from the geometry in Figure 5.6 that the "flatter" is the isoquant from P_0 to P_1, the less will be P_0B relative to P_0C (the greater will be the elasticity of substitution).

As limiting cases, the unit isoquant of a production function having an elasticity of substitution equal to infinity would be perfectly "flat," having no curvature whatever. If the elasticity of substitution were zero, the unit isoquant would be "L-shaped," with its corner corresponding to the technologically invariant k.

The elasticity of substitution can be defined in terms of the elasticities of the interest rate (u) and the wage (v) with respect to the capital-labor ratio. Rewrite (5.15) as

$$\frac{1}{\sigma} \equiv \frac{d(w/r) \cdot r/w}{dk/k}$$

Note that the numerator is a proportional change in the ratio w/r. This is equivalent to the difference between the proportional change in w and the proportional change in r.

Consider the ratio of any two numbers, x and y. We know from above that the first derivative of a natural logarithm is the proportional change. Thus

$$d \log\left(\frac{x}{y}\right) = d\left(\frac{x}{y}\right) \cdot \frac{y}{x}$$

But

$$\log\left(\frac{x}{y}\right) = \log x - \log y$$

so that

$$d \log\left(\frac{x}{y}\right) = d \log x - d \log y$$

$$d \log\left(\frac{x}{y}\right) = \frac{dx}{x} - \frac{dy}{y}$$

The Elasticity of Substitution and the Elasticity of Factor Rewards

Therefore

$$d\left(\frac{x}{y}\right) \cdot \frac{y}{x} = \frac{dx}{x} - \frac{dy}{y}$$

and for the wage-interest rate ratio

$$d\left(\frac{w}{r}\right) \cdot \frac{r}{w} = \frac{dw}{w} - \frac{dr}{r}$$

Thus

$$\frac{1}{\sigma} \equiv \frac{dw}{w} \cdot \frac{k}{dk} - \frac{dr}{r} \cdot \frac{k}{dk}$$

The terms on the right-hand side are nothing more than the elasticities of the wage and the interest rate with respect to the capital-labor ratio as defined in Equations 5.12 and 5.11. Substituting

$$\frac{1}{\sigma} = v + u$$

or

$$\sigma = \frac{1}{u + v} \tag{5.17}$$

The elasticities, u and v, can be thought of as measures of *diminishing marginal returns to proportions*. The greater are these values, the greater is the power of diminishing returns. The greater are u and v, the greater is their sum, and the less is the elasticity of substitution.

Now we can use the relation

$$\frac{u}{v} = \frac{a}{1 - a} \tag{5.13}$$

along with (5.17), to obtain more revealing expressions for u and v. Solving (5.13) for u, and then for v, and substituting into (5.17):

$$u = \frac{a}{\sigma} \tag{5.18}$$

and

$$v = \frac{1 - a}{\sigma} \tag{5.19}$$

98 The Constant Returns to Scale Production Function

These results can be substituted back into (5.11) and (5.12) to obtain

$$\frac{dr}{r} = -\frac{a}{\sigma} \cdot \frac{dk}{k} \tag{5.20}$$

and

$$\frac{dw}{w} = \frac{1-a}{\sigma} \cdot \frac{dk}{k} \tag{5.21}$$

These equations show the consequences of changes in input proportions for changes in factor rewards in terms of (1) the elasticity of substitution and (2) the proportions of output imputed to labor and capital.

Suppose we observe an actual economy in which (1) wages and salaries account for two thirds of national income, (2) the elasticity of substitution is known to be two thirds, and (3) the usual assumptions about the production function and income distribution correspond somewhat to reality. Suppose further that (4) capital deepening occurs so that the capital-labor ratio rises by 0.05 or 5 percent. Then

$$\frac{dr}{r} = -\frac{2/3}{2/3}(0.05) = -0.05 = -5\%$$

$$\frac{dw}{w} = \frac{1/3}{2/3}(0.05) = 0.025 = 2.5\%$$

THE AVERAGE PRODUCTS OF LABOR AND CAPITAL

In this section we shall employ two different, but equivalent, procedures to show how the average products of the inputs change in response to changes in the capital-labor ratio. The first method makes use of the results and techniques already at our disposal. The second introduces a new rule of differentiation.

The average product of labor is

$$\frac{X}{L} = f(k) \tag{5.2}$$

Differentiating with respect to k,

$$d\frac{X}{L} = f'(k)\, dk$$

The Average Products of Labor and Capital

From (5.6), we know that $f'(k) = r$

$$d\frac{X}{L} = r \cdot dk$$

To express the variations in proportional terms, multiply the equation by L/X and divide by k.

$$d\left(\frac{X}{L}\right)\frac{L}{X} = r \cdot \frac{L}{X} \cdot k \cdot \frac{dk}{k}$$

or

$$d\left(\frac{X}{L}\right)\frac{L}{X} = \frac{rK}{X} \cdot \frac{dk}{k}$$

or

$$d\left(\frac{X}{L}\right)\frac{L}{X} = (1-a)\frac{dk}{k} \tag{5.22}$$

The elasticity of the average product-of-labor curve is the proportion of output imputed to capital.

The average product of capital is

$$\frac{X}{K} = \frac{f(k)}{k} \tag{5.3}$$

Differentiating with respect to k,

$$d\frac{X}{K} = \frac{1}{k^2}[k \cdot f'(k)\,dk - f(k)\,dk],$$

or

$$d\frac{X}{K} = -\frac{1}{k^2}[f(k) - k \cdot f'(k)]\,dk$$

From (5.7) we know that the expression in square brackets is equal to w. Thus

$$d\frac{X}{K} = -\frac{w}{k} \cdot \frac{dk}{k}$$

The Constant Returns to Scale Production Function

To express the variations in proportional terms, multiply the equation by K/X.

$$d\left(\frac{X}{K}\right) \cdot \frac{K}{X} = -\frac{w}{k} \cdot \frac{K}{X} \cdot \frac{dk}{k}$$

or

$$d\left(\frac{X}{K}\right) \cdot \frac{K}{X} = -\frac{wL}{X} \cdot \frac{dk}{k}$$

or

$$d\left(\frac{X}{K}\right) \cdot \frac{K}{X} = -a \cdot \frac{dk}{k} \tag{5.23}$$

The elasticity of the average product-of-capital curve is the proportion of output imputed to labor.

These same results can be derived more directly by returning to the production function itself, with the aid of the following rule of differentiation. Let

$$x = f(y, z)$$

where $f(\ )$ is any function whatever. Then

$$dx = \frac{\partial x}{\partial y} \cdot dy + \frac{\partial x}{\partial z} \cdot dz$$

The variation in x can be attributed to

plus
(1) the way x varies when y alone varies ($\partial x/\partial y$), multiplied by the variation in y (dy)

(2) the way x varies when z alone varies ($\partial x/\partial z$), multiplied by the variation in z (dz)

Notice that, as a special case

$$dx = \frac{\partial x}{\partial y} \cdot dy$$

or

$$\frac{dx}{dy} = \frac{\partial x}{\partial y}$$

when there is no variation in z.

The Average Products of Labor and Capital

In terms of the production function,

$$X = f(K, L)$$
$$dX = \frac{\partial X}{\partial L} \cdot dK + \frac{\partial X}{\partial L} \cdot dL \qquad (5.1)$$

Recalling that $\partial X/\partial K = r$ and $\partial X/\partial L = w$,

$$dX = r \cdot dK + w \cdot dL \qquad (5.24)$$

The variation in X is attributed to

(1) the marginal product of capital multiplied by the variation in capital

plus

(2) the marginal product of labor multiplied by the variation in labor

Expressing (5.24) in terms of proportional change,

$$\frac{dX}{X} = \frac{rK}{X} \cdot \frac{dK}{K} + \frac{wL}{X} \cdot \frac{dL}{L}$$

or

$$\frac{dX}{X} = (1-a) \cdot \frac{dK}{K} + a \cdot \frac{dL}{L} \qquad (5.25)$$

The proportional change in X is attributed to the weighted average of the proportional change in the two inputs. The weights are the proportions of output imputed to the two inputs.

To find the proportional change in the average products of labor and capital, subtract the proportional changes of labor and then capital from (5.25).

$$\frac{dX}{X} - \frac{dL}{L} = (1-a)\left(\frac{dK}{K} - \frac{dL}{L}\right)$$

$$\frac{dX}{X} - \frac{dK}{K} = -a\left(\frac{dK}{K} - \frac{dL}{L}\right)$$

We have already seen that, in general,

$$d\left(\frac{x}{y}\right) \cdot \frac{y}{x} = \frac{dx}{x} - \frac{dy}{y}$$

102 The Constant Returns to Scale Production Function

Thus, recalling that $k = K/L$,

$$d\left(\frac{X}{L}\right)\frac{L}{X} = (1 - a)\frac{dk}{k} \qquad (5.22)$$

and

$$d\left(\frac{X}{K}\right)\frac{K}{X} = -a\frac{dk}{k} \qquad (5.23)$$

These are precisely the same results we obtained before.

THE SHARES OF OUTPUT IMPUTED TO LABOR AND CAPITAL

The shares imputed to capital $(1 - a)$ and to labor (a) were defined as

$$1 - a \equiv \frac{rK}{X} \quad \text{and} \quad a \equiv \frac{wL}{X}$$

Put another way, the shares are the marginal products (r and w) divided by the average products (X/K and X/L).

$$1 - a \equiv \frac{r}{X/K} \quad \text{and} \quad a \equiv \frac{w}{X/L}$$

The shares are functions of the capital-labor ratio alone, since the marginal and average products are functions of the capital-labor ratio alone. Substituting (5.6) for r, (5.3) for X/K, (5.7) for w, and (5.2) for X/L, we have

$$1 - a = \frac{k \cdot f'(k)}{f(k)} \qquad (5.26)$$

and

$$a = 1 - \frac{k \cdot f'(k)}{f(k)} \qquad (5.27)$$

One way to find how $1 - a$ and a vary with respect to variations in k would be to differentiate these expressions. Fortunately, there is an easier way. Differentiating the definitions for $1 - a$ and a, we have

$$\frac{d(1 - a)}{1 - a} = \frac{dr}{r} - d\left(\frac{X}{K}\right) \cdot \frac{K}{X} \quad \text{and} \quad \frac{da}{a} = \frac{dw}{w} - d\left(\frac{X}{L}\right) \cdot \frac{L}{X}$$

Since we already have expressions for proportional variations in the average and marginal products in terms of proportional variations in the capital-labor ratio, it should be easy to find the proportional variation in the shares arising out of proportional variations in the capital-labor ratio. Substitute (5.20) and (5.21) for marginal products and (5.22) and (5.23) for average products,

$$\frac{d(1-a)}{1-a} = -\frac{a}{\sigma} \cdot \frac{dk}{k} + a \cdot \frac{dk}{k}$$

$$\frac{da}{a} = \frac{1-a}{\sigma} \cdot \frac{dk}{k} - (1-a) \cdot \frac{dk}{k}$$

or

$$\frac{d(1-a)}{1-a} = -\frac{1-\sigma}{\sigma} \cdot a \cdot \frac{dk}{k} \tag{5.28}$$

$$\frac{da}{a} = \frac{1-\sigma}{\sigma} \cdot (1-a) \cdot \frac{dk}{k} \tag{5.29}$$

Only if σ is precisely equal to one will a change in the capital-labor ratio leave the shares imputed to the two inputs unaffected. The Cobb-Douglas production function ($X = AK^{1-a}L^a$) is the *only* function for which this is true. More generally, capital deepening will lower (raise) the share of labor if σ exceeds (falls short of) one. If σ exceeds one, a rise in capital relative to labor lowers the interest rate (and raises wages), but proportionately lowers the average product of capital even more. As a consequence, the share in capital rises.

A RECAPITULATION

The constant returns to scale assumption implies that (1) the average products of each factor, (2) the marginal products of each factor, and (3) the proportions of output imputed to each factor can be expressed as *functions* of the capital-labor ratio alone. In addition, the marginal and average products, and the shares, have derivatives with respect to the capital-labor ratio. We obtain *elasticities* when these derivatives are expressed in terms of proportional variation.

These functions and elasticities have been derived in the last several pages and they are set out here in Table 5.1 for easy reference. One converts the tabular entries for the functions and elasticities as follows.

1. *Functions.* For example,

$$r = f'(k) \tag{5.6}$$

TABLE 5.1

Average Products, Marginal Products, and Shares as Functions of the Capital-Labor Ratio; Elasticities with Respect to the Capital-Labor Ratio

Variable	Symbol	As a Function of $k \equiv \frac{K}{L}$		Elasticity with Respect to $k \equiv \frac{K}{L}$	
Average product of capital	$\frac{X}{K}$	$\frac{f(k)}{k}$	(5.3)	$-a$	(5.23)
Average product of labor	$\frac{X}{L} \equiv x$	$f(k)$	(5.2)	$1 - a$	(5.22)
Marginal product of capital	$r \equiv \frac{\partial X}{\partial K}$	$f'(k)$	(5.6)	$-\frac{a}{\sigma}$	(5.20)
Marginal product of labor	$w \equiv \frac{\partial X}{\partial L}$	$f(k) - k \cdot f'(k)$	(5.7)	$\frac{1-a}{\sigma}$	(5.21)
Share imputed to capital	$1 - a \equiv \frac{rK}{X}$	$\frac{k \cdot f'(k)}{f(k)}$	(5.26)	$-\frac{1-\sigma}{\sigma} \cdot a$	(5.28)
Share imputed to labor	$a \equiv \frac{wL}{X}$	$1 - \frac{k \cdot f'(k)}{f(k)}$	(5.27)	$\frac{1-\sigma}{\sigma}(1-a)$	(5.29)

2. *Elasticities.* For example,

$$\frac{da}{a} = \frac{1-\sigma}{\sigma} \cdot (1-a) \frac{dk}{k} \qquad (5.29)$$

DYNAMIC PRODUCTION RELATIONS

So far, we have developed the characteristics of the constant-returns-to-scale production function in a timeless context. The set of functions expressing products and shares as functions of the capital-labor ratio are strictly *static* relations. The set of functions expressing the elasticities of products and shares with respect to the capital-labor ratio are *comparative statics* formulations. They show how the variables of concern change from one timeless position to another.

Dynamic relations are set in the context of time. We think of changes occurring in the variables as time passes. Fortunately, we can convert the elasticity relations into dynamic growth equations by specifying that the *changes occur with respect to time.* For example, Equation 5.25 attributes proportionate changes in output to a weighted average of proportionate changes in the two inputs

$$\frac{dX}{X} = (1-a)\frac{dK}{K} + a\frac{dL}{L} \qquad (5.25)$$

As it stands, (5.25) is a comparative statics relation. We can convert it to a dynamic relation by specifying that the changes take place with respect to time

$$\frac{1}{X} \cdot \frac{dX}{dt} = (1-a)\frac{1}{K} \cdot \frac{dK}{dt} + a \cdot \frac{1}{L} \cdot \frac{dL}{dt}$$

Using the asterisk to denote proportional changes with respect to time, we have simply

$$X^* = (1-a)K^* + aL^* \qquad (5.30)$$

If, for example, the share of output imputed to labor is two thirds, capital grows at a rate of 3 percent per annum and labor grows at 2 percent per annum; then

$$X^* = \tfrac{1}{3}(0.03) + \tfrac{2}{3}(0.02)$$
$$X^* = 0.02\tfrac{1}{3}$$
$$X^* = 2\tfrac{1}{3}\%$$

This calculation gives an approximate answer, because it assumes that a is a constant and a generally changes as a consequence of capital deepening. The less the degree of capital deepening, the better the approximation is.

The same procedure can be applied to the elasticity expressions in Table 5.1 to convert them to growth equations. For example, the growth of the output-capital ratio converts from

$$d\left(\frac{X}{K}\right) \cdot \frac{K}{X} = -a\frac{dk}{k} \qquad (5.23)$$

to

$$\frac{d}{dt}\left(\frac{X}{K}\right) \cdot \frac{K}{X} = -a \cdot \frac{1}{k} \cdot \frac{dk}{dt}$$

or

$$\left(\frac{X}{K}\right)^* = -ak^*$$

TABLE 5.2

Dynamic Production Relations

Variable	Growth Equation	
Output	$X^* = (1 - a)K^* + aL^*$	(5.30)
Average product of capital	$(X^* - K^*) = -a(K^* - L^*)$	(5.31)
Average product of labor	$(X^* - L^*) = (1 - a)(K^* - L^*)$	(5.32)
Marginal product of capital	$r^* = -\dfrac{a}{\sigma}(K^* - L^*)$	(5.33)
Marginal product of labor	$w^* = \dfrac{1-a}{\sigma}(K^* - L^*)$	(5.34)
Share imputed to capital	$(1-a)^* = -\dfrac{1-\sigma}{\sigma} \cdot a(K^* - L^*)$	(5.35)
Share imputed to labor	$a^* = \dfrac{1-\sigma}{\sigma}(1-a)(K^* - L^*)$	(5.36)

or

$$(X^* - K^*) = -a(K^* - L^*) \qquad (5.31)$$

The results appear in Table 5.2. These are growth equations for the variables of chief concern, made on the assumption of unchanging technology and constant returns to scale.

EXERCISES

1. Given a Cobb-Douglas production function with constant returns to scale

$$X = K^{1-a}L^a$$

and letting $k \equiv K/L$, derive the following expressions:

$$\dfrac{X}{K} = k^{-a} \qquad (5.37)$$

$$\dfrac{X}{L} = k^{1-a} \qquad (5.38)$$

$$r = (1-a)k^{-a} \qquad (5.39)$$

$$w = ak^{1-a} \qquad (5.40)$$

$$1 - a = \dfrac{rK}{X} \qquad (5.41)$$

$$a = \frac{wL}{X} \tag{5.42}$$

$$\sigma = 1 \tag{5.43}$$

$$X^* = (1 - a)K^* + aL^* \tag{5.44}$$

$$X^* - K^* = -a(K^* - L^*) \tag{5.45}$$

$$X^* - L^* = (1 - a)(K^* - L^*) \tag{5.46}$$

$$r^* = -a(K^* - L^*) \tag{5.47}$$

$$w^* = (1 - a)(K^* - L^*) \tag{5.48}$$

Note. If $x = z^n$, then $dx/dz = nz^{n-1}$.

2. Suppose wages were to rise 1 percent in a competitive economy with production conditions as outlined in this chapter. If the interest rate rises by 1 percent, and if the elasticity of substitution is $\frac{1}{2}$, compute the proportional changes in X/K, X/L, and K/L.

REFERENCES AND SUGGESTIONS FOR FURTHER READING

1. Allen, R. D. G., *Mathematical Analysis for Economists*. London: Macmillan, 1960, Chaps. VI, VII, VIII, and XII.
2. Lewis, J. Parry, *Mathematics for Students of Economics*. London: Macmillan, 1958, Chaps. IX, X, XVIII, XXII, and XIII.
3. Samuelson, P. A., "Parable and Realism in Capital Theory: The Surrogate Production Function." *Review of Economic Studies*, June, 1962.
4. Yamane, Taro, *Mathematics for Economists*, Second Edition. Englewood Cliffs: Prentice-Hall, 1968, Chaps. 3 and 4.

Chapter Six

TECHNOLOGICAL CHANGE

Introduction
Technological Change and the Passing of Time
The Growth of Marginal Products   MP.
The Growth of Output
The Hicks Measure of Bias and the Growth of Marginal Products
The Growth of Average Products   AP.
Changes in Relative Shares
A Recapitulation
Labor-Augmenting Technological Change
The Growth of Marginal Products
The Growth of Output
The Growth of Average Products
Neutrality as Defined by Harrod
Changes in Relative Shares
A Recapitulation
A Comparison of Hicks-Neutral and Harrod-Neutral Technological Change
Exercises
References and Suggestions for Further Reading

INTRODUCTION

Output may increase over time (1) because the quantity of inputs is increasing or (2) because the productivity of the inputs is rising in such a way that output would grow even if the quantity of inputs were unchanging. This latter effect is often attributed to technological change, which is a catch-all term for the sources of all output growth that cannot be accounted for by measured increases in the quantity of inputs.

Studies of growth in the United States and elsewhere have found that measured output growth can be attributed only in part to measured input growth.[1] The rest of output growth is attributed to technological change, the sources of which are not well known, although casual empiricism suggests that the steady advance of knowledge over the years has been a powerful influence in those economies that have grown. New knowledge is manifested in the production function when it is embodied in new and better capital equipment, better educated workers, and more efficient organization of production within and among firms.

In addition, workers and managers are increasingly healthier and perhaps more motivated.

These sources of productivity growth are difficult to identify and measure.[2] It is even more difficult to explain them. As a consequence, the economics of growth generally regards technological advance as exogenous (determined outside the system).

Economists are increasingly dissatisfied with this procedure, because it takes a major source of observed growth to be determined outside the model. Nevertheless, it is useful to trace out the impact of (exogenously determined) technological change on the economic system. To do so, we must introduce technological improvement into the production function.

In this chapter, we shall assume that technological change improves the efficiency of production without having been embodied in new and more efficient machines and men.[3] New (gross) investment is not required to

---

[1] Empirical studies have attempted to isolate the separate influences of input growth (movements along a production function) and technological improvement (shift of the production function). The conclusions of these studies vary. A study by D. W. Jorgenson and Z. Griliches finds that almost all growth in the United States 1945–65 is due to input growth. See "The Explanation of Productivity Change," *Review of Economic Studies* (July 1967). This article contains an excellent bibliography, including references to other studies that have attributed a greater proportion of measured growth to technological change.

[2] For a heroic effort, see E. F. Denison, *Sources of Economic Growth in the United States and the Alternative Before Us*, Supplementary Paper No. 13, The Committee for Economic Development (January 1962).

[3] Embodied technological change has been particularly studied. Two articles are recommended to suggest the flavor of the embodied approach: R. M. Solow, "Investment and Technical Progress," Chap. 7 of K. J. Arrow, S. Karlin, and P. Suppes (Eds.), *Mathematical Methods in the Social Sciences* (Stanford: Stanford University Press, 1960) and E. F. Denison, "The Unimportance of the Embodied Question," *American Economic Review* (March 1964). Embodiment bears on the larger issue of the existence of aggregate capital stocks and aggregate production functions. See F. M. Fisher, "The Existence of Aggregate Production Functions," *Econometrica* (October 1969).

transmit better techniques into production processes; new entrants to the labor force are not required to bring new knowledge to bear. This kind of technical change is called disembodied. It affects all existing capital and labor equally with new machines and new entrants to the labor force.

Even after making this assumption, we must recognize that technological advance may not be neutral, but may be biased, changing the marginal productivity of capital and labor unequally. Two definitions of bias will be employed in subsequent sections; the first to be explored was originated by Sir J. R. Hicks and the second by Sir Roy Harrod.

TECHNOLOGICAL CHANGE AND THE PASSING OF TIME

The Growth of Marginal Products

Technological change occurs with the passing of time. Output must be thought of as depending not only upon the inputs, but also upon time. Thus

$$X = F(K, L, t) \tag{6.1}$$

This new production function is assumed to be homogeneous of the first degree (constant returns to scale) in capital and labor. However, the inclusion of time (t) means that it is not homogeneous of the first degree in all its arguments, including time. Constant returns to scale in K and L means that

$$q \cdot X = F(q \cdot K, q \cdot L, t)$$

is a true statement for any value of q. Letting q equal $1/L$,

$$\frac{X}{L} = F\left(\frac{K}{L}, 1, t\right)$$

and we can define a new function, $f(\ )$, that absorbs the constant, 1.

$$\frac{X}{L} = f\left(\frac{K}{L}, t\right)$$

or

$$X = L \cdot f(k, t), \qquad k \equiv \frac{K}{L} \tag{6.2}$$

The average product of labor depends on the capital-labor ratio, as before, and also on time. If technology is improving over time, the average product of labor will be rising for any given capital-labor ratio.

Technological Change

The marginal product of capital is the first partial derivative of (6.2) with respect to capital. The rules of ordinary differentiation are employed, but we must take care to hold labor and time constant.

$$\frac{\partial X}{\partial K} = L \cdot f_k(k, t) \cdot \frac{\partial k}{\partial K}$$

Labor, L, is regarded as a constant. The expression $f_k(\ )$ indicates partial differentiation of the function $f(\ )$, where k is allowed to vary but t is held constant. The last factor, $\partial k/\partial K$, indicates that we have yet to partially differentiate k with respect to K. Note that we first used the product rule and the rule for differentiating a constant.

IN GENERAL	SPECIFICALLY
$y = a \cdot f(x)$	$X = L \cdot f(k, t)$
$\dfrac{dy}{dx} = a \cdot \dfrac{d}{dx} \cdot f(x)$	$\dfrac{\partial X}{\partial K} = L \cdot \dfrac{\partial}{\partial K} f(k, t)$

Second, we used the function-of-a-function rule.

IN GENERAL	SPECIFICALLY
$x = f(y)$	$\dfrac{X}{L} = f(k, t)$
$y = g(z)$	$k = \dfrac{K}{L}$
$\dfrac{dx}{dy} = \dfrac{d}{dy} f(y) \cdot \dfrac{d}{dz} g(z)$	$\dfrac{\partial}{\partial K} f(k, t) = \dfrac{\partial}{\partial k} f(k, t) \cdot \dfrac{\partial}{\partial K} k$
	$= f_k(k, t) \cdot \dfrac{\partial k}{\partial K}$

Put another way, the partial derivative of the function

$$X = L \cdot f(k, t), \qquad k \equiv \frac{K}{L}$$

with respect to K,

$$\frac{\partial X}{\partial K}$$

is equal to a "constant"

$$L$$

multiplied by the way $f(k, t)$ varies when k alone varies,

$$f_k(k, t)$$

multiplied by the way k varies when K alone varies,

$$\frac{\partial k}{\partial K}$$

Now we must evaluate this last factor.

$$\frac{\partial k}{\partial K} = \frac{\partial}{\partial K} \cdot \frac{K}{L} = \frac{1}{L}$$

Substituting this into our previous result, we finally obtain

$$\frac{\partial X}{\partial K} = f_k(k, t)$$

Recall that, in the last chapter, time was not an argument in the production function. There,

$$\frac{\partial X}{\partial K} = f'(k) \qquad (5.6)$$

Here, the passage of time impinges on the production relation and upon the marginal-product-of-capital function. But the marginal product of capital is the partial derivative of output with respect to capital alone. Thus, we indicate partial differentiation with the subscript.

For notational convenience, denote the marginal product of capital by r (the "interest rate").

$$r = f_k(k, t) \qquad (6.3)$$

It is left as an exercise to show that the marginal product of labor, denoted by w (the "wage rate"), is

$$w = f(k, t) - k \cdot f_k(k, t) \qquad (6.4)$$

114   Technological Change

Moving on, we wish to know how the marginal products of capital and labor vary over time. The time path of r is found by differentiating (6.3) with respect to time. We follow the rule for differentiating an implicit function as before, but now we differentiate with respect to time. Using a dot over a variable to denote the first time derivative,

IN GENERAL	SPECIFICALLY
$x = f(y, z)$	$r = f_k(k, t)$
$\dot{x} = \dfrac{\partial x}{\partial y} \cdot \dot{y} + \dfrac{\partial x}{\partial z} \cdot \dot{z}$	$\dot{r} = \dfrac{\partial r}{\partial k} \cdot \dot{k} + \dfrac{\partial r}{\partial t} \cdot \dfrac{dt}{dt}$
	$\dot{r} = \dfrac{\partial r}{\partial k} \cdot \dot{k} + \dfrac{\partial r}{\partial t}$

Expressing this derivative in proportional terms,

$$\frac{\dot{r}}{r} = \frac{\partial r}{r} \cdot \frac{k}{\partial k} \cdot \frac{\dot{k}}{k} + \frac{1}{r} \cdot \frac{\partial r}{\partial t}$$

and denoting proportional changes through time with an asterisk, we have

$$r^* = \frac{\partial r}{r} \cdot \frac{k}{\partial k} \cdot k^* + \frac{1}{r} \cdot \frac{\partial r}{\partial t}$$

The first term shows how proportional changes in the capital-labor ratio alone give rise to proportional changes in the marginal product of capital. It is (minus) the (partial) elasticity of the marginal product of capital with respect to the capital-labor ratio. In the last chapter we designated this elasticity as u and found that

$$u = \frac{a}{\sigma} \tag{5.18}$$

where a is the proportion of output imputed to labor and σ is the elasticity of substitution in production. (Note: u is a positive number).

The second term shows how changes in time alone give rise to proportional changes in the marginal product of capital. Define

$$\pi_K \equiv \frac{1}{r} \cdot \frac{\partial r}{\partial t}$$

Thus, we have for the growth of capital's marginal product

$$r^* = -\frac{a}{\sigma} k^* + \pi_K \tag{6.5}$$

If the share of product imputed to labor is two thirds, the elasticity of substitution equals one third, the capital-labor ratio rises 2 percent, and in addition, technical improvement alone raises the marginal product by 1 percent, then

$$r^* = -\frac{2/3}{1/3}(0.02) + 0.01$$

$$r^* = -0.04 + 0.01 = -0.03$$

The effect of capital deepening is to lower the interest rate. This effect is partially offset by technological change, which raises the interest rate. The net effect in this numerical example is a fall in the interest rate.

Proportional changes in the wage rate can also be decomposed into changes in the capital-labor ratio and technical progress due to the passage of time.

$$w^* = v \cdot k^* + \pi_L$$

where

$$v = \frac{\partial w}{w} \cdot \frac{k}{\partial k} \quad \text{and} \quad \pi_L = \frac{1}{w} \cdot \frac{\partial w}{\partial t}$$

Again, v is the (partial) elasticity of the wage with respect to the capital-labor ratio. We know from Chapter Five that

$$v = \frac{1-a}{\sigma} \tag{5.19}$$

where $1 - a$ is the proportion of output imputed to capital and σ is as before. Thus

$$w^* = \frac{1-a}{\sigma} k^* + \pi_L \tag{6.6}$$

expresses the growth of labor's marginal product.

The Growth of Output

The production function can be differentiated with respect to time, using the usual procedure. Differentiating (6.1) with respect to time,

$$\dot{X} = \frac{\partial X}{\partial K} \cdot \dot{K} + \frac{\partial X}{\partial L} \cdot \dot{L} + \frac{\partial X}{\partial t}$$

Converting to proportional changes and denoting marginal products by w and r,

$$\frac{\dot{X}}{X} = \frac{rK}{X} \cdot \frac{\dot{K}}{K} + \frac{wL}{X} \cdot \frac{\dot{L}}{L} + \frac{1}{X} \cdot \frac{\partial X}{\partial t}$$

Denoting the share of output imputed to capital as $1 - a$, the share imputed to labor as a, and the proportional increase in output due to the passage of time alone by π, we have

$$\frac{\dot{X}}{X} = (1-a)\frac{\dot{K}}{K} + a\frac{\dot{L}}{L} + \pi$$

or

$$X^* = (1-a)K^* + aL^* + \pi \qquad (6.7)$$

It is useful to consider changes in output from the point of view of payments imputed to the factors of production. Recall that the constant returns to scale property of production ensures that payments to factors based on their marginal productivities exactly exhaust total product.

$$X = wL + rK \qquad (5.8)$$

Differentiating with respect to time,

$$\dot{X} = w \cdot \dot{L} + L \cdot \dot{w} + r \cdot \dot{K} + K \cdot \dot{r}$$

or

$$X^* = (1-a)K^* + a \cdot L^* + (1-a)r^* + a \cdot w^*$$

Substituting (6.5) for r^* and (6.6) for w^*,

$$X^* = (1-a)K^* + aL^* + (1-a)\left(-\frac{a}{\sigma}k^* + \pi_K\right) + a\left(\frac{1-a}{\sigma}k^* + \pi_L\right)$$

or

$$X^* = (1-a)K^* + aL^* + (1-a)\pi_K + a\pi_L \qquad (6.8)$$

Comparing this result with (6.7), we have

$$\pi = (1 - a)\pi_K + a\pi_L \qquad (6.9)$$

The increase in output due to the sole influence of technological change can be decomposed into a weighted average of increases in the marginal products of the inputs due to the passage of time alone. The weights are the proportions of output imputed to the inputs.

The Hicks Measure of Bias and the Growth of Marginal Products

If the marginal products of the inputs increase in precisely the same proportions due to technological change alone ($k^* = 0$), then we say that technological progress is *Hicks neutral*.[4] More generally,

$$\beta \equiv \pi_K - \pi_L \qquad (6.10)$$

where β is a measure of bias in the sense of Hicks. If, at a given ratio of capital to labor ($k^* = 0$), technological change raises the marginal product of capital more than that of labor, we say that progress is *capital-using* or *labor-saving*.

This terminology is most appropriate when thinking of a competitive firm that adopts new technology. If π_K is greater than π_L, the firm will be induced to hire more capital relative to labor at given factor prices, because the marginal product of capital has risen relative to that of labor at the original capital-labor ratio.

Precisely the opposite happens if π_L is greater than π_K. This is called *labor-using* or *capital-saving* technological change because the marginal product of labor has risen more than that of capital at the original capital-labor ratio, thus inducing the firm to hire more labor relative to capital at given factor prices.

If π_K equals π_L, there is no incentive for a firm adopting the new technology to change factor proportions, since the ratio of marginal products has not changed at the original capital-labor ratio. Such a technological change is *neutral*.

For a closed economy, the capital-labor ratio is fixed at any given time, so labor or capital "saving" or "using" cannot be manifested in changed factor proportions. Instead, capital-using or labor-saving technological progress will induce firms to bid up the return on capital relative to wages. The opposite change in relative factor rewards would occur in the labor-using

[4] J. R. Hicks, *The Theory of Wages* (London: 1932), p. 121. The concept of bias is used here to refer to the *initial* impact of a change. The ultimate impact will depend on the equilibrium properties of the system. See Chapter Seven.

or capital-saving case. No change would occur in the neutral case; wages and the interest rate would rise in the same proportion.

The case of neutrality in the sense of Hicks has special importance in economic theory. Hicks'-neutral change magnifies or "blows up" the marginal productive power of capital and labor in the same proportion. If there are constant returns to scale, the marginal products depend upon the capital-labor ratio alone. We might guess, therefore, that $f(k, t)$ could be replaced by another expression, $A(t) \cdot g(k)$. Here, $A(t)$ is a productivity index that rises as time goes on. The function $g(k)$ has the usual properties, $g'(k) > 0$ and $g''(k) < 0$. The new production function is

$$\frac{X}{L} = A(t) \cdot g\left(\frac{K}{L}\right)$$

or

$$x = A(t) \cdot g(k)$$

We ask if a rising $A(t)$ portrays technological progress that is neutral in the sense of Hicks. Specifically, is

$$\beta = \pi_K - \pi_L = 0$$

or

$$\beta = \frac{1}{r} \cdot \frac{\partial r}{\partial t} - \frac{1}{w} \cdot \frac{\partial w}{\partial t} = 0?$$

To find out, we must first find expressions for r and w, and then find out how these vary as time passes and $A(t)$ increases.

The marginal physical product of capital is the partial derivative of X with respect to K in

$$X = L \cdot A(t) \cdot g\left(\frac{K}{L}\right)$$

We treat L and t as if they were constants.

$$\frac{\partial X}{\partial K} = L \cdot A(t) \cdot g'\left(\frac{K}{L}\right) \cdot \frac{\partial}{\partial K}\left(\frac{K}{L}\right)$$

$$= L \cdot A(t) \cdot g'(k) \cdot \frac{1}{L}$$

$$r = A(t) \cdot g'(k)$$

Technological Change and the Passing of Time 119

The reader can confirm that the marginal physical product of labor is

$$w = A(t) \cdot [g(k) - k \cdot g'(k)]$$

To find π_K and π_L, we differentiate partially with respect to time and express the partial derivative as a proportion.

$$\frac{\partial r}{\partial t} = g'(k) \frac{dA}{dt} = g'(k) \cdot \dot{A}$$

$$\frac{1}{r} \cdot \frac{\partial r}{\partial t} = \frac{1}{A} \cdot \frac{dA}{dt} = \frac{\dot{A}}{A} = A^*$$

$$\pi_K = A^*$$

Likewise, for the marginal product of labor,

$$\pi_L = A^*$$

Thus,

$$\beta = \pi_K - \pi_L = A^* - A^* = 0$$

For example, if A is equal to 100 at a point in time, and rises to 102, then $A^* = 0.02$ or 2 percent. With no change in $k \equiv K/L$, both w and r rise by 2 percent. The technological improvement is Hicks neutral ($\pi_K = \pi_L; k^* = 0$).

Hicks neutrality is illustrated in Figure 6.1. The unit isoquant corresponding to the original technology is designated by $X = 1$. The resource base of the economy consists of $0G$ of capital and $0H$ of labor, and the capital-labor ratio is k. With output at the unit level, and with product exhausted by factor payments,

$$1 = w_0 L + r_0 K$$

Consequently

$$K = \frac{1}{r_0} - \frac{w_0}{r_0} \cdot L$$

is the equation of the line CAE, tangent to the unit isoquant at A. Its slope is the ratio of wages to the interest rate. Its intercept on the vertical axis ($L = 0$) is $1/r_0$, or the distance $0C$. Its intercept on the horizontal axis ($K = 0$) is $1/w_0$, or the distance $0E$.

Technological improvement is denoted by a shift of the unit isoquant toward the origin—the unit of output can be produced with less inputs, *or more than unit output can be produced with the same resource endowment.*

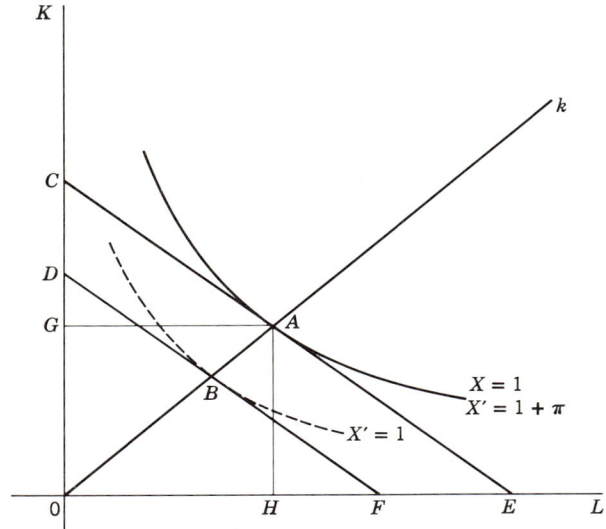

Figure 6.1 Hicks-neutral technological change.

In Figure 6.1, the unit isoquant corresponding to the new technology is labelled $X' = 1$. The unit output can now be produced with less capital and labor. If $0G$ of capital and $0H$ of labor continue to be employed, output increases from $X = 1$ to $X' = 1 + \pi$, where π is the proportional increase in output due to technological improvement alone.

Technological change is Hicks neutral if, at any capital-labor ratio, the ratio of wages to the interest rate is unaffected. This is shown in the figure by constructing the new unit isoquant at point B on ray $0k$, with the same slope as at point A on the old unit isoquant. The tangent line DBF has the same slope as the tangent line CAE, indicating that the ratio of factor rewards has not changed at the capital-labor ratio k as a consequence of the improvement. The isoquants have merely been renumbered.

The output increase due to the technological change alone is AB along the ray $0k$. In proportional terms,

$$\pi = \frac{AB}{0B}$$

The increase in the interest rate can be measured along the vertical axis. Recall that the reciprocal of the original interest rate was $0C$. That is,

$$r_0 = \frac{1}{0C}$$

By analogy, the new interest rate is

$$r_1 = \frac{1}{OD}$$

The rise in the interest rate is thus

$$r_1 - r_0 = \frac{1}{OD} - \frac{1}{OC}$$

$$= \frac{OC - OD}{OC \times OD}$$

In proportional terms,

$$\pi_K = \frac{r_1 - r_0}{r_0} = OC \cdot \frac{OC - OD}{OC \times OD} = \frac{OC - OD}{OD}$$

or

$$\pi_K = \frac{CD}{OD}$$

In addition, since the triangles OCE and ODF are geometrically similar, it can be easily proved that

$$\pi_K = \pi_L$$

or

$$\beta = 0$$

The case of capital-saving or labor-using technical progress is illustrated in Figure 6.2. The initial position is as before, and the production point is at A. As a consequence of the improvement, the unit isoquant shifts toward the origin, as before, but this time it "tilts" and becomes "steeper" so that the tangent at B on the ray Ok becomes "steeper" as well. This means that wages rise relative to the interest rate, as indicated by the slope of DBF being greater than the slope of CAE where these lines intersect the ray Ok. If resources remain fully employed, the output point remains at A, with wages having risen relative to the interest rate. The proportional rise in output is

$$\pi = \frac{AB}{OB}$$

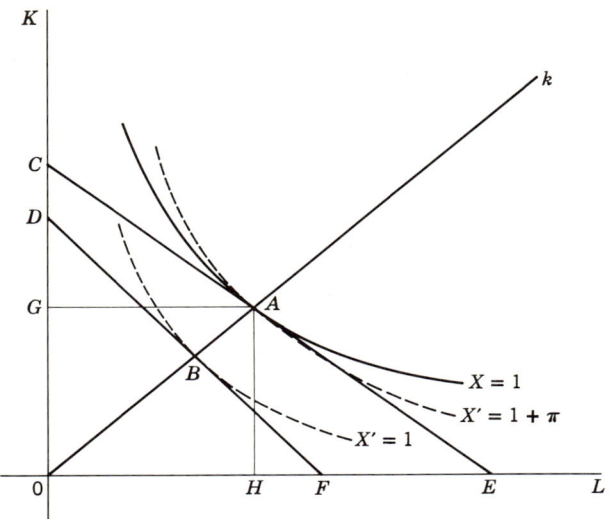

Figure 6.2 Labor-using or capital-saving technological change in the sense of Hicks.

The proportional rise in the interest rate is

$$\pi_K = \frac{CD}{OD}$$

and the wage increase is

$$\pi_L = \frac{EF}{OF}$$

Clearly

$$\pi_L > \pi_K$$

or

$$\beta < 0$$

The case of labor-saving or capital-using technical progress is not illustrated. Its development would be precisely analogous to the opposite case just presented. The axes in Figure 6.2 need only to be reversed.

We can now return to the growth equations for marginal products and reinterpret them in terms of the measure of bias, β. Recall that

$$r^* = -\frac{a}{\sigma} k^* + \pi_K \tag{6.5}$$

and

$$w^* = \frac{1-a}{\sigma} k^* + \pi_L \qquad (6.6)$$

Moreover, we found in the last section that

$$\pi = (1-a)\pi_K + a\pi_L \qquad (6.9)$$

In this section, we defined

$$\beta \equiv \pi_K - \pi_L \qquad (6.10)$$

By combining (6.9) and (6.10) we can express the growth of the marginal products due to technological change alone in terms of the growth of output due to progress alone and the bias of the change.

$$\pi_K = \pi + a\beta \qquad (6.11)$$

$$\pi_L = \pi - (1-a)\beta \qquad (6.12)$$

Substituting these expressions into (6.5) and (6.6) we have, finally,

$$r^* = -\frac{a}{\sigma} k^* + \pi + a\beta \qquad (6.13)$$

$$w^* = \frac{1-a}{\sigma} k^* + \pi - (1-a)\beta \qquad (6.14)$$

Capital deepening ($k^* > 0$) suppresses the interest rate but raises wages. Output increase due to technological progress alone ($\pi > 0$) tends to raise both the interest rate and wages. However, if progress is capital-using or labor-saving, ($\beta > 0$), the interest rate rises more, and the wage less, than if the bias were zero.

We can confirm that (6.13) and (6.14) embody the concept of Hicks neutrality. When progress is neutral ($\beta = 0$), the ratio of wages to the interest rate does not change ($w^* - r^* = 0$) when the capital-labor ratio is constant ($k^* = 0$). Subtract (6.13) from (6.14).

$$w^* - r^* = -\beta + \frac{1}{\sigma} k^*$$

When

$$k^* = \beta = 0$$

we have

$$w^* - r^* = 0$$

The Growth of Average Products

Growth equations for the average products of capital and labor are easily obtained by subtracting the growth of capital (K^*) and the growth of labor (L^*) from (6.7).

$$X^* - K^* = -ak^* + \pi \tag{6.15}$$

$$X^* - L^* = (1 - a)k^* + \pi \tag{6.16}$$

The growth of average products is not affected by whatever bias there may be in technological improvement. Average products always rise in the same proportion as output (π) as the consequence of technical progress. Capital deepening ($k^* > 0$), as before, always reduces the average product of capital and raises the average product of labor.

Changes in Relative Shares

Recall that the share of output imputed to an input is the input's marginal product divided by its average product. The share of an input will rise if the growth of its marginal product exceeds the growth of its average product.

We can find a growth equation for the share of capital by subtracting the growth of capital's average product, Equation 6.15, from the growth of its marginal product, Equation 6.13.

$$(1 - a)^* = a\beta - a \cdot \frac{1 - \sigma}{\sigma} k^* \tag{6.17}$$

A similar expression for the share of labor can be found by subtracting (6.14) from (6.16).

$$a^* = -(1 - a)\beta + (1 - a)\frac{1 - \sigma}{\sigma} k^* \tag{6.18}$$

With the exception of the terms containing the measure of bias, these expressions are identical with those obtained before, when technology was assumed to be unchanging: Equations 5.28 and 5.29. Capital deepening will reduce (increase) capital's share, and raise (lower) labor's share, if the elasticity of substitution is less (greater) than one. Now the additional effect of any bias in technological change must be taken into account. Capital-using or labor-saving bias will unambiguously tend to raise capital's share and reduce labor's share.

TABLE 6.1

Growth Equations When Technological Change is Biased in the Sense of Hicks

Variable		Growth Equation			
Output	$X^* =$	$(1-a)K^* + aL^* + \pi$			(6.7)
Average product of capital	$X^* - K^* =$	$-ak^* +$	π		(6.15)
Average product of labor	$X^* - L^* =$	$(1-a)k^* +$	π		(6.16)
Marginal product of capital	$r^* =$	$-\dfrac{a}{\sigma}k^* + \pi +$		$a\beta$	(6.13)
Marginal product of labor	$w^* =$	$\dfrac{1-a}{\sigma}k^* + \pi$	$- (1-a)\beta$		(6.14)
Share imputed to capital	$(1-a)^* =$	$-a \cdot \dfrac{1-\sigma}{\sigma}k^*$	$+$	$a\beta$	(6.17)
Share imputed to labor	$a^* =$	$(1-a)\dfrac{1-\sigma}{\sigma}k^*$	$-(1-a)\beta$		(6.18)

A Recapitulation

Growth equations for output, average and marginal products, and relative shares are collected below in Table 6.1. They show proportional changes in the variables as a consequence of proportional changes in the capital-labor ratio and of technological change.

LABOR-AUGMENTING TECHNOLOGICAL CHANGE

The Growth of Marginal Products

There is a second method of introducing technological change into the production function which is less general than the one we have been working with but very useful in growth theory. In the last section, we assumed that technological progress was linked to time, and time was inserted into the production function in a very general way. Here, we will also assume that technological progress occurs as time passes, but that progress can be described as *labor-augmenting*. This concept of technological change was employed in Chapter Three, where growth in an advanced economy was introduced. Specifically, if technological change can be described as labor-augmenting through time, then

$$X = F(K, Q \cdot L)$$

where Q is an efficiency coefficient associated with the labor input, which becomes larger as time goes on. If 100 workers, this year, can produce, with the same amount of capital, the same output that required 102 workers last year, then the rate of labor-augmenting technological progress is about 2 percent.

This concept of technological progress does *not* imply that progress is "embodied in" workers or that workers become "better" in some way. Rather, we merely want to allow for the possibility that technological progress has the *effect* of magnifying the labor input. For example, suppose that a neighborhood laundry rearranges its washing and drying machines (at negligible cost) so that the flow pattern of work in process becomes more efficient, and fewer workers are required for the machine-to-machine transfers of the laundry. The capital input (K) is unchanged. But now the same output (X) can be produced with less labor of the same average quality. Suppose only 10 workers are now required to produce the same output that 12 workers produced before the change. Then the efficiency coefficient has risen from, say, 100 to 120. The change is an organizational improvement, due to neither "better" machines nor labor. But the change has had the *effect* of magnifying labor's productive power while leaving that of capital unchanged.

It is convenient to think of labor as "*efficiency labor*" or labor measured in "*efficiency units*," when labor, measured in conventional units, is multiplied by its associated efficiency index. Define

$$\hat{L} \equiv Q \cdot L$$

where $\hat{L}$ is efficiency labor. Furthermore, we can think of labor efficiency as growing at a constant proportional rate, m, and equal to unity in the initial period. Thus, in general,

$$Q \equiv e^{mt}$$

When t equals zero, Q equals unity.

Now, the production relation can be written

$$X = F(K, \hat{L}), \qquad \hat{L} = e^{mt} \cdot L \qquad (6.19)$$

which is homogeneous of the first degree in capital and efficiency labor, so that

$$q \cdot X = F(q \cdot K, q \cdot \hat{L})$$

is a true statement for any positive q. Letting q equal $1/\hat{L}$,

$$\frac{X}{\hat{L}} = F\left(\frac{K}{\hat{L}}, 1\right)$$

Labor-Augmenting Technological Change

and we can define a new function, $f(\ )$, that absorbs the constant, 1.

$$\frac{X}{\hat{L}} = f\left(\frac{K}{\hat{L}}\right)$$

or

$$X = \hat{L} \cdot f(\hat{k}), \qquad \hat{k} \equiv \frac{K}{\hat{L}}, \qquad \hat{L} \equiv e^{mt} \cdot L \qquad (6.20)$$

The marginal products of capital and labor, measured in natural units, are $\partial X/\partial K = r$ and $\partial X/\partial L = w$ as before. It is left to the reader to show that

$$r = f'(\hat{k}) \qquad (6.21)$$

and

$$w = e^{mt}[f(\hat{k}) - \hat{k} \cdot f'(\hat{k})] \qquad (6.22)$$

The interest rate is constant if the ratio of capital to efficiency labor ($\hat{k}$) is constant. However, the wage rate would be increasing in the same circumstances at the constant proportional rate at which labor efficiency improves. Wages paid per efficiency unit of labor are, however, constant, if $\hat{k}$ is constant. Wages paid per efficiency worker are

$$\hat{w} = \frac{wL}{\hat{L}} = w \cdot e^{-mt}$$

Thus

$$\hat{w} = f(\hat{k}) - \hat{k} \cdot f(\hat{k})$$

To find expressions for the growth of r and w, we differentiate (6.21) and (6.22) with respect to time. For the interest rate,

$$\frac{d}{dt}r = f''(\hat{k})\frac{d\hat{k}}{dt}$$

Expressed in terms of proportional variation,

$$\frac{1}{r} \cdot \frac{dr}{dt} = f''(\hat{k})\frac{\hat{k}}{r} \cdot \frac{1}{\hat{k}} \cdot \frac{d\hat{k}}{dt}$$

Technological Change

The factor, $f''(\hat{k})\hat{k}/r$, relates changes in r associated with changes in $\hat{k}$. Denote this factor by $-u$, where u is the elasticity of r with respect to $\hat{k}$. (*Note.* u is a positive number.)

$$u \equiv -f''(\hat{k}) \cdot \frac{\hat{k}}{r}$$

Using the asterisk to denote proportional change through time,

$$r^* = -u \cdot \hat{k}^*$$

The growth of k can be decomposed into the growth of the capital-labor ratio and the growth of labor efficiency.

$$\hat{k} = \frac{K}{e^{mt} \cdot L} = k \cdot e^{-mt}$$

Taking logarithms,

$$\log \hat{k} = \log k - mt$$

Differentiating with respect to time,

$$\hat{k}^* = k^* - m$$

Finally

$$r^* = -u \cdot k^* + um \tag{6.23}$$

The rate of interest is depressed by capital deepening, but raised by increases in labor efficiency.

Differentiating (6.22) with respect to time, we obtain an expression for the growth of the wage.

$$w^* = -\hat{k} \cdot f''(\hat{k}) \cdot \frac{\hat{k}}{w} \cdot \hat{k}^* \cdot e^{mt} + m$$

From our derivation of the growth of the interest rate, we have

$$f''(\hat{k}) \cdot \hat{k} = -u \cdot r$$

Thus

$$w^* = \hat{k} \cdot u \cdot \frac{r}{w} \cdot \hat{k}^* \cdot e^{mt} + m$$

Labor-Augmenting Technological Change

which can be further simplified by recalling that $\hat{k} = (K/L)e^{-mt}$.

$$w^* = u \cdot \frac{rK}{wL} \cdot \hat{k}^* + m$$

or

$$w^* = u \cdot \frac{1-a}{a} \cdot \hat{k}^* + m$$

where $1 - a$ is the share of output imputed to capital and a is the share imputed to labor. Notice that the first term indicates the proportional change in the wage with respect to the proportional change in the ratio of capital to efficiency labor. We can define

$$v \equiv u \cdot \frac{1-a}{a}$$

as the elasticity of the wage with respect to the ratio of capital to efficiency labor.

$$w^* = v \cdot \hat{k}^* + m$$

Decomposing $\hat{k}^*$ as before,

$$\hat{k}^* = k^* - m$$

we have, at last,

$$w^* = vk^* + (1-v)m \tag{6.24}$$

The growth equations for r (6.23) and w (6.24) can be reinterpreted in terms of relative shares and the elasticity of substitution. In Chapter Five, we found that the elasticities, u and v, were:

$$u \equiv \frac{a}{\sigma} \tag{5.18}$$

$$v \equiv \frac{1-a}{\sigma} \tag{5.19}$$

where the elasticity of substitution (σ) was defined as

$$\sigma \equiv \frac{dk/k}{d(w/r) \cdot r/w} \tag{5.15}$$

Technological Change

In this section we have defined u and v as the elasticities of r and w with respect to $\hat{k}$, not to k (as in Chapter Five). But it is easy to show that we can replace k with $\hat{k}$ in (5.15) without changing the definition of σ. That is, the elasticity of substitution, which indicates how the capital-*labor* ratio changes when relative factor prices change, has the same value when indicating how the capital-*efficiency labor* ratio changes when relative factor prices change.

To show this, we need only prove that the numerator of (5.15) has the same value when expressed in terms of k or $\hat{k}$. It is sufficient to show that

$$\frac{d\hat{k}}{\hat{k}} = \frac{dk}{k}$$

Recall that $\hat{L} = Q \cdot L$, where Q was defined as e^{mt}, which is a parameter, a constant at any point in time and not dependent on the ratio of wages to the interest rate. Thus,

$$d\hat{k} = d\frac{K}{Q \cdot L} = \frac{1}{Q} dk$$

and

$$\hat{k} = \frac{1}{Q} \cdot \frac{K}{L} = \frac{1}{Q} \cdot k$$

Therefore

$$\frac{d\hat{k}}{\hat{k}} = \frac{dk}{k}$$

This is a very convenient result. Now we can apply (5.18) and (5.19) in the current context, where labor is expressed in efficiency units. We can rewrite (6.23) and (6.24), using (5.18) and (5.19).

$$r^* = -\frac{a}{\sigma} k^* + \frac{a}{\sigma} m \tag{6.25}$$

$$w^* = \frac{1-a}{\sigma} k^* + \left(\frac{a}{\sigma} - \frac{1-\sigma}{\sigma}\right) m \tag{6.26}$$

These are the final growth equations for the interest rate and wages. Note that technological progress by itself does not necessarily raise wages. In fact, the effect of labor-augmenting technological progress alone is to lower wages if $1 - \sigma$ exceeds a.

The Growth of Output

The production function was defined in terms of capital and efficiency labor.

$$X = F(K, \hat{L}), \qquad \hat{L} = e^{mt} \cdot L \qquad (6.19)$$

To find out how output grows over time, we can differentiate (6.19) with respect to time, using the same techniques we used before.

$$\frac{dX}{dt} = \frac{\partial X}{\partial K} \cdot \frac{dK}{dt} + \frac{\partial X}{\partial \hat{L}} \cdot \frac{d\hat{L}}{dt}$$

The expression $\partial X / \partial \hat{L}$ is the wage per efficiency worker, or the "efficiency wage." We know from the previous section that

$$\hat{w} = w \cdot e^{-mt}$$

The expression $d\hat{L}/dt$ is the increase in efficiency labor, which can be decomposed into changes in the labor force itself, and changes in its efficiency.

$$\frac{d\hat{L}}{dt} = \frac{d}{dt}(e^{mt} \cdot L)$$

$$= e^{mt} \cdot \frac{dL}{dt} + L \cdot \frac{d}{dt} e^{mt}$$

$$\frac{d\hat{L}}{dt} = e^{mt} \cdot \frac{dL}{dt} + mLe^{mt}$$

The second term of the differentiated production function is thus nothing more than

$$\frac{\partial X}{\partial \hat{L}} \cdot \frac{d\hat{L}}{dt} = w \cdot e^{-mt} \left[e^{mt} \cdot \frac{dL}{dt} + mLe^{mt} \right]$$

$$= w \cdot \frac{dL}{dt} + m \cdot wL$$

Therefore, letting $\partial X / \partial K \equiv r$ and substituting back into the differential production function

$$\frac{dX}{dt} = r \cdot \frac{dK}{dt} + w \cdot \frac{dL}{dt} + m \cdot wL$$

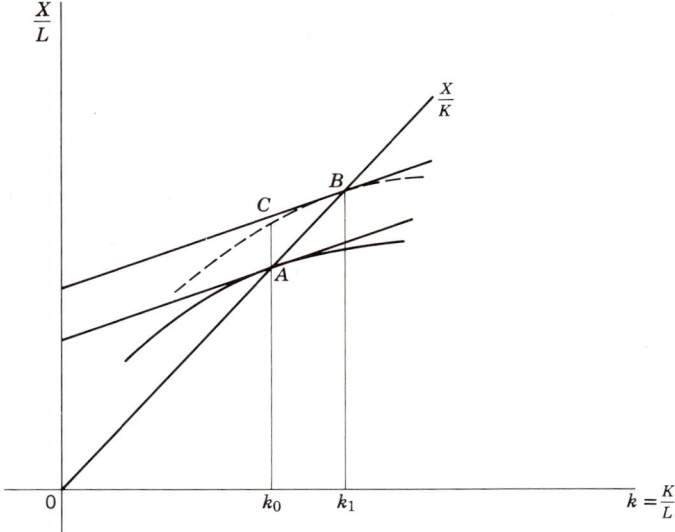

Figure 6.3a Harrod-neutral technological progress.

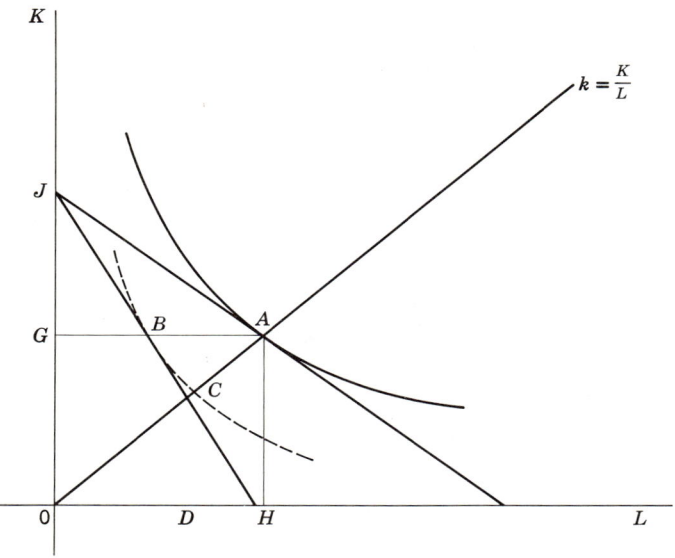

Figure 6.3b Harrod-neutral technological progress.

Labor-Augmenting Technological Change

In terms of proportional changes, and letting $1 - a \equiv rK/X$ and $a \equiv wL/X$,

$$X^* = (1 - a)K^* + aL^* + a \cdot m \qquad (6.27)$$

Note that the greater the power of labor augmentation to raise output, the greater is the share of output imputed to labor. This is what we should expect, since labor augmentation is like labor-force growth from the point of view of production.

The Growth of Average Products

Growth equations for the average products of capital and labor are obtained by subtracting K^*, and then L^*, from (6.27).

$$X^* - K^* = -ak^* + a \cdot m \qquad (6.28)$$
$$X^* - L^* = (1 - a)k^* + a \cdot m \qquad (6.29)$$

The average product of capital (labor) is depressed (increased) by capital deepening. Labor-augmenting technological change has the same impact on the average products of both inputs.

Neutrality as Defined by Harrod

In this section we show that labor-augmenting technological change is Harrod neutral.[5] If technological change is neutral in the sense of Harrod, the marginal product of capital is unchanged at a constant ratio of output to capital.[6]

This concept of neutrality is illustrated in Figure 6.3, which shows the production function (6.19) rewritten in such a way that the average product of labor depends on the capital-labor ratio, with labor measured in natural units. To accomplish this, we must return to the production function that allows for labor augmentation over time,

$$X = F(K, \hat{L}), \qquad \hat{L} = e^{mt} \cdot L \qquad (6.19)$$

and to recall that constant returns to scale permitted us to write

$$q \cdot X = F(q \cdot K, q \cdot \hat{L})$$

---

[5] The converse can also be shown. See H. Uzawa, "Neutral Inventions and the Stability of Growth Equilibrium," *Review of Economic Studies* (February, 1961).

[6] R. E. Harrod, *Towards a Dynamic Economics* (London: Macmillan, 1948), p. 23.

where q has any value. We want to express the left-hand side of the equation as the average product of labor, so we let $q = 1/L$.

$$\frac{X}{L} = F\left(\frac{K}{L}, \frac{\hat{L}}{L}\right)$$

or

$$\frac{X}{L} = F(k, e^{mt})$$

Now we can define a new function, $h(\ )$, which absorbs the exponential component.

$$\frac{X}{L} = h(k)$$

The function $h(\ )$ is *not* a stable function; it is constantly shifting through time. However, *at any point in time* the function is "frozen," and we can regard it in the usual way.

The function is plotted in Figure 6.3a. The reader can show that the slope of the function is the marginal product of capital.

$$\frac{\partial X}{\partial K} = r = h'(k)$$

Moreover, any ray out of the origin is the output-capital ratio.

Harrod neutrality requires that r be constant for any constant X/K subsequent to a shift in the function $h(\ )$. In the present analysis, this shift would be due to the passage of time, which shifts the function from that shown by the solid line to the dotted line just above it. The initial production point is at A, which moves to B subsequent to the technological improvement. The change is Harrod neutral because A and B are on the same ray (X/K constant), and the slope of the two functions is the same (r constant). If the change is everywhere Harrod neutral, a move between points like A and B must be possible for all output-capital ratios.

Equations 6.25 and 6.28 show that *labor augmentation is Harrod-neutral technological change*. In (6.25), Harrod-neutral change requires $r^* = 0$.

$$0 = -\frac{a}{\sigma}k^* + \frac{a}{\sigma}\cdot m$$

or

$$k^* = m$$

In (6.28), Harrod-neutral change requires $X^* - K^* = 0$.

$$0 = -ak^* + a \cdot m$$

or

$$k^* = m$$

The same proportional increase in the capital-labor ratio satisfies the dual requirement for neutrality, that $r^* = 0$ and that $X^* - K^* = 0$. In Figure 6.3a, the proportional increase in k is $k_0 k_1 / 0 k_0$.

For an economy as a whole, the capital-labor ratio is fixed at any point in time by its resource endowment. If the resource base is locked in at $0k$, the production point moves from A to C as a consequence of Harrod-neutral change. The output-capital ratio rises and the interest rate rises as well, since the slope of the function is greater at C than at A. This result is contained in (6.25), and (6.28) as well. If the capital-labor ratio is constant ($k^* = 0$) we have

$$r^* = \frac{a}{\sigma} \cdot m$$

and

$$X^* - K^* = a \cdot m$$

Harrod-neutral technological change can also be illustrated with the familiar isoquant map. This is done in Figure 6.3b.[7] The initial production point on the original unit isoquant is at A. The distance $0J$ equals $1/r$, as before. The capital-output ratio is the distance $0G$, since $0G$ measures capital, and output is at the unit level.

Labor-augmenting (Harrod neutral) technological change magnifies the productive power of the existing labor force. One way to show the change would then be to simply renumber the horizontal axis, indicating that the same output can be produced with less labor but the same capital. For example, given $0G$ of capital and $0H = 100$ workers, one unit of output is produced at A before the change. After the change, $0G$ of capital and $0H = 70$ workers can produce the same unit output at A.

Another way to show the change is to retain the same scale on the labor axis and "shrink" the unit isoquant with respect to that axis. The new unit isoquant is shown by the dotted line. The production point is at B, where $0G$ of capital and, for example, $0D = 70$ workers produce a unit of output.

---

[7] The diagrammatic treatment is due to R. W. Jones, "'Neutral' Technological Change and the Isoquant Map," *American Economic Review*, **55**: 848–55 (September 1965).

The improvement is Harrod neutral because the same interest rate ($r = 1/0J$) prevails after the change as before, at the same capital-output ratio ($K/X = 0G$) as before.

Again, for an entire economy, the capital-labor ratio is given at any point in time. So the production point remains at A on a new isoquant (not shown) corresponding to the new and better technology. From (6.27) we know that the proportional increase in output is $a \cdot m$. In terms of the diagram,

$$a \cdot m = \frac{AC}{0A}$$

What has happened to the wage-interest rate ratio as a consequence of the technological change? This ratio is the slope of the new isoquant (not shown) that passes through the point A. Because of constant returns to scale, the ratio of factor rewards is the same along any ray like $0k$. The unit isoquant passing through point C tells us everything we have to know about the new technology, except the volume of output. As a consequence, if we know the slope of the isoquant at point C corresponding to the new technology, we know the slope of the new isoquant (not shown) passing through point A. To find out what happens to the ratio of factor rewards, we need only compare the slope at point A, corresponding to the old technology, with the slope at point C, corresponding to the new technology.

The movement from A (old technology) to C (new technology) can be decomposed into a movement from A to B, and then from A to C. From A to B, the slope clearly increases, indicating that w/r rises. But there is substitution of labor for capital moving along the dotted isoquant from B to C, indicating that w/r falls as a consequence of that move. What is the net effect? Economic intuition tells us that the magnitude of the fall of w/r when moving from B to C is linked to elasticity of substitution.

In fact, the total effect on w/r depends crucially on the elasticity of substitution. Subtracting (6.25) from (6.26), we have

$$w^* - r^* = \frac{k^*}{\sigma} - \frac{1-\sigma}{\sigma} \cdot m$$

Holding the capital-labor ratio constant ($k^* = 0$),

$$w^* - r^* = -\frac{1-\sigma}{\sigma} \cdot m$$

The proportional change in the ratio of wages to the interest rate is positive if the elasticity of substitution exceeds unity. But the effect of Harrod-neutral technological change is to lower wages relative to the interest rate if the elasticity of substitution is less than one. These conclusions hold so long as the capital-labor ratio is constant. For example, suppose labor efficiency rises by 2 percent ($m = 0.02$) and the elasticity of substitution is one half ($\sigma = 0.5$). Then at a constant capital-labor ratio ($k^* = 0$), wages fall relative to the interest rate by 2 percent ($w^* - r^* = -0.02$).

Changes in Relative Shares

Expressions for the growth of relative shares are obtained directly from growth equations for marginal and average products that have already been derived. The growth of a share is the growth of its average product subtracted from the growth of its marginal product. The growth of the share of output imputed to capital is found by subtracting (6.28) from (6.25).

$$(1-a)^* = -\frac{1-\sigma}{\sigma} \cdot ak^* + \frac{1-\sigma}{\sigma} \cdot am \tag{6.30}$$

The growth of labor's share is found by subtracting (6.29) from (6.24).

$$a^* = \frac{1-\sigma}{\sigma}(1-a)k^* - \frac{1-\sigma}{\sigma}(1-a)m \tag{6.31}$$

The effect of labor augmentation (Harrod-neutral technological change) alone is to raise labor's share only if the elasticity of substitution is greater than one. As before, capital deepening will raise labor's share if the elasticity of substitution is less than one.

A Recapitulation

Growth equations for the variables of chief interest are set out below for the case of labor-augmenting (Harrod-neutral) technological change occurring at the constant proportional rate, m.

A COMPARISON OF HICKS-NEUTRAL AND HARROD-NEUTRAL TECHNOLOGICAL PROGRESS

Two concepts of bias and neutrality of technological change have just been explored. If technological change is neutral in the sense of Hicks, the ratio of marginal products remains unaltered at a constant capital-labor ratio. If technological change is neutral in the sense of Harrod, the marginal product of capital is unaltered at a constant capital-output ratio.

It should be emphasized that these are but *definitions* of neutrality, and others are conceivable. The definitions are useful because they permit us

138 Technological Change

to classify, at least conceptually, kinds of technological change, and to trace out their impacts on the rest of the economic system.

Classification schemes are most useful when they are related to one another. It would benefit us to know if conditions exist such that Hicks and Harrod neutrality amount to the same thing.

We can put the question in two equivalent ways:

1. Do conditions exist such that Hicks-neutral change leaves the marginal product of capital constant at an unaltered capital-output ratio?

2. Do conditions exist such that Harrod-neutral change leaves the ratio of marginal products unaltered at a constant capital-labor ratio?

To explore the first approach, we exploit Table 6.1. Technological change is Hicks neutral when $\beta = 0$. It is also Harrod neutral if the output-capital ratio is preserved at a constant marginal product of capital. The growth equation for the output-capital ratio when change is Hicks neutral is (6.15). Setting $X^* - K^*$ equal to zero,

$$X^* - K^* = 0 = -ak^* + \pi$$

The growth equation for the marginal product of capital when change is Hicks neutral is (6.13). Setting $\beta = 0$ and $r^* = 0$,

$$r^* = 0 = -\frac{a}{\sigma}k^* + \pi$$

For both of these equations to hold simultaneously, the elasticity of substitution, σ, must equal one. Hicks and Harrod neutrality amount to the same thing when $\sigma = 1$.

As a check on this discovery, we can turn to Table 6.2, which contains growth equations for Harrod neutrality, and explore the second approach. Hicks neutrality requires that $w^* - r^* = 0$ when $k^* = 0$. Subtracting (6.25) for r^* from (6.26) for w^*, setting the difference equal to zero and letting $k^* = 0$, we have

$$w^* - r^* = 0 = -\frac{1-\sigma}{\sigma}m$$

again, the conditions hold only when $\sigma = 1$.

The argument can be illustrated graphically in terms of the isoquant map that we have used twice before in this chapter to illustrate separately Hicks neutrality (Figure 6.1) and Harrod neutrality (Figure 6.3b). The diagram was also used in the last chapter (Figure 5.6) to illustrate the elasticity of substitution. We can now bring these concepts together to show the links

A Comparison of Hicks-Neutral and Harrod-Neutral Technological Progress

TABLE 6.2

Growth Equations When Technological Change is Neutral in the Sense of Harrod

Variable	Growth Equation	
Output	$X^* = (1-a)K^* + aL^* + am$	(6.27)
Average product of capital	$X^* - K^* = -ak^* + am$	(6.28)
Average product of labor	$X^* - L^* = (1-a)k^* + am$	(6.29)
Marginal product of capital	$r^* = -\dfrac{a}{\sigma}k^* + \dfrac{a}{\sigma}m$	(6.25)
Marginal product of labor	$w^* = \dfrac{(1-a)}{\sigma}k^* + \left(\dfrac{a}{\sigma} - \dfrac{1-\sigma}{\sigma}\right)m$	(6.26)
Share imputed to capital	$(1-a)^* = -\dfrac{1-\sigma}{\sigma}ak^* + \dfrac{1-\sigma}{\sigma}am$	(6.30)
Share imputed to labor	$a^* = \dfrac{1-\sigma}{\sigma}(1-a)k^* - \dfrac{1-\sigma}{\sigma}(1-a)m$	(6.31)

between Hicks and Harrod neutrality and the elasticity of substitution.[8] The technological change is indicated in Figure 6.4 by a shrinking of the unit isoquant toward the origin from the solid isoquant, passing through points A and B, to the dotted one, passing through points C and E. The change is Hicks neutral because, starting from A, the slope of the new unit isoquant is unchanged at E, which lies on the same ray, $0k$, as does A. The change is also Harrod neutral because, starting from point B, the marginal product of capital ($r = 1/0J$) is unchanged at a constant capital-output ratio ($0G$).

It was demonstrated in the last chapter that the elasticity of substitution is the ratio of two line segments. The first, AC here, was formed by the counterclockwise rotation of the ray $0k$ to $0k'$, cutting the horizontal line GA, first at A, and then at C. The second line segment was formed by the clockwise rotation of the tangent line, anchored at point J, to a position where it was parallel with the tangent line at point B. The tangent cut the line GA first at A, and then at some point to the left of A on GA. In this case, that point is C. Thus, the two line segments are equal; their ratio is one; the elasticity of substitution is unity; and Hicks and Harrod neutrality amount to the same thing when $\sigma = 1$.

Figure 6.4, in fact, portrays a Cobb-Douglas production function ($\sigma = 1$), and it is instructive to show that technological change is both Hicks and Harrod neutral in Cobb-Douglas technology. To take the case of Hicks

---

[8] The diagrammatic presentation is based on R. W. Jones, *op. cit.*

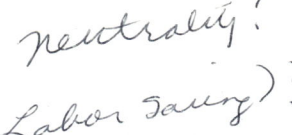
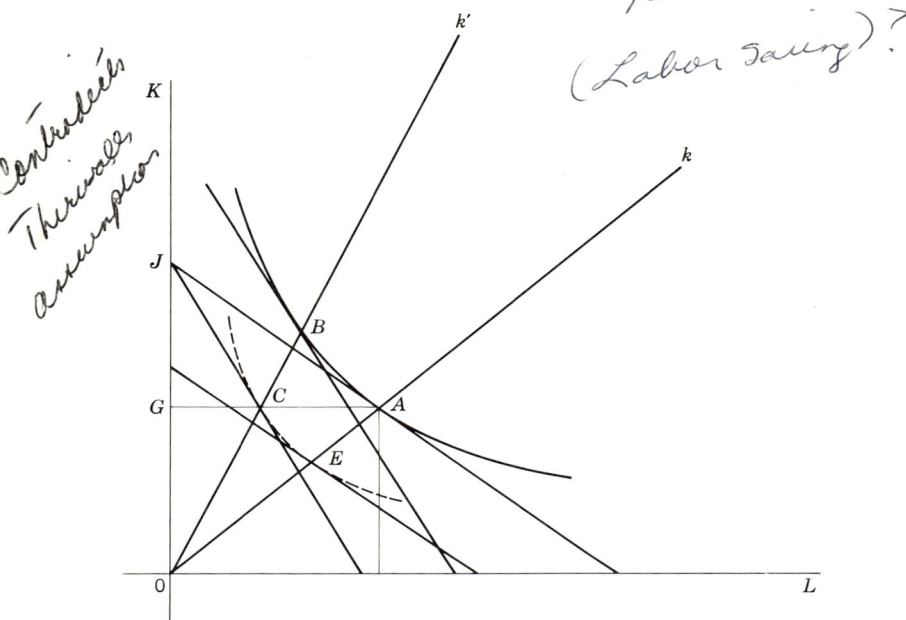

Figure 6.4 Hicks neutrality, Harrod neutrality, and the elasticity of substitution.

neutrality first, recall that in general, Hicks-neutral technological change results if

$$\frac{X}{L} = A(t) \cdot g\left(\frac{K}{L}\right)$$

or

$$x = A(t) \cdot g(k)$$

The special case of Cobb-Douglas is therefore written

$$X = A(t)K^{1-a}L^a$$

or

$$\frac{X}{L} = A(t)\left(\frac{K}{L}\right)^{1-a}$$

or

$$x = A(t)k^{1-a}$$

Harrod-neutral technological change is the same thing as labor augmentation. Letting the augmentation index (Q) depend on the passage of time, we have in general

$$\frac{X}{Q(t)L} = f\left(\frac{K}{Q(t)L}\right)$$

or

$$x = f\left(\frac{k}{Q(t)}\right)Q(t)$$

The special case of Cobb-Douglas is therefore written

$$x = \left(\frac{k}{Q(t)}\right)^{1-a} Q(t)$$

or

$$x = Q(t)^a k^{1-a}$$

Clearly, x is related to k in the same way by $A(t)$ and $Q(t)^a$. Since both marginal products and the average product of capital depend upon k alone, equal shifts in $A(t)$ and $Q(t)^a$ will have identical effects.

It has been shown that technological change is both Hicks and Harrod neutral in Cobb-Douglas technology. It can be shown that the Cobb-Douglas case is the only case where the two coincide, but that demonstration is not made here.

EXERCISES

1. If $X = F(K, L, t)$, show that the average product of capital is $f(k, t)/k$ where $k \equiv K/L$.
2. If $X = L \cdot f(k, t)$ and $k \equiv K/L$, show that the marginal product of labor is $f(k, t) - k \cdot f_k(k, t)$.
3. If $X = \hat{L} \cdot f(\hat{k})$, $\hat{k} \equiv K/\hat{L}$, and $\hat{L} = e^{mt} \cdot L$, show that $\partial X/\partial K = r = f'(\hat{k})$ and that $w = e^{mt}[f(\hat{k}) - \hat{k} \cdot f'(\hat{k})]$.
4. Draw a figure similar to 6.3a but illustrating a technological change that is neutral in the sense of Hicks.

REFERENCES AND SUGGESTIONS FOR FURTHER READING

1. Denison, E. F., "The Unimportance of the Embodied Question." *American Economic Review*, March, 1964.
2. Denison, E. F., *Sources of Economic Growth in the United States and the Alternatives Before Us.* Supplementary Paper No. 13, The Committee for Economic Development, January 1962.
3. Fisher, F. M., "The Existence of Aggregate Production Functions." *Econometrica*, October 1969.
4. Harrod, R. E., *Towards A Dynamic Economics.* London: Macmillan, 1948.
5. Hicks, J. R., *The Theory of Wages.* London: Macmillan, 1932.
6. Jones, R. W., "'Neutral' Technological Change and the Isoquant Map." *American Economic Review*, September 1965.
7. Jorgenson, D. W. and Z. Griliches, "The Explanation of Productivity Change." *Review of Economic Studies.* July 1967.
8. Solow, R. M., "Investment and Technical Progress." Chap. 7 of K. J. Arrow, S. Karlen, and P. Suppes (Eds.), *Mathematical Methods in the Social Sciences.* Stanford: Stanford University Press, 1960.
9. Uzawa, H., "Neutral Inventions and the Stability of Growth Equilibrium." *Review of Economic Studies*, February 1961.

Chapter Seven

GROWTH WITH TECHNOLOGICAL CHANGE

Comparative Dynamics
Technological Change in an Advanced Economy
Continuous Labor Augmentation
Continuous Improvement with Bias as Defined by Hicks
A Single Improvement
An Explicit Solution
Technological Change in a Primitive Economy
A Single Improvement
An Explicit Solution
Exercises
References and Suggestions for Further Reading

COMPARATIVE DYNAMICS

The last two chapters have explored the static, comparative static and dynamic properties of constant returns to scale production in some detail. Growth equations for output, average and marginal products, and relative shares have been derived in terms of the rate of capital deepening (k^*), the elasticity of substitution (σ), the measures of technological change (π, β, m) and labor's share of product (a). For our purposes, we shall regard the elasticity of substitution and technological change to be *exogenous*, or determined outside the framework of analysis.[1] The remaining variables are *endogenous*, to be determined within the context of the growth models.

In this chapter, we shall first link up the characteristics of equilibrium growth for an advanced economy (Chapter Three) and a primitive economy (Chapter Four) with the more detailed view of the production function (Chapter Five) and the way it shifts when technological change occurs (Chapter Six). Second, a specific production function will be employed that will permit an explicit solution of differential equations of growth for the two economies.

This second approach permits more to be said about interequilibrium transitions. The first approach focuses attention on equilibrium growth states, and compares one with another.

The concept of *comparative dynamics* has already been introduced in Chapters Three and Four, where we compared one moving equilibrium with another. Each equilibrium growth path was associated with a particular set of values for the relevant parameters (exogenous variables). Examples of these parameters were the saving ratio, population growth rate for the advanced economy, and the crude death rate for the primitive economy. In those earlier chapters, we were able to trace the consequences for certain endogenous variables when one of these parameters changed. We were able to *compare* one *dynamic* equilibrium with another, and could make such qualitative statements as "a rise in the saving ratio increases per capita income..." in the advanced economy.

The model links per capita income (one of the endogenous variables) to the saving ratio (one of the exogenous variables or parameters) along an equilibrium growth path. A higher level of per capita income is associated with a higher saving ratio along another equilibrium growth path. In comparative dynamics, we compare the qualities of the two equilibrium growth paths.

This procedure largely overlooks the mechanism that leads the economy from the original equilibrium to the new one. In this respect, comparative dynamics is akin to the more familiar comparative statics.

An example of the latter is the usual supply and demand analysis of a market for a single consumer good. The model of the market links price and quantity (the endogenous variables) to several exogenous variables,

---

[1] More complete analyses treat these variables as endogenous. For a model that views technological change as an economic activity that absorbs resources, see K. Shell, "Toward a Theory of Inventive Activity and Capital Accumulation," *American Economic Review* (May 1966). An attempt to explain the bias of technological change is made by P. A. Samuelson, "A Theory of Induced Innovation Along Kennedy-Weisäcker Lines," *The Review of Economics and Statistics* (November 1965).

including, say, income. We are able to *compare* one *static* equilibrium with another, and make such statements as "a rise in income increases price and quantity." Not much attention is paid in the usual analysis to *how* the new equilibrium is established, or even to whether it is possible to *get to* the new equilibrium. It is simply assumed that the new equilibrium *is* established, at least eventually.

To illustrate *comparative dynamics* procedure, we return to the model of growth in an advanced economy without technological change. Let us re-examine the consequences of a rise in the saving ratio or a fall in the rate of population growth. We know from Chapter Three that both these events will lead to a higher capital-labor ratio along the new moving equilibrium. Moreover, per capita income will rise, so long as the interest rate is positive (and we assume that it is); now we can use the characteristics of the production function developed in Chapter Five to obtain a more detailed comparison of the new and old moving equilibria.

Table 5.1 shows how the variables of chief concern respond to a change in the capital-labor ratio (k). Can we discover *how much* k changes from one equilibrium to another as a consequence of changes in the saving ratio (s) or the growth rate (g)? If so, we can recompute Table 5.1 in terms of these exogenous changes.

The other source of information, in addition to Table 5.1, is the equilibrium growth property of the model discovered in Chapter Three: all variables grow at the same constant proportional rate, g. Recall the saving and investment relation.

$$K^* = s\frac{X}{K} \quad (3.2)$$

But in equilibrium,

$$K^* = g$$

Thus, for *any* equilibrium growth path with no technological change,

$$g = s\frac{X}{K}$$

or

$$\frac{X}{K} = \frac{g}{s} \quad (7.1)$$

If g or s should change, the *equilibrium* value of the output-capital ratio will change in proportion. Taking logarithms of (7.1),

$$\log \frac{X}{K} = \log g - \log s$$

Differentiating the *equilibrium condition*,

$$d\left(\frac{X}{K}\right)\frac{K}{X} = \frac{dg}{g} - \frac{ds}{s} \qquad (7.2)$$

But from the *production function*, we have a link between changes in the output-capital ratio and changes in k.

$$d\left(\frac{X}{K}\right)\cdot\frac{K}{X} = -a\cdot\frac{dk}{k} \qquad (5.23)$$

Equating the right-hand sides of (7.2) and (5.23), we combine our knowledge of (1) equilibrium growth relations, and (2) production relations, to obtain an expression for the change in the capital-labor ratio from one equilibrium to another.

$$\frac{dk}{k} = \frac{1}{a}\cdot\frac{ds}{s} - \frac{1}{a}\cdot\frac{dg}{g} \qquad (7.3)$$

Now we can recompute Table 5.1 to show how average products, marginal products, and relative shares change in response to a change in s or g, when comparing one equilibrium with another.

Table 7.1 reveals that a rise in the saving ratio or a fall in the growth rate results in capital deepening, a fall in the average product of capital, a rise in the average product of labor, a fall in the interest rate, and a rise in wages. The consequence for relative shares depends on the elasticity of substitution: the distribution of income shifts in favor of capital if the elasticity of substitution is greater than one. This is what we should expect as the consequence of capital deepening.

A word of caution is in order with respect to the use of Table 7.1, and others like it. In most cases, the *magnitude* of the response of an endogenous variable to changes in an exogenous variable depends on the relative share of labor. But the share of labor itself changes unless the elasticity of substitution equals unity. In general, the results are *approximations*, but the smaller the change in s or g, the smaller is the error of approximation. For example, suppose:

$$a = \tfrac{2}{3}$$
$$\sigma = 0.8$$
$$\frac{ds}{s} = \frac{0.01}{0.10} = 0.10 = 10\%$$
$$\frac{dg}{g} = \frac{0.0015}{0.03} = 0.05 = 5\%$$

TABLE 7.1

Comparative Dynamics: Changes in the Saving Ratio and the Growth of Labor

Variable		
Capital-labor ratio	$\dfrac{dk}{k} = \dfrac{1}{a} \cdot \dfrac{ds}{s} - \dfrac{1}{a} \cdot \dfrac{dg}{g}$	(7.3)
Output-capital ratio	$d\dfrac{X}{K} \cdot \dfrac{K}{X} = -\dfrac{ds}{s} + \dfrac{dg}{g}$	(7.2)
Output-labor ratio	$d\dfrac{X}{L} \cdot \dfrac{L}{X} = \dfrac{1-a}{a} \cdot \dfrac{ds}{s} - \dfrac{1-a}{a} \cdot \dfrac{dg}{g}$	(7.4)
Interest rate	$\dfrac{dr}{r} = -\dfrac{1}{\sigma} \cdot \dfrac{ds}{s} + \dfrac{1}{\sigma} \cdot \dfrac{dg}{g}$	(7.5)
Wage rate	$\dfrac{dw}{w} = \dfrac{1-a}{a} \cdot \dfrac{1}{\sigma} \cdot \dfrac{ds}{s} - \dfrac{1-a}{a} \cdot \dfrac{1}{\sigma} \cdot \dfrac{dg}{g}$	(7.6)
Share imputed to capital	$\dfrac{d(1-a)}{1-a} = -\dfrac{1-\sigma}{\sigma} \cdot \dfrac{ds}{s} + \dfrac{1-\sigma}{\sigma} \cdot \dfrac{dg}{g}$	(7.7)
Share imputed to labor	$\dfrac{da}{a} = \dfrac{1-a}{a} \cdot \dfrac{1-\sigma}{\sigma} \cdot \dfrac{ds}{s} - \dfrac{1-a}{a} \cdot \dfrac{1-\sigma}{\sigma} \cdot \dfrac{dg}{g}$	(7.8)

The *approximate* change in labor's share is:

$$\frac{da}{a} = \frac{1}{2} \cdot \frac{1 - 0.08}{0.08}(0.10 - 0.05)$$

$$\frac{da}{a} = \frac{0.05}{8} = 0.00625$$

$$\frac{da}{a} = 0.625\%$$

and the *approximate* change in per capita income is:

$$d\left(\frac{X}{L}\right) \cdot \frac{L}{X} = \tfrac{1}{2}(0.05) = 0.025$$

$$d\left(\frac{X}{L}\right) \cdot \frac{L}{X} = 2.5\%$$

when *comparing* one *dynamic* equilibrium with another. We shall employ similar techniques when working out the consequences of technological change in sections that follow.

TECHNOLOGICAL CHANGE IN AN ADVANCED ECONOMY

Continuous Labor Augmentation

It was found in Chapter Three that if technological change can be described as labor-augmenting, then equilibrium is marked by all variables growing apace with labor when labor is measured in efficiency units. In terms of the notation introduced in Chapter Six, the model was:

$$X = F(K, \hat{L}), \quad \hat{L} = e^{mt}L \tag{7.9}$$

$$K^* = s\frac{X}{K} \tag{7.10}$$

$$\hat{L}^* = g + m \tag{7.11}$$

The production function shows that output depends on capital and labor (measured in efficiency units). As before, the production function has constant returns to scale, so we can write

$$X = \hat{L} \cdot f(\hat{k}), \quad \hat{k} = \frac{K}{\hat{L}}$$

Moreover, positive but diminishing marginal products are assumed. We saw in Chapter Six that this implies declining average and marginal products of capital as more capital is combined per unit of efficiency labor. Thus, we can obtain a solution in the same way as was done in Figure 2.7, except that now labor is measured in efficiency units. A solution is illustrated in Figure 7.1.

Equilibrium is established at $\hat{k}$ with all variables growing at the rate $g + m$ (the rate of growth of labor plus the rate of growth of its efficiency). Thus

$$\hat{k}^* = 0$$

where

$$\hat{k}^* = K^* - \hat{L}^*$$

but

$$\hat{L}^* = L^* + m$$

so

$$\hat{k}^* = K^* - L^* - m$$

or

$$\hat{k}^* = k^* - m$$

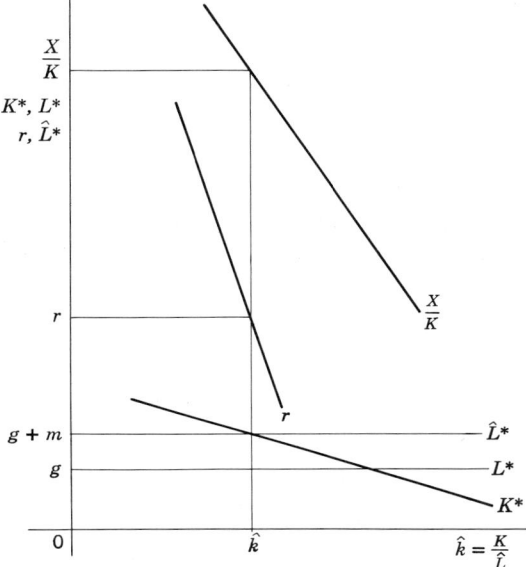

Figure 7.1 The equilibrium rate of growth with labor-augmenting technological change.

Therefore

$$k^* = m$$

The ratio of capital to labor measured in natural units grows at a rate equal to the rate of growth of labor efficiency. In terms of natural labor, there is capital deepening along an equilibrium growth path with improving labor efficiency.

We can now use this *equilibrium* condition

$$k^* = m \qquad (7.12)$$

along with the growth equations derived from the *production function* to recompute Table 6.2 and confirm that the economy grows as we had imagined in our graphical analysis. Substituting $k^* = m$ and $L^* = g$ into Table 6.2, we obtain Table 7.2. The table shows equilibrium growth rates for the variables of concern. *Comparing* one *equilibrium* with another, we conclude that the *rate of growth* of the marginal and average products of capital is zero and insensitive to the rate of labor augmentation. The shares imputed to the two inputs are also constant. But the *rate of growth* of wages and per capita income increases in proportion to the *rate of growth* of labor efficiency. For example, in the case of wages,

$$\frac{dw^*}{w^*} = \frac{dm}{m}$$

comparing one *dynamic* equilibrium growth state with another.

However, *comparing* one *dynamic* equilibrium with another, the equilibrium *values* of the endogenous variables are different for different rates of growth of efficiency labor. This is evident in Figure 7.1. If the rate of growth

TABLE 7.2

Growth with Labor-Augmenting Technological Change: Labor Measured in Natural Units

Variable	Growth Equation	
Output	$X^* = m + g$	(7.13)
Output-capital ratio	$X^* - K^* = 0$	(7.14)
Output-labor ratio	$X^* - L^* = m$	(7.15)
Interest rate	$r^* = 0$	(7.16)
Wage rate	$w^* = m$	(7.17)
Share imputed to capital	$(1 - a)^* = 0$	(7.18)
Share imputed to labor	$a^* = 0$	(7.19)

of labor efficiency (m) or the rate of growth of labor (g) should increase, a new equilibrium will be eventually established with a lower ratio of capital to efficiency labor ($\hat{k}$). Other variables are likely to change as well.

Since Figure 7.1 shows a solution of the model in terms of $\hat{k}$, let us match our algebraic results in Table 6.2 with the graphical analyses in Figure 7.1, by expressing Table 6.2 in terms of labor measured in efficiency units by substituting

$$L^* = \hat{L}^* - m$$

and

$$k^* = \hat{k}^* + m$$

into Table 6.2. Note that the average and marginal products of labor now appear in Table 7.3 in terms of efficiency labor.

The graphical solution of the model in Figure 7.1 indicates that $\hat{k}^*$ equals zero in long-run equilibrium. When $\hat{k}^*$ equals zero, the entries in Table 7.3

TABLE 7.3

Growth with Labor-Augmenting Technological Change: Labor Measured in Efficiency Units

Variable	Growth Equation	
Output	$X^* = (1 - a)K^* + a\hat{L}^*$	(7.20)
Output-capital ratio	$X^* - K^* = -a\hat{k}^*$	(7.21)
Output-labor ratio	$X^* - \hat{L}^* = (1 - a)\hat{k}^*$	(7.22)
Interest rate	$r^* = -\dfrac{a}{\sigma}\hat{k}^*$	(7.23)
Wage rate	$\hat{w}^* = \dfrac{1-a}{\sigma}\hat{k}^*$	(7.24)
Share imputed to capital	$(1-a)^* = -\dfrac{1-\sigma}{\sigma}a\hat{k}^*$	(7.25)
Share imputed to labor	$a^* = \dfrac{1-\sigma}{\sigma}(1-a)\hat{k}^*$	(7.26)

are precisely the same as those in Table 7.2. Along an equilibrium growth path, capital and output grow at the same proportional rate as efficiency labor.

We are now in a position to *compare* one *dynamic* equilibrium with another. We have the *equilibrium condition* that capital grows at the same rate as efficiency labor.

$$K^* = g + m$$

But

$$K^* = s\frac{X}{K}$$

Thus

$$s\frac{X}{K} = g + m \qquad (7.27)$$

must be true along *any* equilibrium growth path. There is a particular value of the output-capital ratio (an endogenous variable) associated with given values of the saving ratio, the growth of labor, and the growth of its efficiency (exogenous variables). Consequently, *changes* in s, g, or m will give rise to *changes* in X/K, comparing one equilibrium with another. Changes in s and g were explored earlier in this chapter, so here we concentrate on changes in the rate of labor-augmenting technological change.

Growth with Technological Change

To find out how the *equilibrium* value of X/K changes when m changes, we can differentiate (7.27), regarding s and g as constants.

$$s \cdot d\left(\frac{X}{K}\right) = dm$$

Divide this expression by (7.27) to obtain the derivative in proportional terms.

$$d\left(\frac{X}{K}\right) \cdot \frac{K}{X} = \frac{m}{g+m} \cdot \frac{dm}{m} \tag{7.28}$$

As a numerical example, suppose that an initial equilibrium were marked by efficiency labor growing at 4 percent per annum, with labor-force growth equal to 2 percent and labor augmentation growing at 2 percent. Then, if the rate of labor augmentation were to rise to 2.1 percent, a new equilibrium would eventually be established with a higher ratio of output to capital. In proportional terms, the increase would be

$$d\left(\frac{X}{K}\right)\frac{K}{X} = \frac{0.02}{0.04} \cdot \frac{0.001}{0.020} = 0.025$$

or

$$d\left(\frac{X}{K}\right)\frac{K}{X} = 2.5\%$$

The next step is to link together (7.28) with what we already know about the production function. When the output-capital ratio changes, how do the other variables change? To find out, we can interpret the *growth* equations in Table 7.3 as *comparative statics* relations. For example,

$$X^* - K^* = -a\hat{k}^* \tag{7.21}$$

shows the *growth* of X/K in relation to the *growth* of $\hat{k}$. Recall that the asterisk was used to denote proportional change *through time*. For example,

$$X^* = \frac{1}{X} \cdot \frac{dX}{dt}$$

Thus, another way to write (7.21) is

$$\frac{1}{X} \cdot \frac{dX}{dt} - \frac{1}{K} \cdot \frac{dK}{dt} = -a\frac{1}{\hat{k}} \cdot \frac{d\hat{k}}{dt}$$

When *comparing* one *dynamic* equilibrium with another, we are making a *timeless* comparison, just as *comparative statics* does not involve time explicitly. Thus, we can multiply by dt to obtain

$$\frac{dX}{X} - \frac{dK}{K} = -a\frac{d\hat{k}}{\hat{k}}$$

or

$$d\left(\frac{X}{K}\right)\frac{K}{X} = -a\frac{d\hat{k}}{\hat{k}}$$

This is a *timeless* proposition. It tells how much X/K changes when $\hat{k}$ changes. This is a property of the production function that is *always* true. But (7.28) tells us how much X/K changes when m changes, comparing one dynamic equilibrium with another. Thus, by substitution, we can find out how much $\hat{k}$ changes when m changes, comparing one dynamic equilibrium with another. We had

$$d\left(\frac{X}{K}\right)\frac{K}{X} = -a \cdot \frac{d\hat{k}}{\hat{k}}$$

Solving for the proportional change in $\hat{k}$,

$$\frac{d\hat{k}}{\hat{k}} = -\frac{1}{a} \cdot d\left(\frac{X}{K}\right)\frac{K}{X}$$

But the dynamic equilibrium condition was

$$d\left(\frac{X}{K}\right)\frac{K}{X} = \frac{m}{g+m} \cdot \frac{dm}{m} \qquad (7.28)$$

Substituting,

$$\frac{d\hat{k}}{\hat{k}} = -\frac{1}{a} \cdot \frac{m}{g+m} \cdot \frac{dm}{m} \qquad (7.29)$$

An increase in the growth of labor efficiency reduces the ratio of capital to efficiency labor. The less is labor's share of output, and the greater is labor augmentation as a component of the growth rate, the greater will be the proportional effect.

Now that we know how a change in the rate of labor augmentation affects the equilibrium value of the ratio of capital to efficiency labor, it is easy to compute how other variables in the system change. We interpret the remaining growth equations in Table 7.3 as comparative statics relations, and

TABLE 7.4

Comparative Dynamics: A Change in Rate of Labor Augmentation

Variable			
Capital-labor ratio	$\dfrac{d\hat{k}}{\hat{k}} = -\dfrac{1}{a}$	$\dfrac{m}{g+m} \cdot \dfrac{dm}{m}$	(7.29)
Output-capital ratio	$d\left(\dfrac{X}{K}\right) \cdot \dfrac{K}{X} =$	$\dfrac{m}{g+m} \cdot \dfrac{dm}{m}$	(7.28)
Output-labor ratio	$d\left(\dfrac{X}{\hat{L}}\right) \cdot \dfrac{\hat{L}}{X} = -\dfrac{1-a}{a} \cdot$	$\dfrac{m}{g+m} \cdot \dfrac{dm}{m}$	(7.30)
Interest rate	$\dfrac{dr}{r} =$	$\dfrac{1}{\sigma} \cdot \dfrac{m}{g+m} \cdot \dfrac{dm}{m}$	(7.31)
Wage rate	$\dfrac{d\hat{w}}{\hat{w}} = -\dfrac{1-a}{a} \cdot$	$\dfrac{1}{\sigma} \cdot \dfrac{m}{g+m} \cdot \dfrac{dm}{m}$	(7.32)
Share imputed to capital	$\dfrac{d(1-a)}{1-a} = \dfrac{1-\sigma}{\sigma} \cdot$	$\dfrac{m}{g+m} \cdot \dfrac{dm}{m}$	(7.33)
Share imputed to labor	$\dfrac{da}{a} = -\dfrac{1-\sigma}{\sigma} \cdot \dfrac{1-a}{a} \cdot$	$\dfrac{m}{g+m} \cdot \dfrac{dm}{m}$	(7.34)

insert the comparative dynamics value of $d\hat{k}/\hat{k}$, which has just been found. The results are set out in Table 7.4.

An increase in the labor-augmentation rate raises the equilibrium value of the output-capital ratio and lowers the output-efficiency labor ratio. The marginal products move in opposite directions, the rate of interest rising and the efficiency wage falling. With average and marginal products moving in opposite directions, shares imputed to the inputs will rise or fall, depending on whether the elasticity of substitution exceeds or falls short of unity. A rise in the rate of labor augmentation results in capital shallowing (in terms of efficiency labor) which, as was seen before, increases the share of capital if the elasticity of substitution is less than one.

Taken together, Tables 7.4 and 7.2 present a more complete view of the comparative dynamics properties of the model. Table 7.2 shows the *growth rate* of the variables while moving along an equilibrium growth path. Simple differentiation reveals how the growth rates change (in response to a change in the rate of technological improvement) when one equilibrium growth path is compared with another. Table 7.4 shows how the *values* of the variables differ when equilibrium growth paths are compared. For example, Equation 7.16 in Table 7.2 shows that the interest rate is *constant* when *moving along* any equilibrium growth path. Equation 7.31 in Table 7.4 indicates that the interest rate is *higher* as a consequence of *shifting between* growth paths. A higher equilibrium rate of interest is associated with a higher rate of technological progress.

Continuous Improvement with Bias as Defined by Hicks

The broad historical record of growing economies suggests rising trends of per capita income and wages, with shares of income along with the interest rate remaining relatively constant by comparison.[2] We have just seen that labor-augmenting technological change will produce these results. Is there an equivalent continuous improvement in technology with bias as defined by Hicks?

We can begin by noticing that a constant interest rate and a constant share of capital implies a constant output-capital ratio. Since

$$1 - a = r \cdot \frac{X}{K}$$

it follows that

$$\log(1 - a) = \log r + \log X - \log K$$

and, differentiating,

$$(1 - a)^* = r^* + (X^* - K^*)$$

Turning to Table 6.1, we can find out when the interest rate and the output-capital ratio are constant.

$$r^* = 0 = -\frac{a}{\sigma} k^* + \pi + a\beta \qquad (6.13)$$

$$X^* - K^* = 0 = -ak^* + \pi \qquad (6.15)$$

The first condition is satisfied when

$$k^* = \frac{\sigma}{a} \cdot \pi + \sigma\beta$$

and the second condition is satisfied when

$$k^* = \frac{\pi}{a}$$

---

[2] The facts are still in dispute, and there are questions of interpretation. In any case, all statements about trend are abstracted from short-run movements, especially over the business cycle.

It follows that both conditions are satisfied when

$$\beta = \frac{1-\sigma}{\sigma} \cdot \frac{\pi}{a} \qquad (7.35)$$

and

$$k^* = \frac{\pi}{a} \qquad (7.36)$$

When these values are substituted into Table 6.1, the reader can discover that the average and marginal products of capital are constant along the growth path, while the average and marginal products of labor are rising at the rate π/a. With labor growing at the rate g, output growth is given by

$$X^* = \frac{\pi}{a} + g \qquad (7.37)$$

In an economy with technological improvement ($\pi > 0$), steady growth is marked by constant relative shares, rising per capita income, and a constant interest rate. Technological change must be of a particular variety: if the elasticity of substitution (σ) is less than one, technological change must be capital-using or labor-saving ($\beta > 0$); if the elasticity of substitution is greater than one, technological change must be labor-using or capital-saving.

If the *rate* of technological change should increase, its *bias* must also increase if a steady growth path is to be reestablished. Once achieved, the *growth rate* of output, per capita income, and wages are permanently higher. Note, however, that there is no mechanism in the model to ensure that technological change has required bias (Equation 7.35).[3] For that matter, we have not shown that the required rate of capital deepening (Equation 7.36) will be achieved. For these reasons, the concept of technological change as labor-augmenting is more useful when we are considering *continuous* technological improvement, as was done in the last section.

A Single Improvement

The consequences of a single technological improvement can be analyzed in terms of its intensity (π) and bias (β). We can bring to bear the characteristics of equilibrium growth along with the results of our analysis of the production function and the way it shifts when technological change occurs.

---

[3] It was shown in Chapter Six that Hicks and Harrod neutrality are both consistent with technological change in a Cobb-Douglas production function ($\sigma = 1$). In that case, β is zero in (7.35), and we are back to the case of labor augmentation.

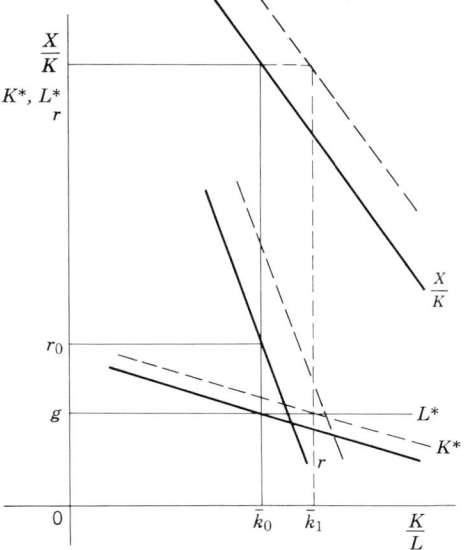

Figure 7.2 A single technological improvement.

An initial equilibrium is depicted in Figure 7.2 for an economy that is growing with no technological change. The equilibrium growth path is the one described in Chapter Three, Figure 3.7, with an equilibrium capital-labor ratio established at $\bar{k}_0$. Capital and labor are growing at the same rate, g. With a constant proportion (s) of income being saved and invested, the equilibrium growth condition is as before

$$K^* = s\frac{X}{K}$$

or

$$g = s\frac{X}{K}$$

The *equilibrium* ratio of output to capital is given by the saving ratio and the growth of labor *irrespective of the state of technology.*

$$\frac{X}{K} = \frac{g}{s}$$

158 Growth with Technological Change

Consequently, if there is a *single* improvement in technology, but no change in g or s, the new equilibrium will be marked by precisely the same output-capital ratio as the old one.

The next step is to reinterpret Table 6.1 as expressing comparative statics relationships. For example, (6.15) now reads as a growth equation.

$$X^* - K^* = -ak^* + \pi \qquad (6.15)$$

or

$$\frac{1}{X} \cdot \frac{dX}{dt} - \frac{1}{K} \cdot \frac{dK}{dt} = -a \cdot \frac{1}{k} \cdot \frac{dk}{dt} + \pi$$

The comparison of one equilibrium with another is a timeless exercise. We obtain the comparative statics counterpart of (6.15) by multiplying by dt.

$$\frac{dX}{X} - \frac{dK}{K} = -a \cdot \frac{dk}{k} + \pi$$

Now π is interpreted as the proportional increase in output, as the consequence of a once-and-for-all improvement.

But we know that the output-capital ratio must be the same, once the new equilibrium is established. Thus, comparing one moving equilibrium with another,

$$0 = -a \cdot \frac{dk}{k} + \pi$$

or

$$\frac{dk}{k} = \frac{\pi}{a} \qquad (7.38)$$

The capital-labor ratio will be higher in the new equilibrium. This information can be used with Table 6.1 to find out how the other variables change. The results are set out in Table 7.5, where $dk/k = \pi/a$ has been substituted for k^*.

The improvement leads to capital deepening and a rise in per capita income. The interest rate will tend to fall if the elasticity of substitution is less than one, but this effect will be offset if the new technology is more capital-using than the old. A labor-saving improvement will dampen the rise in wages. The distribution of income will tend to move in favor of labor if the elasticity of substitution is less than one. But this effect is countered by a capital-using bias.

Technological Change in an Advanced Economy   159

TABLE 7.5

Comparative Dynamics: A Single Technological Improvement

Variable		
Capital-labor ratio	$\dfrac{dk}{k} = \dfrac{\pi}{a}$	(7.38)
Output-capital ratio	$d\left(\dfrac{X}{K}\right) \cdot \dfrac{K}{X} = 0$	(7.39)
Output-labor ratio	$d\left(\dfrac{X}{L}\right) \cdot \dfrac{L}{X} = \dfrac{\pi}{a}$	(7.40)
Interest rate	$\dfrac{dr}{r} = -\dfrac{1-\sigma}{\sigma}\pi + a\beta$	(7.41)
Wage rate	$\dfrac{dw}{w} = \left(1 + \dfrac{1-a}{a}\cdot\dfrac{1}{\sigma}\right)\pi - (1-a)\beta$	(7.42)
Share imputed to capital	$\dfrac{d(1-a)}{1-a} = -\dfrac{1-\sigma}{\sigma}\pi + a\beta$	(7.43)
Share imputed to labor	$\dfrac{da}{a} = \dfrac{1-a}{a}\cdot\dfrac{1-\sigma}{\sigma}\pi - (1-a)\beta$	(7.44)

The transition to the new equilibrium can be traced with the aid of Figure 7.2. The initial equilibrium is marked with solid lines. An improvement in technology increases the output-capital ratio and the interest rate at the existing capital-labor ratio. The new average and marginal product curves are shown by dotted lines. The magnitude of the shift is given by (6.15) and (6.13), interpreted as comparative-statics propositions.

$$d\frac{X}{K}\left(\frac{K}{X}\right) = -a\frac{dk}{k} + \pi$$

$$\frac{dr}{r} = -\frac{a}{\sigma}\cdot\frac{dk}{k} + \pi + a\beta$$

At the existing capital-labor ratio, $dk/k = 0$ so that the shifts at that point are:

$$d\frac{X}{K}\left(\frac{K}{X}\right) = \pi$$

and

$$\frac{dr}{r} = \pi + a\beta$$

160 Growth with Technological Change

The proportional shift of the output-capital ratio exceeds that of the interest rate if the change is capital-using or labor-saving. Consequently, the initial change in capital's share of output depends on the bias as well.

$$\frac{d(1-a)}{1-a} = \frac{dr}{r} - d\left(\frac{X}{K}\right)\frac{K}{X} = a\beta$$

The K^* line rises proportionately to the upward shift of the X/K line. Capital is growing faster than labor at the initial capital-labor ratio. There is now capital deepening, which will go on until a new equilibrium is achieved at $\bar{k}_1$.

Note that the interest rate rose initially, and proportionately more than the average product of capital. From this we conclude that the change was capital-using or labor-saving ($\beta > 0$). However, subsequent capital deepening lowered the interest rate below its original level. A glance at (7.41) in Table 7.5 informs us that the elasticity of substitution must be less than one.

An Explicit Solution

So far we have relied on graphical techniques to find solutions of the growth models. An alternative is to specify a production function and obtain a *differential* equation of growth that can be solved explicitly. Some generality is foregone when a production function is specified. On the other hand, new insights into growth processes are provided by the explicit algebraic solutions made possible by assuming a less-general production function.

A differential equation relates the *derivatives* of a variable to the *value* of the variable. In growth economics, one usually encounters differential equations of the *first order*, and the derivatives are commonly with respect to time. These equations relate the *value* of a variable *at a point in time* to the *first* time *derivative* (its rate of change) *at that same point in time*.

One of the simplest of all differential equations was introduced in Chapter Two. If a variable grows at a constant proportional rate, g,

$$x^* \equiv \frac{\dot{x}}{x} \equiv \frac{1}{x} \cdot \frac{dx}{dt} = g$$

or

$$\dot{x} \equiv \frac{dx}{dt} = g \cdot x$$

This is a *first-order* differential equation because it relates the *first* time derivative ($\dot{x}$) of the variable to its *value* at the same point in time (x).

The equation is also *linear* and *homogeneous*. We can multiply the variable on the right-hand side by any constant number q and the variable on the left-hand side by q^n, factor out the q, and find that $n = 1$.

$$\frac{d}{dt}(x) = g(x)$$

$$\frac{d}{dt}(q^n \cdot x) = g \cdot (q \cdot x)$$

$$q^n \cdot \dot{x} = q \cdot g \cdot (x)$$

$$\therefore \quad n = 1$$

By way of contrast, the differential equation

$$\dot{x} = g \cdot x^3$$

is homogeneous, but of the third degree, and therefore not linear.

$$\frac{d}{dt}(q^n \cdot x) = g(q \cdot x)^3$$

$$q^n \cdot \dot{x} = q^3 g(x^3)$$

$$\therefore \quad n = 3$$

The differential equations

$$\dot{x} = g \cdot x + h$$

or

$$\dot{x} = g \cdot x + H(t)$$

are linear in x but not homogeneous of any degree in x.

Finally, the differential equation has a constant coefficient, since g is a constant and not a function of time. Contrast

$$\dot{x} = G(t)x$$

which is linear and homogeneous in x, but has a nonconstant coefficient. To sum up, the differential equation, first encountered in Chapter Two,

$$\dot{x} = gx$$

is *homogeneous* of the *first degree* with a *constant coefficient*.

162 Growth with Technological Change

We will see that the growth models encountered in Chapters Three and Four can be reduced to differential equations of the form

$$\dot{x} + hx = j$$

which is nonhomogeneous (due to $j \neq 0$) but of the first degree. Since many growth models can be reduced to this form, it is worthwhile to explore a general method of solution so that we can express x as an explicit and known function of time. For example, the *homogeneous* differential equation of Chapter Two,

$$\dot{x} = gx$$

or

$$\dot{x} - gx = 0$$

had the *solution*

$$x = ae^{gt}$$

We want to find the *solution* of the more general, *nonhomogeneous* form

$$\dot{x} + hx = j \tag{7.45}$$

where h and j are constants.

Suppose for now that h is positive. Then higher *values* of the variable (x) are associated with lower *growth rate* ($\dot{x}$). The greater x is, the more slowly it grows; the smaller x is, the faster it grows. This suggests that x converges toward some equilibrium value where x doesn't grow at all ($\dot{x} = 0$). This can be confirmed in a *phase diagram* of (7.45). (A phase diagram shows how the *growth of* a variable depends on its *value*.) Equation 7.45 is plotted in Figure 7.3 for an (arbitrarily chosen) positive value of j.

$$\dot{x} = j - hx \tag{7.45}$$

When x is zero, $\dot{x}$ is j and $\dot{x}$ declines as x increases according to the slope $(-h)$.

The value of x is stationary where the equation crosses the horizontal axis. At that point, $\dot{x}$ equals zero and we can label the associated x as

$$\bar{x} \equiv \text{the equilibrium value of } x$$

Note that x will approach $\bar{x}$ from any initial value of x, $x(0)$. Suppose that $x(0)$ were greater than $\bar{x}$; then $\dot{x}$ would be negative, and *falling*. Suppose that $x(0)$ were *less* than $\bar{x}$; then $\dot{x}$ would be positive, and *rising*.

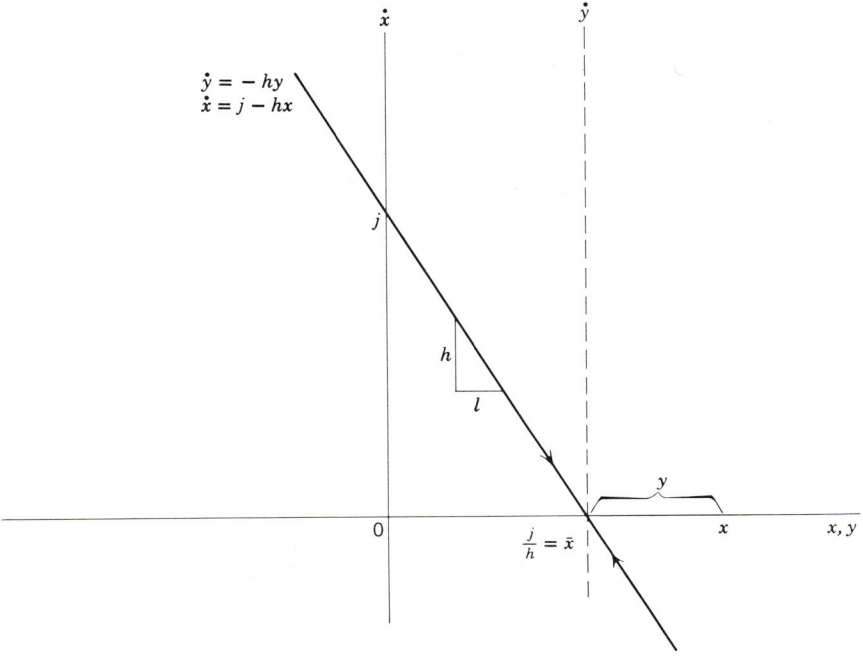

Figure 7.3 A phase diagram of a first order, nonhomogeneous, linear differential equation with a constant coefficient.

Armed with this result, we can solve for $\bar{x}$ in (7.45). Setting $\dot{x}$ to equal 0,

$$\bar{x} = \frac{j}{h}$$

Now we can *define y*, a new variable, as the difference between the value of x that may happen to exist at any moment (x) and its equilibrium value ($\bar{x}$).

$$y \equiv x - \bar{x} \tag{7.46}$$

Since $\bar{x}$ is a constant, it is also true that

$$\dot{y} \equiv \dot{x}$$

We can now write out a new equation for y, the difference between x and its equilibrium value. Since

$$\dot{x} \equiv \dot{y}$$

Growth with Technological Change

and

$$x \equiv y + \bar{x}$$

we can substitute back into (7.45) to obtain

$$\dot{y} = j - h(y - \bar{x})$$

or

$$\dot{y} = j - h\left(y - \frac{j}{h}\right)$$

or

$$\dot{y} = j - hy - j$$

or

$$\dot{y} = -hy$$

We already know how to solve this equation. It is *homogeneous* of *the first degree* with a *constant coefficient*, so the time path of y is given by

$$y = y(0)e^{-ht}$$

As time goes on, y disappears.

In terms of Figure 7.3, we have simply created a new axis for y (the vertical dotted line) by plotting y along with x on the horizontal axis, but the origin of y is at $\bar{x}$. Clearly, if we know what is happening to y, we have complete information on x as well.

We have defined

$$x \equiv y + \bar{x}$$

Substituting,

$$x = y(0)e^{-ht} + \bar{x}$$

But $y(0)$ is simply the difference between the initial x, $x(0)$, and the equilibrium x, $\bar{x}$.

$$y(0) = x(0) - \bar{x}$$

Finally, the *solution* of (7.45) is

$$x = [x(0) - \bar{x}]e^{-ht} + \bar{x} \qquad (7.47)$$

or

$$x = \left[x(0) - \frac{j}{h}\right]e^{-ht} + \frac{j}{h} \quad ^4 \qquad (7.47)$$

As time goes on, e^{-ht} becomes smaller and smaller and the difference disappears between the initial x and its equilibrium. The term in square brackets gradually vanishes and we are left with $x = j/h = \bar{x}$ as time becomes very large.

We get a slightly different interpretation of (7.47) by rearranging it.

$$x = x(0)e^{-ht} + (1 - e^{-ht}) \cdot \frac{j}{h} \qquad (7.47')$$

As time goes on, the initial value of x, $x(0)$, loses its power over x because e^{-ht} is disappearing. Meanwhile, the coefficient in brackets is approaching unity, and for the same reason. The value of x gradually approaches $\bar{x} = j/h$ with the passing of time.

This gradual approach toward equilibrium is illustrated in Figure 7.4, where the left-hand portion is the phase diagram of the *differential equation* flipped on its side, and the right-hand side is the corresponding time-path *solution*. If the initial value of x is $0A$, less than $\bar{x} = 0E$, then the corresponding $\dot{x}$ is positive and equal to $0a$. As time goes on, x continues to rise and its rate of growth to fall. For example, when x reaches point C, closer to $\bar{x}$, $\dot{x}$ has fallen to $0c$, less than $0a$.

If the initial value of x is $0B$, greater than $\bar{x} = 0E$, then the corresponding $\dot{x}$ is negative and equal to $0b$. As time goes on, x continues to fall and its rate of growth becomes less negative. For example, when x reaches point D, closer to $\bar{x}$, $\dot{x}$ is less negative at $0d$ than it was originally at $0b$.

If x starts out from its equilibrium value, $\bar{x} = 0E$, it maintains that value on through time.

The fact that x converges to an equilibrium is due to the algebraic sign of h. In the differential equation (7.45), h appears with a positive sign on the left-hand side. This means that as the *value* of x becomes *larger*, its *growth* ($\dot{x}$) becomes *smaller*, to maintain the equality. This suggests a convergence of x toward an equilibrium. Convergence is confirmed in the solution of the equation. As time goes on, any difference between initial and equilibrium values gradually disappears as an influence on x.

By contrast, suppose h were negative in the differential equation (7.45). Then, as the *value* of x becomes *larger*, its *growth* ($\dot{x}$) becomes *larger*. This

---

[4] A check on the assertion that (7.47) is the solution of (7.45) is to differentiate (7.47) to see if (7.45) emerges. $\dot{x} = -h[x(0) - j/h]e^{-ht}$. From (7.47), $[x(0) - j/h]e^{-ht}$ equals $x - j/h$. Substituting, $\dot{x} = j - hx$.

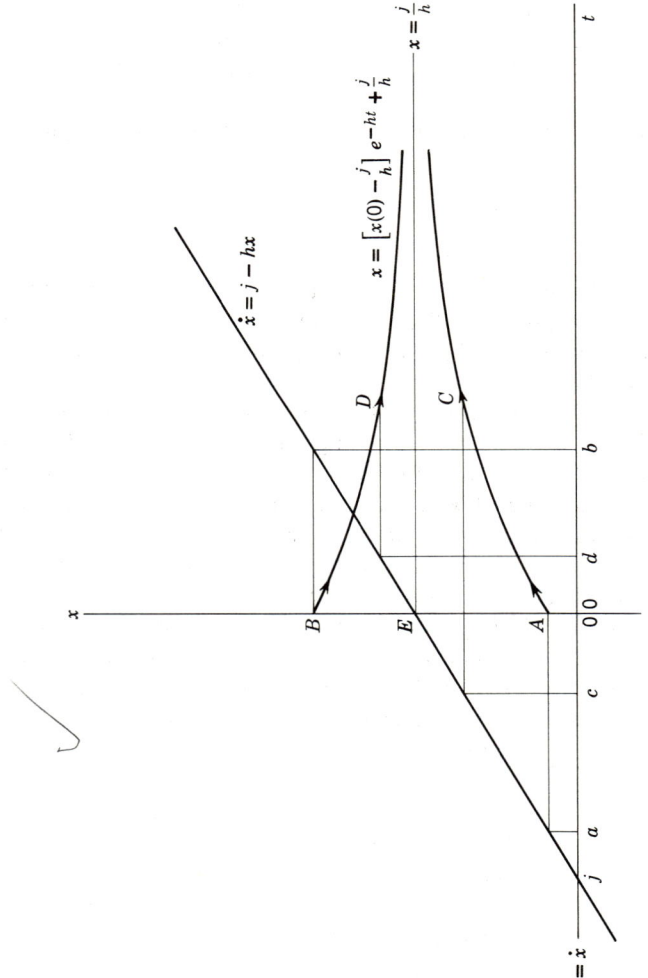

Figure 7.4 A phase diagram and approaches to equilibrium.

suggests an explosive growth process, with x becoming ever larger, and never converging toward any finite value. The suggestion is confirmed in the solution that indicates an explosive path of x if h appears with a positive sign in the exponent(s).

The differential equation of constant proportional growth introduced in Chapter Two is a special case of (7.45), where $j = 0$ and $h = -g$. It is left as an exercise to show that (7.47) or (7.48) yields the (explosive) solution

$$x = x(0)e^{gt}$$

The first obvious application of the solution procedure is to the model of an advanced economy, which was initially presented in Chapter Three. The first step is to reduce the three equations of the model

$$X = F(K, L)$$
$$\dot{K} = sX$$
$$L^* = g$$

to a single differential equation in the standard form

$$\dot{x} + hx = j \tag{7.45}$$

We must first specify the algebraic form of the production function. Let us assume that Cobb-Douglas conditions prevail ($\sigma = 1$).

$$X = AK^{1-a}L^a$$

We can think of A as growing at the constant proportional rate π, indicating continuous Hicks-neutral progress.

$$X = e^{\pi t}K^{1-a}L^a$$

Alternatively, we can imagine that labor augmentation is proceeding at the rate m, indicating continuous Harrod-neutral progress.

$$X = K^{1-a}(e^{mt}L)^a$$

or

$$X = e^{amt}K^{1-a}L^a$$

Clearly, these methods are equivalent with Cobb-Douglas technology ($\sigma = 1$).[5] We shall employ the labor-augmenting formulation.

[5] They are not equivalent in general. See Chapter Six.

Growth with Technological Change

As an exercise, the reader should obtain a differential equation in k. It is

$$\dot{k} + gk = sAk^{1-a}$$

or

$$\dot{k} + gk = se^{amt}k^{1-a}$$

and clearly not in the standard form of (7.45). Thus one cannot apply our present procedure to this equation, although other methods can be used.

A little experimentation will reveal that a standard-form differential equation can be obtained in the capital-output ratio (K/X).[6] Take logarithms of the production function and differentiate with respect to time.

$$\log X = amt + (1-a)\log K + a\log L$$

$$X^* = am + (1-a)K^* + aL^*$$

With labor growing at a constant proportional rate, g, and with the growth of capital given by $K^* = sX/K$, we obtain by substitution

$$X^* = am + s(1-a)\frac{X}{K} + ag$$

Subtract this from $K^* = sX/K$.

$$K^* - X^* = as\frac{X}{K} - (am + ag)$$

where

$$K^* - X^* \equiv \left(\frac{K}{X}\right)^* \equiv \left(\frac{\dot{K}}{X}\right)\frac{X}{K} \equiv \frac{d}{dt}\frac{K}{X} \cdot \frac{X}{K}$$

Thus

$$\left(\frac{\dot{K}}{X}\right) + a(m+g)\frac{K}{X} = as \tag{7.48}$$

is the standard-form differential equation, which can be solved in the usual

---

[6] In his seminal article, T. W. Swan obtains a graphical solution for X/K. See "Economic Growth and Capital Accumulation," *Economic Record* (November 1956). Here, we solve for the reciprocal K/X and do it algebraically.

way. Using what we know already:

	IN GENERAL		SPECIFICALLY	
If		If		

$$\dot{x} + hx = j \quad (7.45) \qquad \left(\frac{\dot{K}}{X}\right) + a(m+g)\frac{K}{X} = as \quad (7.48)$$

then then

$$x = \left[x(0) - \frac{j}{h}\right]e^{-ht} + \frac{j}{h} \quad (7.47) \qquad \frac{K}{X} = \left[\frac{K}{X}(0) - \frac{s}{m+g}\right]e^{-a(m+g)t}$$

$$+ \frac{s}{m+g} \quad (7.49)$$

or or

$$x = x(0)e^{-ht} + (1 - e^{-ht}) \cdot \frac{j}{h} \qquad \frac{K}{X} = \frac{K}{X}(0)e^{-a(m+g)t}$$

$$(7.47') \qquad \qquad + (1 - e^{-a(m+g)t}) \cdot \frac{s}{m+g} \quad (7.49')$$

The equivalent solution equations (7.49) or (7.49') indicate that the *speed of adjustment* is $a(m + g)$. This is the proportional rate at which the difference between the initial and the equilibrium values of the capital-output ratio disappears in (7.49). The growth rate of labor is g and the growth of its efficiency is m. The labor exponent on the production function is a. This is also labor's share of output, as we have defined it before.[7] The adjustment rate is greater, the greater is the rate of labor's growth and technological change, and the greater is labor's share of output. This is what we should expect. The greater labor's rate of growth (g), the more rapidly the system as a whole will move through time. It is reasonable to expect more rapidly moving systems to adjust more quickly. Moreover, the greater labor's share, the less capital must be "made up" or "worked off" if there is a "deficiency" or "surplus" of capital with respect to the equilibrium capital-labor ratio.

The adjustment toward equilibrium is illustrated in Figure 7.5, which is a simultaneous display of the differential equation (7.48) and its solution (7.49). The *differential equation* relates the *change* in K/X (horizontal axis)

---

[7] If $X = AK^{1-a}L^a$, the wage is $w \equiv \partial X/\partial L = aA(K/L)^{1-a}$ and the average product of labor is $X/L = A(K/L)^{1-a}$. Labor's share is $wL/X = a$.

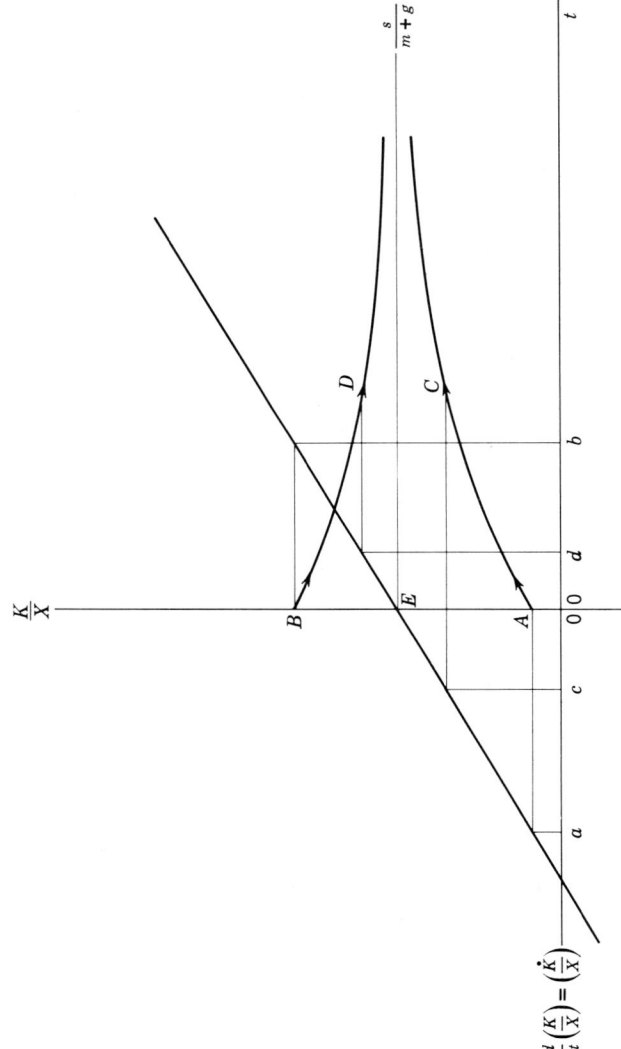

Figure 7.5 A phase diagram and approaches to equilibrium.

to the *value* of K/X (vertical axis). The *solution* relates the *value* of K/X (vertical axis) to *time* (horizontal axis) and the *initial value* of K/X.

The equilibrium value of K/X is s/(m + g). This is the value of K/X when its change (d/dt K/X) is zero in the differential equation (7.48). For values of K/X in excess of s/(m + g), the change is negative; for values of K/X less than s/(m + g), the change is positive. The linear differential equation is a linear relation between K/X and its change, so the equation has a constant slope, downward to the left.

The solution of the differential equation indicates a time path of K/X that converges to s/(m + g) from any initial starting position at t = 0. The *slope* of the time path is d/dt · K/X or precisely the corresponding value of d/dt · K/X shown by the differential equation. For example, the slope of the time path at point A is 0a, on the horizontal axis. Point A is *below* the equilibrium value of K/X and 0a is positive, indicating that K/X is *rising*. At point D the value of K/X is *above* its equilibrium value. But the associated change in K/X is 0d, which is negative, indicating that K/X is falling. If the initial point happened to be at E, with K/X = s/(m + g), the change would be zero, and K/X would maintain its equilibrium value.

With the capital-output ratio constant in equilibrium, and with capital's share (1 − a) always constant, the rate of interest must also be constant in equilibrium. The average product of labor and wages is, however, rising so long as technological change is positive. From the production function, the average product of labor

$$\frac{X}{L} = e^{amt}\left(\frac{K}{L}\right)^{1-a}$$

is growing at the rate

$$\left(\frac{K}{L}\right)^* = am + (1-a)(K^* - L^*)$$

with

$$K^* = s\frac{X}{K} = s \cdot \frac{a(m+g)}{as} = m + g$$

in equilibrium and L^* always equal to g. Therefore,

$$\left(\frac{X}{L}\right)^* = X^* - L^*$$
$$= am + (1-a)(m + g - g)$$
$$= m$$

172   Growth with Technological Change

With labor's share (a) always constant, wages must be growing apace with labor's average product.

Finally, output growth is the growth of labor's average product plus the growth of labor.

$$X^* - L^* = m$$
$$X^* = m + g$$

Now that we have an explicit solution for the model, an interequilibrium transition can be traced more precisely. Suppose the economy is in balanced growth equilibrium when a thrift campaign raises the saving ratio. What will happen to the capital-output ratio?

The initial equilibrium value of K/X is $s/(m + g)$. As a numerical example, if

$$a = \tfrac{2}{3} \qquad g = 0.015$$
$$m = 0.01 \qquad s = 0.10$$

then the initial K/X is

$$\frac{K}{X}(0) = \frac{0.10}{0.025} = \frac{100}{25} = 4$$

If the new saving ratio is 0.125, then the ultimate capital-output ratio is

$$\left(\frac{K}{X}\right) = \frac{0.12}{0.025} = \frac{125}{25} = 5$$

In addition, the speed of adjustment is

$$a(m + g) = \tfrac{2}{3}(0.025) = 0.017 \quad \text{approximately}$$

The time path of the capital-output ratio is given by substitution of these numerical values into (7.49).

$$\frac{K}{X} = 5 + (4 - 5)e^{-0.017t}$$

When $t = 0$ (the time when the saving ratio rises), the capital-output ratio is momentarily unaffected.

$$\frac{K}{X} = 5 + (4 - 5) = 4$$

But the increased proportion of income that is now saved and invested will gradually raise the capital-output ratio. The difference between the initial and final equilibrium values of K/X is disappearing at the rate of 1.7 percent per period due to the constant proportional rate of change of the "die-away factor" ($e^{-0.017t}$). Its absolute rate of change is

$$\frac{d}{dt}e^{-0.017t} = -0.017e^{-0.017t}$$

Thus, its proportional rate of change is -0.017.[8]

TECHNOLOGICAL CHANGE IN A PRIMITIVE ECONOMY

A Single Improvement

The consequences of a single technological change in a primitive economy were tentatively explored in Chapter Four. We were able to conclude that the model

$$X = F(L, N) \tag{4.1}$$

$$L^* = B \cdot \frac{X}{L} - D \tag{4.7a}$$

$$L^* = M - D \tag{4.7b}$$

$$N^* = 0 \tag{4.8}$$

could be solved for the equilibrium level of per capita income

$$\frac{X}{L} = \frac{D}{B} \tag{4.9}$$

without reference to production information. *Comparing* one *equilibrium* with another, we see that an improvement in technology would support a population increment with no change in average income. This information can be combined with the more detailed view of the production function (Chapter Five) and the way it shifts (Chapter Six). In this section, we will trace out the effects of a once-and-for-all improvement with bias as defined by Hicks.

The production function information is derived from Table 7.1, which was based on the production function

$$X = F(K, L)$$

---

[8] Recall that 0.017 is nothing but the coefficient of the variable in the original differential equation, or its slope.

174 Growth with Technological Change

The key variable was the capital-labor ratio.

$$k \equiv \frac{K}{L}$$

For the primitive economy we have

$$X = F(N, L)$$

In view of our analysis in Chapter Four, it is natural to choose

$$n \equiv \frac{L}{N}$$

as the key variable here. To convert the notation in Table 5.1, we substitute land for capital, so that, for example, the change in the average product of land is

$$d\left(\frac{X}{N}\right) \cdot \frac{N}{X} = -a\frac{dk}{k} + \pi, \qquad k \equiv \frac{N}{L}$$

instead of

$$d\left(\frac{X}{K}\right) \cdot \frac{K}{X} = -a\frac{dk}{k} + \pi, \qquad k \equiv \frac{K}{L}$$

The next step is to convert changes in $k \equiv N/L$ to changes in $n \equiv L/N$. Taking logarithms and differentiating

$$\frac{dk}{k} \equiv \frac{dN}{N} - \frac{dL}{L}$$

and

$$\frac{dn}{n} \equiv \frac{dL}{L} - \frac{dN}{N}$$

so that

$$\frac{dk}{k} = -\frac{dn}{n}$$

the proportional change in the average product of land is

$$d\left(\frac{X}{N}\right) \cdot \frac{N}{X} = a\frac{dn}{n} + \pi$$

TABLE 7.6

Comparative Statics: A Single Technological Improvement in a Primitive Economy

Variable		
Output-land ratio	$d\left(\dfrac{X}{N}\right) \cdot \dfrac{N}{X} = a\dfrac{dn}{n} + \pi$	(7.50)
Output-labor ratio	$d\left(\dfrac{X}{L}\right) \cdot \dfrac{L}{X} = -(1-a)\dfrac{dn}{n} + \pi$	(7.51)
Rental rate	$\dfrac{dr}{r} = \dfrac{a}{\sigma}\dfrac{dn}{n} + \pi + a\beta$	(7.52)
Wage rate	$\dfrac{dw}{w} = -\dfrac{1-a}{\sigma} \cdot \dfrac{dn}{n} + \pi - (1-a)\beta$	(7.53)
Share imputed to land	$\dfrac{d(1-a)}{1-a} = a \cdot \dfrac{1-\sigma}{\sigma} \cdot \dfrac{dn}{n} + a\beta$	(7.54)
Share imputed to labor	$\dfrac{da}{a} = -(1-a)\dfrac{1-\sigma}{\sigma} \cdot \dfrac{dn}{n} - (1-a)\beta$	(7.55)

The average product of land rises if there is labor deepening or technological change.

Finally, we interpret a positive β to denote a land-using or labor-saving bias in technological change. Rental per unit of land is r, and a remains the relative share of labor.

The results of making these changes in Table 5.1 are described in Table 7.6. Labor-deepening raises the average product of land and lowers the average product of labor. The marginal products tend to move in the same direction as average products. The greater the magnitude of the movement, the less is the elasticity of substitution. Land-using bias will accentuate the rise in rental rates and dampen the rise in wages. Labor-deepening will shift relative shares in favor of landlords if the elasticity of substitution is less than one.

This comparative statics information on the production function can now be linked with the rest of the model, which suggests that labor's average product cannot change as a consequence of technological improvement, when one equilibrium is compared with another. That is,

$$d\left(\dfrac{X}{L}\right) \cdot \dfrac{L}{X} = 0$$

Using this information in (7.51),

$$0 = -(1-a)\dfrac{dn}{n} + \pi$$

or

$$\frac{dn}{n} = \frac{1}{1-a}\pi \qquad (7.56)$$

Now we know how much the population (and labor force) increase from one equilibrium to another as a consequence of the improvement.

$$\frac{dn}{n} = \frac{dL}{L} - \frac{dN}{N}$$

But the land supply does not change. Thus,

$$\frac{dL}{L} = \frac{1}{1-a}\pi$$

If the increase in output due to the technological change alone is five percent, and landlords take one half of national income, then the labor force (and population) rise by about ten percent between the initial and the final equilibrium.

To find out what happens to the other variables of concern, we can substitute into Table 5.1 the *comparative dynamics* value of n (7.56) to find *comparative dynamics* values for the other variables of concern. The results are set out in Table 7.7.

TABLE 7.7

Comparative Dynamics: A Single Technological Improvement in a Primitive Economy

Variable		
Output-land ratio	$d\left(\frac{X}{N}\right) \cdot \frac{N}{X} = \frac{1}{1-a}\pi$	(7.57)
Output-labor ratio	$d\left(\frac{X}{L}\right) \cdot \frac{L}{X} = 0$	(7.58)
Rental rate	$\frac{dr}{r} = \left(\frac{a}{1-a} \cdot \frac{1}{\sigma} + 1\right)\pi + a\beta$	(7.59)
Wage rate	$\frac{dw}{w} = -\frac{1-\sigma}{\sigma}\pi - (1-a)\beta$	(7.60)
Share imputed to land	$\frac{d(1-a)}{1-a} = \frac{a}{1-a} \cdot \frac{1-\sigma}{\sigma}\pi + a\beta$	(7.61)
Share imputed to labor	$\frac{da}{a} = -\frac{1-\sigma}{\sigma}\pi - (1-a)\beta$	(7.62)

The rental on land is sure to rise as a consequence of the improvement, unless it is very land-saving or labor-using. This we would expect, since we know that the improvement results in labor deepening on the land. Wages will fall if the elasticity of substitution is less than one, unless the effects of labor deepening are offset by sufficient labor-using or land-saving bias. Finally, the distribution of income will tend to shift in favor of labor if the elasticity of substitution is greater than one, but land-using bias could be a sufficient offset.

An Explicit Solution

In this section, we shall work out the consequences of continuous technological change in a primitive economy where the production function can be described as Cobb-Douglas. We shall find that a continuous stream of improvement can raise the equilibrium *level* of per capita income, but *not* its *growth* rate, unless the maximum rate of births has been reached. If this maximum rate obtains, however, it is likely that the rate of growth of per capita income will be continuous.

As before, we hope to obtain a differential equation of growth by assuming Cobb-Douglas technology. But this time, let us assume that technological change proceeds at the Hicks-neutral rate of π.

$$X = e^{\pi t} N^{1-a} L^a$$

Assume for the moment that per capita income is sufficiently low so that the birth rate rises with per capita income.

$$L^* = B \cdot \frac{X}{L} - D$$

Since the output-labor ratio appears in this equation, it would seem natural to attempt to formulate a differential equation in that variable.

Differentiating the production function,

$$X^* = \pi + (1-a)N^* + aL^*$$

Subtracting L^* from either side and letting $N^* = 0$ yields

$$X^* - L^* = \pi - (1-a)L^*$$

or

$$\frac{d}{dt}\left(\frac{X}{L}\right)\frac{L}{X} = \pi - (1-a)L^*$$

Growth with Technological Change

Substituting in the growth-of-labor relation

$$\frac{d}{dt}\left(\frac{X}{L}\right)\frac{L}{X} = \pi - (1-a)\left(B \cdot \frac{X}{L} - D\right)$$

or

$$\frac{d}{dt}\left(\frac{X}{L}\right)\frac{L}{X} = \pi + (1-a)D - (1-a)B \cdot \frac{X}{L}$$

or

$$\frac{d}{dt}\left(\frac{X}{L}\right) + (1-a)B\left(\frac{X}{L}\right)^2 = [\pi + (1-a)D]\frac{X}{L} \qquad (7.63)$$

This will be recognized as a nonlinear form because (X/L) appears squared. The standard linear form is obtained by transforming the variable into its reciprocal.

$$\frac{X}{L} = \frac{1}{L/X}$$

Evaluating its derivative, the first term in (7.63) above, is

$$\frac{d}{dt}\frac{X}{L} = \frac{d}{dt}\frac{1}{L/X} = -\frac{1}{(L/X)^2} \cdot \frac{d}{dt}\frac{L}{X}$$

Substituting these expressions into (7.63),

$$-\frac{1}{(L/X)^2} \cdot \frac{d}{dt}\frac{L}{X} + (1-a)B\frac{1}{(L/X)^2} = [\pi + (1-a)D] \cdot \frac{1}{(L/X)}$$

Multiplying by $(L/X)^2$,

$$-\frac{d}{dt}\frac{L}{X} + (1-a)B = [\pi + (1-a)D]\frac{L}{X}$$

or

$$\frac{d}{dt}\frac{L}{X} + [\pi + (1-a)D]\frac{L}{X} = (1-a)B \qquad (7.64)$$

Technological Change in a Primitive Economy

This equation is in the standard form of (7.45)

$$\dot{x} + hx = j \tag{7.45}$$

which has the solution

$$x = \bar{x} + [\dot{x}(0) - \bar{x}]e^{-ht}$$

$$\bar{x} = \frac{j}{h}$$

The solution of (7.64) is therefore

$$\frac{L}{X} = \frac{(1-a)B}{\pi + (1-a)D} + \left[\frac{L}{X}(0) - \frac{(1-a)B}{\pi + (1-a)D}\right]e^{-[\pi + (1-a)D]t} \tag{7.65}$$

As time goes on, the second term on the right-hand side disappears, so that the *equilibrium* value of per capita income is

$$\frac{X}{L} = \frac{\pi + (1-a)D}{(1-a)B} \tag{7.66}$$

Recall from Chapter Four that

$$\frac{X}{L} = \frac{D}{B} \tag{4.9}$$

in equilibrium with no technological change. Thus (4.9) is a special case of (7.66) when $\pi = 0$.

Figure 7.6 illustrates the differential equation (7.64) and its solution (7.65) for the primitive economy. It is to be interpreted in the same way as Figure 7.5, with one exception. The equations are based on the assumption that the birth rate responds to changes in per capita income. But we have assumed that there is a level of per capita income above which the birth rate reaches a maximum (M), so that the population growth becomes a constant

$$L^* = M - D$$

and the differential equation and its solution no longer apply. This area is marked off in the figure by the horizontal dotted line. Below that line, per capita incomes are "too high," and we must formulate a new model, based on a constant (maximum) rate of population growth.

Let there be a sufficiently high rate of continuous technological improvement to move the equilibrium labor-output ratio down to the dotted line.

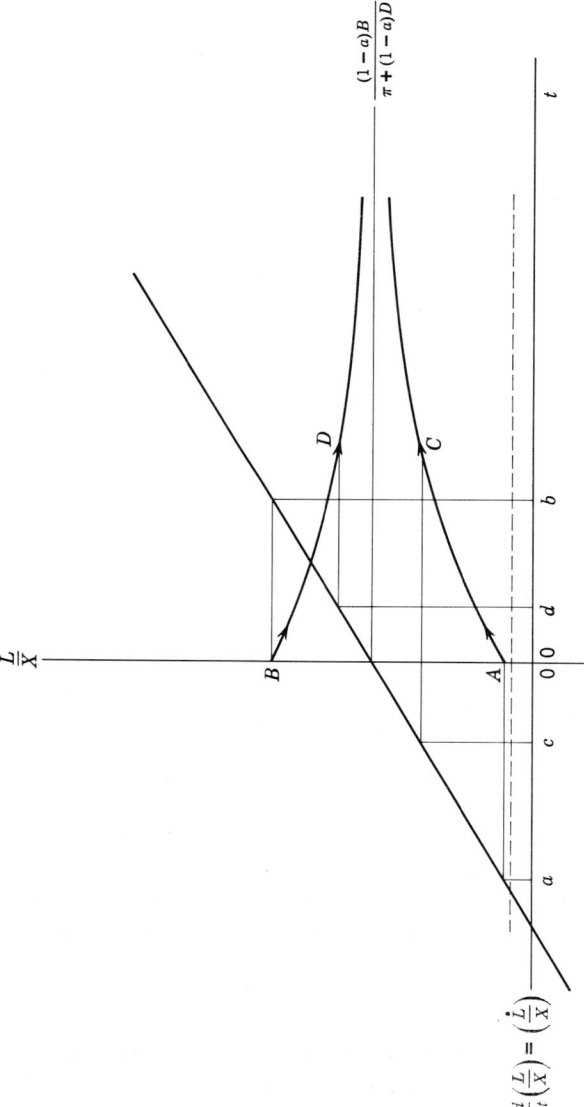

Figure 7.6 The adjustment of the labor-output ratio toward equilibrium.

For higher rates of technological change the model is:

$$X = e^{\pi t} N^{1-a} L^a$$
$$L^* = M - D$$
$$N^* = 0$$

Differentiating the production function, and substituting for L^* and N^*,

$$X^* = \pi + a(M - D)$$

In per capita terms,

$$X^* - L^* = \pi - (1 - a)(M - D)$$

The rate of technological change that will just keep per capita income constant is

$$\pi = (1 - a)(M - D)$$

Suppose M is 4 percent, D is 1 percent, and one half of national income accrues to land. Then technological improvement must occur at a rate of $1\frac{1}{2}$ percent to hold per capita income steady. A higher rate will yield steadily rising average incomes. A lower rate will cause per capita income to degenerate toward the level below which the birth rate again becomes sensitive to income. At that point, the model, as originally solved, applies again.

EXERCISES

Referring to the advanced economy:

1. Comparing one equilibrium with another, what would happen to the share imputed to capital if the saving ratio rose by 1 percent and the growth of population fell by 2 percent? Assume that the elasticity of substitution equals one half and that there is no technological change.

2. Comparing one equilibrium with another, suppose we observe that as a consequence of a single technological improvement:
   (a) r falls by 1 percent.
   (b) π is 5 percent.
   c) a is $\frac{3}{4}$ initially.
   (d) a rises by 2.5 percent.

   What was the value of the (constant) elasticity of substitution (σ)? What was the capital-using bias?

3. Let $\hat{L} = e^{mt}L$ and $X = K^{1-a}\hat{L}^a$. Find the differential equation for $k \equiv K/L$. Can you solve it graphically? Algebraically?

REFERENCES AND SUGGESTIONS FOR FURTHER READING

1. Allen, R. D. G., *Macro-Economic Theory*. London: Macmillan. 1967, pp. 259–274.
2. Allen, R. D. G., *Mathematical Analysis for Economists*. London: Macmillan, 1960, pp. 412–425.
3. Baumol, W. J., *Economic Dynamics*. New York: Macmillan, 1959, pp. 279–285, 311–317.
4. Samuelson, P. A., "A Theory of Induced Innovation Along Kennedy-Weisäcker Lines." *Review of Economics and Statistics*, November 1965.
5. Shell, K., "Toward a Theory of Inventive Activity and Capital Accumulation." *American Economic Review*, May 1966.
6. Swan, T., "Economic Growth and Capital Accumulation." *Economic Record*, November 1956.
7. Yamane, T., *Mathematics for Economists*. Englewood Cliffs: Prentice-Hall, 1968, Chap. 8.

Chapter Eight

BALANCED AND UNBALANCED GROWTH

Introduction
One Variable
Existence, Uniqueness, and Stability of Balanced Growth Paths
Disequilibrium Growth in an Advanced Economy
Low-Level Equilibrium Traps
A Saving Trap
A Population Trap
Two Variables
Systems of Equations
A Model of Explosive Growth
Exercises
References and Suggestions for Further Reading

INTRODUCTION

The existence of balanced growth equilibrium is not always guaranteed. But if it exists, it has this property: every included variable, if it grows at all, grows at the same proportional rate as all the others. The model advanced economy reached balanced growth equilibrium when output and capital grew at the same rate as efficiency labor. The output-capital ratio stabilized as did income per efficiency worker. The model primitive economy reached balanced "growth" equilibrium when nothing grew at all in the absence of technological change. A balanced growth equilibrium is sometimes called a *Golden Age*. The concept of a Golden Age is to growth economics what the concept of equilibrium prices and quantities is to static microeconomics. Once equilibrium is reached, prices and quantities never change in the latter, and everything grows proportionately in the former.

If equilibria were always obtained, and obtained quickly, there would be little interest in the study of disequilibrium. But we shall see that:

1. Model economies converge rather slowly toward growth equilibrium, even if the equilibrium is stable and unique.
2. Model economies may have more than one equilibrium growth configuration, some of which may be stable and others unstable.
3. Model economies may have no equilibrium which is stable. These economies are likely to explode or decay in an unbalanced fashion.

If our models are to give us insights on economies as we observe them, we should be prepared to analyze unbalanced (disequilibrium) growth states. This chapter is an introduction to that analysis.

ONE VARIABLE

Existence, Uniqueness, and Stability of Balanced Growth Paths

The models so far have been reducible to a single differential equation in one variable (for example, the capital-labor ratio or the ratio of labor to land). We have been assuming, for simplicity, that one stable balanced growth equilibrium exists. Now we want to allow for multiple equilibria and instability.

Consider the following first-order differential equation in any variable x.

$$\frac{dx}{dt} = \dot{x} = g(x)$$

It states that the *rate of change* of x ($dx/dt = \dot{x}$) depends upon the *value* of x. The *solution* of (8.1) shows how the *value* of x depends upon its initial value and upon time

$$x = h[x(0), t]$$

The solution is often difficult or impossible to obtain in analytic form. It is therefore fortunate that a good deal can be discovered about the behavior of x over time from a *phase diagram* (a graphical depiction of the differential equation).

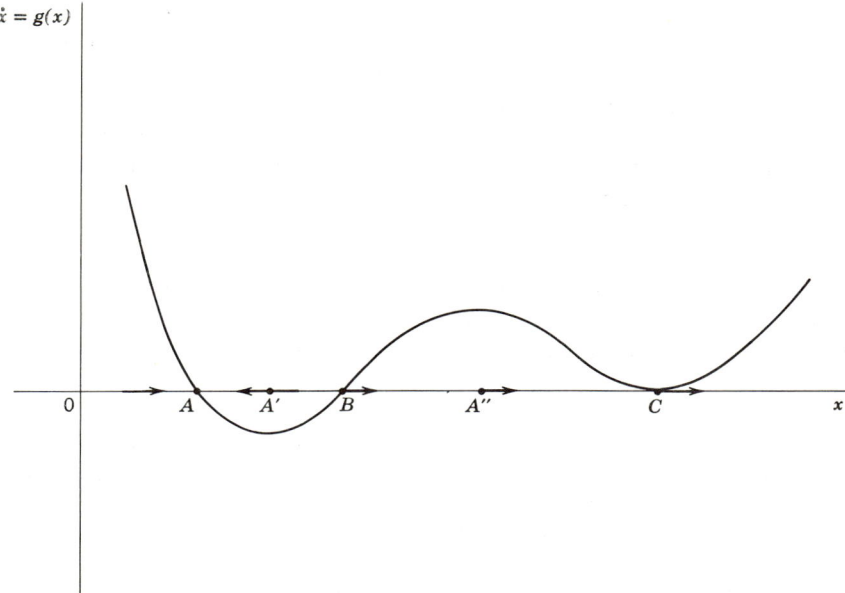

Figure 8.1 A phase diagram depicting a first-order differential equation with multiple particular solutions.

An example of $\dot{x} = g(x)$ is plotted in Figure 8.1. Observe that:

1. x is *growing* ($\dot{x} > 0$) everywhere *above* the x axis; x is *declining* ($\dot{x} < 0$) everywhere *below* the x axis.

2. x is stationary ($\dot{x} = 0$) whenever $\dot{x} = g(x)$ crosses, or is tangent to, the x axis. A value of x for which $\dot{x} = 0$, is called the *particular solution* of the differential equation. A particular solution is an *equilibrium* value of x.

3. A particular solution exists if there is an x such that $g(x) = 0$.

4. There may be more than one particular solution. But if there is only one, the particular solution, or equilibrium x, is *unique*.

In Figure 8.1, a particular solution exists for three values of x:

$$x = A$$
$$x = B$$
$$x = C$$

The function $f(x)$ *crosses* the x axis at $x = A$ and $x = B$. It is *tangent* to the x axis at $x = C$.

An equilibrium is locally *stable* if the function is falling from left to right as it crosses the x axis. For values of x sufficiently close to a stable equilibrium, higher values of x are associated with lower values of its growth. The variable tends to return to its equilibrium value from some other value that is sufficiently close to the particular solution in question. A locally stable equilibrium is illustrated at point A. If $x = A'$, greater than A, we note that $\dot{x}$ is everywhere negative between A' and A. The value of x will recede toward A from A'. However, if x is displaced from A to A'', greater than A *and* greater than A', $\dot{x}$ is positive at A'' and x will increase away from A. Thus, A is but *locally* stable.

The particular solution at B is *unstable*. At this equilibrium, the function crosses the horizontal axis rising from left to right. For values of x sufficiently near this equilibrium higher (lower) values of x are associated with higher (lower) values of its growth. Once displaced from a solution like B, x will never return.

The tangency equilibrium at C is locally stable for displacements of x to the left of C, but locally unstable for displacements of x to the right of C. Tangency equilibria are called unstable.

An equilibrium is *globally* stable if the value of the variable always converges toward equilibrium from *any* value of x permitted by the function. Figure 8.2 illustrates a globally stable equilibrium at $x = A$. The line illustrates a function for which $\dot{x}$ is always positive for values of x less than A, and always negative for values of x greater than A. Moreover, for the illustrated function,

$$\lim_{x \to 0} g(x) = \infty$$

$$g'(x) < 0$$

and

$$g''(x) > 0$$

For this function, we are assured that a globally stable solution exists and that it is unique for all positive values of x.

The variable x might be the ratio of two economic variables ($x = y/z$). For example, x could be the ratio of employment in two different production sectors, or the ratio of capital to output. There is *balanced growth* if $dx/dt = \dot{x} = 0$. In that case,

$$\frac{d}{dt}\left(\frac{y}{z}\right) = 0$$

or

$$-\frac{y \cdot \dot{z} - z \cdot \dot{y}}{z^2} = 0$$

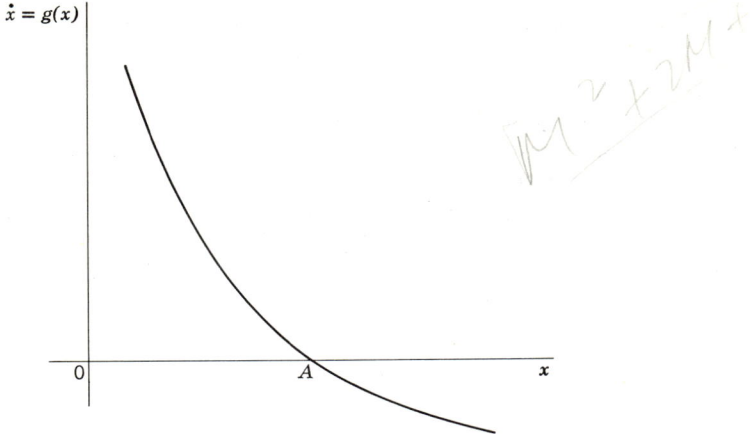

Figure 8.2 A phase diagram depicting a first-order differential equation with a globally stable solution.

or

$$-\frac{y}{z} \cdot \frac{\dot{z}}{z} + \frac{1}{z} \cdot \dot{y} = 0$$

or

$$-\frac{y}{z} \cdot z^* + \frac{y}{z} y^* = 0$$

or

$$z^* = y^*$$

The variables z and y grow apace at the same time proportional rate, once an equilibrium growth path is attained.

But the movement toward equilibrium is typically slow in models of economic growth. If only 5 percent of the difference between the current value of an economic variable and its equilibrium value is eliminated each year, then we ought to be concerned with disequilibrium growth states.

Disequilibrium Growth in an Advanced Economy

In Chapters Three and Seven we explored, for the advanced economy, some of the consequences of changes in the saving ratio, the growth of labor, and the growth of its efficiency. The impact of a single technological change was also analyzed. If the economy was initially growing along a balanced growth path, a change in one of the parameters will set in motion an adjustment process, during which some variables grow faster than others until

188   Balanced and Unbalanced Growth

a new equilibrium is attained. There is *disequilibrium growth* while the economy converges toward its new equilibrium-growth configuration.

There would be little reason to study disequilibrium growth of this kind, were it not for the typically slow adjustment speeds that we expect on *a priori* grounds. For example, we discovered in Chapter Seven that the capital-output ratio closed the gap between its actual and its equilibrium value at the proportional rate $a(m + g)$. In the (not unrealistic) numerical example there, the speed was 1.7 percent per period (year). To simplify matters, let us suppose that the speed of adjustment is 2 percent per period (year). Then the time path of the capital-output ratio is given by

$$\frac{K}{X} = 5 + (4 - 5)e^{-0.02t}$$

where the initial K/X is 4 and the equilibrium K/X is 5.

The reciprocal of the speed of adjustment is called the *time constant* of the system.

$$\text{time constant} \equiv \frac{1}{\text{speed of adjustment}}$$

In our example,

$$\text{time constant} = \frac{1}{0.02} = 50$$

The time constant has the following interpretation. Suppose $1/0.02 = 50$ years have passed since the initial disturbance. Then

$$\frac{K}{X}(50) = 5 + (4 - 5)e^{-(0.02)50}$$

$$= 5 + (4 - 5)e^{-1}$$

$$= 5 + (4 - 5) \cdot \frac{1}{e}$$

Since $e = 2.7183$ (approximately), its reciprocal is 0.3678 (approximately), or a little more than one third. Thus, a little less than two thirds of the difference between the initial (4) and the ultimate (5) values of K/X has been eliminated after 50 years.

$$\frac{K}{X}(50) = 5 + (4 - 5) \cdot \tfrac{1}{3} \quad \text{roughly}$$

$$= 5 - \tfrac{1}{3} = 4\tfrac{2}{3} \quad \text{roughly}$$

For the linear differential equation, the speed of adjustment is the (constant) slope of the equation. In this case,

$$\left(\frac{\dot{K}}{X}\right) = as - a(m + g)\frac{K}{X} \tag{7.48}$$

The time constant is simply one over the slope. In this case, $a(m + g) = 0.02$, so the economy requires 50 periods (years) to achieve close to two thirds of the required adjustment. Put another way, if the saving ratio fell permanently in 1929, over one third of the consequent fall in the capital-output ratio would remain to be effected in 1979. Thus, what are "short-run" interequilibrium adjustments in the model, can easily appear to be "long-run" secular movements in the real world. Solution equations like (7.48) are useful devices for understanding these protracted adjustment periods.

More generally, the slope of a differential equation is different for different values of the variable, as in Figures 8.1 and 8.2. But in general, we can conclude that if disturbances, like changes in the saving ratio, are large and frequent, relative to (typically slow) adjustment speeds, the chances of observing an equilibrium growth state would seem slight. An *observed* growth situation will be closer to an equilibrium path if more recent disturbances have been comparatively small.

Low-Level Equilibrium Traps

A Saving Trap. Thus far we have assumed that a constant proportion of income is saved, and is not dependent on income, the rate of interest, the demographic structure, or anything else. Our graphical analysis of growth with capital accumulation (introduced in Figure 3.7) is quite versatile, however, and the consequences of alternate assumptions about saving behavior can be analyzed. One such assumption is illustrated in Figure 8.3.

It has been alleged by some observers that the early stages of development in some modern underdeveloped countries is marked by a period of "rising expectations." An important manifestation of this expectational phenomenon is an attempt to emulate the private and public consumption standards of more developed countries by consuming more and saving less.[1]

In Figure 8.3 we portray an underdeveloped economy that has adopted primarily capital-using production techniques, so the model of the advanced economy (introduced in Chapter Three) is the more appropriate basic model. The initial capital-labor ratio is k_0, where growth prospects would be quite good if the initial saving ratio could be maintained. In that case, the capital-growth relation would be the dotted K^* line, and the capital-labor ratio (k)

---

[1] R. Nurske, *Problems of Capital Formation in Underdeveloped Countries and Patterns of Trade and Development* (New York: Oxford University Press, 1967), pp. 57–70.

190 Balanced and Unbalanced Growth

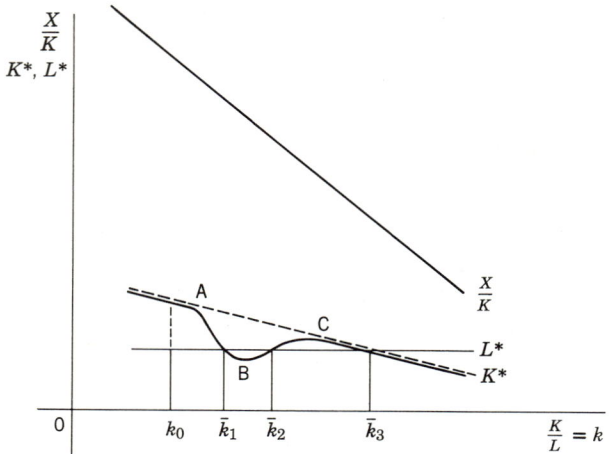

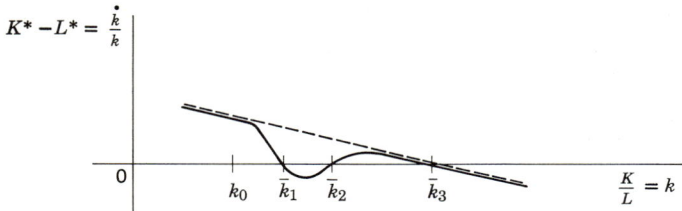

Figure 8.3   Growth with a variable saving function.

would eventually rise to $\bar{k}_3$. Per capita incomes would rise smoothly along with k.[2]

However, as per capita incomes begin to rise, the saving ratio begins to fall. The marginal propensity to save is less than the average propensity to save, and so the average falls. This occurs at point A in the diagram, and continues to point B. Per capita incomes continue to rise so long as capital growth (K^*) exceeds labor growth (L^*). But capital deepening is less rapid than it would have been if the initial saving ratio had been maintained. As it is, the development process grinds to a halt at an equilibrium $\bar{k}_1$, where capital growth has slowed to the rate of labor growth. The equilibrium at $\bar{k}_1$ is *locally stable*, which can be established in the usual way in Figure 8.3. The labor-growth relation (L^*) has been subtracted from the capital-growth relation (K^*) in the lower panel of Figure 8.3. For a capital-labor ratio locally larger (smaller) than $\bar{k}_1$, the capital-labor ratio is declining (growing). The

---

[2] Assume for now that the labor force and population grow at a constant proportional rate throughout the growth process. This assumption will be dropped in the next section. The relation of the saving ratio and per capita income may not be reversible. Moreover, it may not be stable for other reasons.

equilibrium at $\bar{k}_1$ could be called a *low-level equilibrium trap*. It is one (of three) particular solutions of the differential equation illustrated in the diagram.

From point B to point C, in Figure 8.3, the marginal propensity to save exceeds the average propensity to save and the saving ratio rises. One might imagine that a "confrontation with reality" occurs at point B, whereby the links between current saving and future income become clearer to individuals and to their government.

With the saving ratio higher for higher capital-labor and output-labor ratios, capital growth will rise between B and C. In this example, capital growth rises with capital deepening to equal labor growth at $\bar{k}_2$, and then continues to rise for a time with further capital deepening. The capital-labor ratio at $\bar{k}_2$ is a particular solution of the differential equation. It is an *equilibrium* capital-labor ratio. But it is *unstable*. The slightest displacement of k to either side of $\bar{k}_2$ will be magnified as time goes on. For values of k between $\bar{k}_1$ and $\bar{k}_2$, labor growth (L^*) exceeds capital growth (K^*), and k recedes toward the low-level equilibrium trap at the locally stable equilibrium, $\bar{k}_1$.

However, if a k is achieved that exceeds $\bar{k}_2$ by even a little bit, k will continue to rise toward the "high-level equilibrium trap." This is the locally stable equilibrium capital-labor ratio at $\bar{k}_3$. Between $\bar{k}_2$ and C, the marginal saving ratio continues to exceed the average saving ratio, so the average ratio is rising. For even higher values of k, the saving ratio is a constant, as the country finally emerges as an advanced economy.

To sum up, the saving behavior illustrated in Figure 8.3 implies the possibility of multiple particular solutions. As depicted, there are two locally stable equilibria, one at a lower level of capital and output relative to labor and the other at a higher level. Capital-labor ratios in between cannot be sustained at an unstable equilibrium.

A once-and-for-all infusion of foreign aid capital or private investment that establishes a k between $\bar{k}_1$ and $\bar{k}_2$ will have disappointing results. Domestic saving cannot keep ahead of labor growth in this range, and the capital-labor ratio will recede toward the low-level trap. On the other hand, a *big push* that injects sufficient capital to drive k past $\bar{k}_2$, will lead to sustained growth until the "high-level trap" is attained.

A Population Trap. Another possible source of multiple specific solutions is the population-growth function. Suppose that population growth responds to higher levels of per capita income when per capita income is low, reaches a maximum for a range of higher average incomes,[3] and then falls and stabilizes at a constant lower rate for even higher levels of per capita income.

---

[3] This part of the function was employed in the analysis of the primitive economy in Chapter Six. Here, as there, we identify the labor force with the population. This procedure overlooks a number of practically important and analytically fascinating problems having to do with the demographic structure of the population. For example, a rise in the birth rate leads to a greater labor force only with a lag. The dependency ratio is particularly high during the lag period.

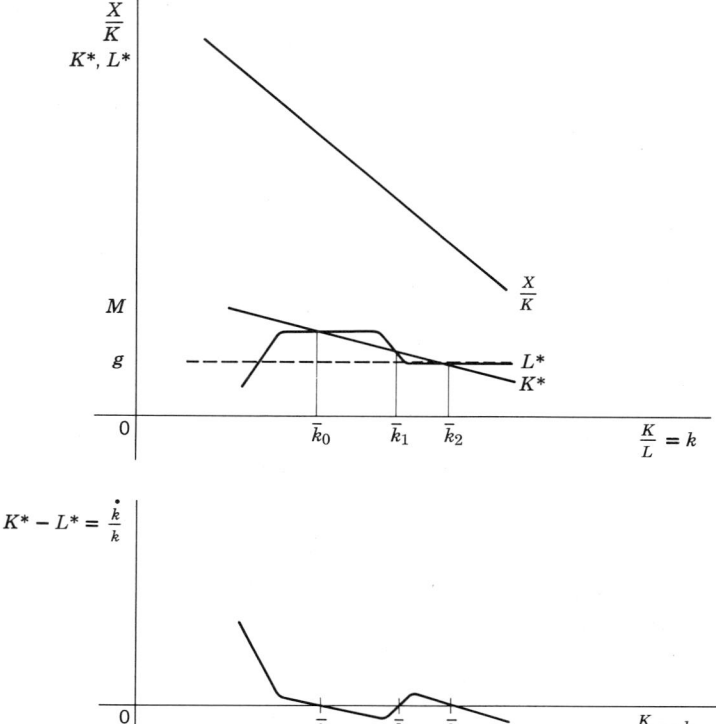

Figure 8.4 Growth with a variable population-growth function.

A population growth function with these characteristics is employed in Figure 8.4. Per capita income rises with the capital-labor ratio (k), plotted on the horizontal axis. If population growth (L^*) were insensitive to average income, it would be a horizontal line, like the dotted line in the figure. As it is, L^* rises at first as k increases at lower levels of k, reaches a maximum (equal to $0M$) for higher levels of k, then finally falls to a constant and lower rate (equal to $0g$) for even higher levels of k and average incomes.

A glance at the upper panel of Figure 8.4 shows the possibility of three particular solutions for k: $\bar{k}_0$, $\bar{k}_1$, and $\bar{k}_2$. One of these, $\bar{k}_1$, is unstable. The value of k will migrate toward $\bar{k}_0$ (or $\bar{k}_2$) if its current value is less (or greater) than $\bar{k}_1$. The same behavior for k is predicted from the lower panel of 8.4. The (locally) stable solutions for k are either the low-level trap at $\bar{k}_0$ or the "high-level trap" at $\bar{k}_2$.

Again, infusions of capital from abroad, that carry k past $\bar{k}_0$ but short of $\bar{k}_1$, will not lead to growth or even sustain k. Labor growth (L^*) will exceed capital growth (K^*) in this range and k will recede toward $\bar{k}_0$.

This analysis suggests once again the crucial role played by population growth in models of this kind. The middle income range, corresponding to $\bar{k}_0$, is marked by high birth rates, and consequent high population growth, compared with the high income range corresponding to $\bar{k}_2$. Higher income has been associated before with a lower population growth rate, where the rate has been exogenously determined. Here, the rate is endogenously determined and the link between proliferation tendencies and material well-being is even more apparent.

TWO VARIABLES

Systems of Equations

Many models of economic growth cannot be reduced to a *single* differential equation, but they can be reduced to a *system* of differential equations. In general, a system of simultaneous differential equations in a number of variables $(x, y, \ldots, z)$ can be written

$$\dot{x} = f(x, y, \ldots, z)$$
$$\dot{y} = g(x, y, \ldots, z)$$
$$\vdots \qquad \vdots$$
$$\dot{z} = h(x, y, \ldots, z)$$

The *time rate of change* of *each* variable *depends upon* the *level* of the variables that appear in the system.

We shall explore here the special case where there are only two variables.

$$\dot{x} = f(x, y) \qquad (8.1a)$$

$$\dot{y} = g(x, y) \qquad (8.1b)$$

Equations 8.1a and 8.1b are a system of first-order simultaneous differential equations. We wish to know how x and y move through time. Do they grow ever larger? Or smaller? Or will they approach constant values as time goes on?

We assume that Equations 8.1a and 8.1b possess continuous first partial derivatives everywhere, and that these partial derivatives have the same algebraic sign everywhere. For example, if we increase the *level* of x in (8.1a) and hold y constant, the *rate of change of* x will smoothly increase or decrease (or remain unchanged), depending upon the algebraic sign of $\partial \dot{x}/\partial x$. Let us denote this partial derivative by f_x. It is *always* positive or *always* negative (or *always* zero).

In the same way, if we increase the *level* of y in (8.1a) and hold x constant, the *rate of change* of x will smoothly increase or decrease (or remain unchanged) depending on the algebraic sign of $\partial \dot{x}/\partial y = f_y$.

The *total* effect on $\dot{x}$ of changing *both* x and y is found by taking the total differential of (8.1a).

$$d\dot{x} = f_x \cdot dx + f_y \cdot dy$$

The change in $\dot{x}$ is equal to the way $\dot{x}$ changes when x alone changes, multiplied by the change in x, plus the way $\dot{x}$ changes when y alone changes, multiplied by the change in y.

We would like to be able to plot (8.1a) and others like it, in two dimensions. Now we can use these concepts to do so. Since we have three dimensions ($\dot{x}$, x, and y), one of them must be sacrificed. Let us use the old technique familiar from production theory. There, we could portray output depending on inputs, $x = f(a, b)$, by plotting *isoquants*: combinations of a and b that yield given values of x. The isoquants were *contours* of a *production* surface.

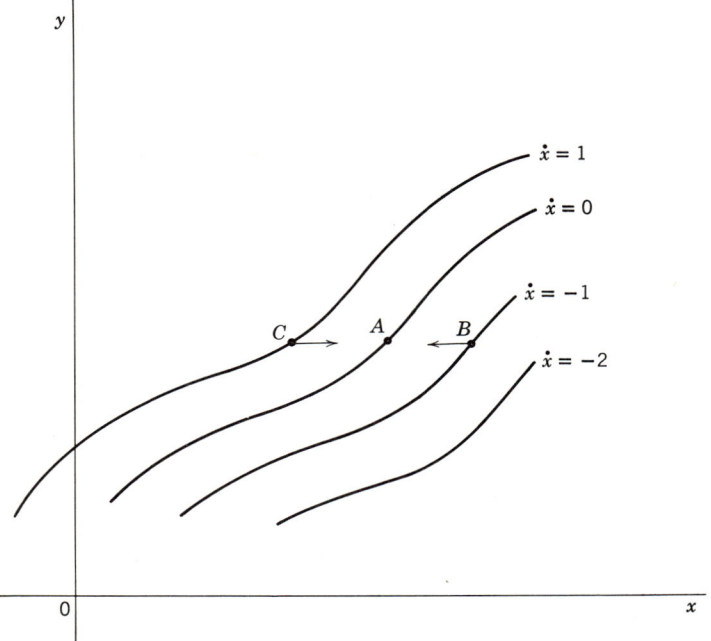

Figure 8.5   Isokines on a growth surface.

Here, we can portray the time derivative of x depending on x and y, $\dot{x} = f(x, y)$, by plotting *isokines* (*iso* [equal] plus *kine* [move]), combinations of x and y that yield given values of $\dot{x}$. The isokines are *contours* on a *growth* surface.

A portion of a growth surface of (8.1a) is illustrated in Figure 8.5. We will be most interested in the $\dot{x} = 0$ contour: the combinations of x and y for which x grows not at all. As illustrated, higher values of y are required to compensate for higher values of x in order to keep $\dot{x} = 0$. The $\dot{x} = 0$ isokine slopes upward. In addition, if x is increased (by moving from, say, A to B), x declines back toward the $\dot{x} = 0$ isokine. If x is decreased (by moving from, say, A to C) x grows forward toward the $\dot{x} = 0$ isokine. These are, of course, particular examples. Let us examine the $\dot{x} = 0$ isokine in more detail.

If we set $\dot{x}$ to equal zero in (8.1a), we can solve for combinations of x and y for which x is unchanging. If we have to solve the implicit function

$$0 = f(x, y)$$

we must know at least the *slope* of the required relation of y to x. Recalling the rule for differentiating an implicit function, we can write as before

$$d\dot{x} = f_x \cdot dx + f_y \cdot dy$$

Now, suppose we could choose a point on the function where $\dot{x} = 0$; for example, point A in Figure 8.6a. If x is increased ($dx > 0$), holding y constant ($dy = 0$), $\dot{x}$ will become positive (negative) if f_x is positive (negative). Thus, to restore $\dot{x}$ to zero, it is necessary to make some change in y. If increasing x caused $\dot{x}$ to become positive, then to restore $\dot{x}$ to zero, we must increase y ($dy > 0$) if f_y is negative, or decrease y ($dy < 0$) if f_y is positive. We conclude that $0 = f(x, y)$ *has a positive slope if f_x and f_y have opposite signs*. In that case, an increase (or decrease) in both x and y is required to have the desired offsetting effects on $\dot{x}$, maintaining its value at zero.

Similar reasoning leads to the conclusion that $0 = f(x, y)$ *has a negative slope if f_x and f_y have the same sign*. In that case, an increase in x would have to be offset by a decrease in y to maintain $\dot{x} = 0$.

To illustrate, suppose that

$$\dot{x} = -ax + by, \quad a > 0, \quad b > 0$$

so that $\dot{x} = 0$ when

$$y = \frac{a}{b} x$$

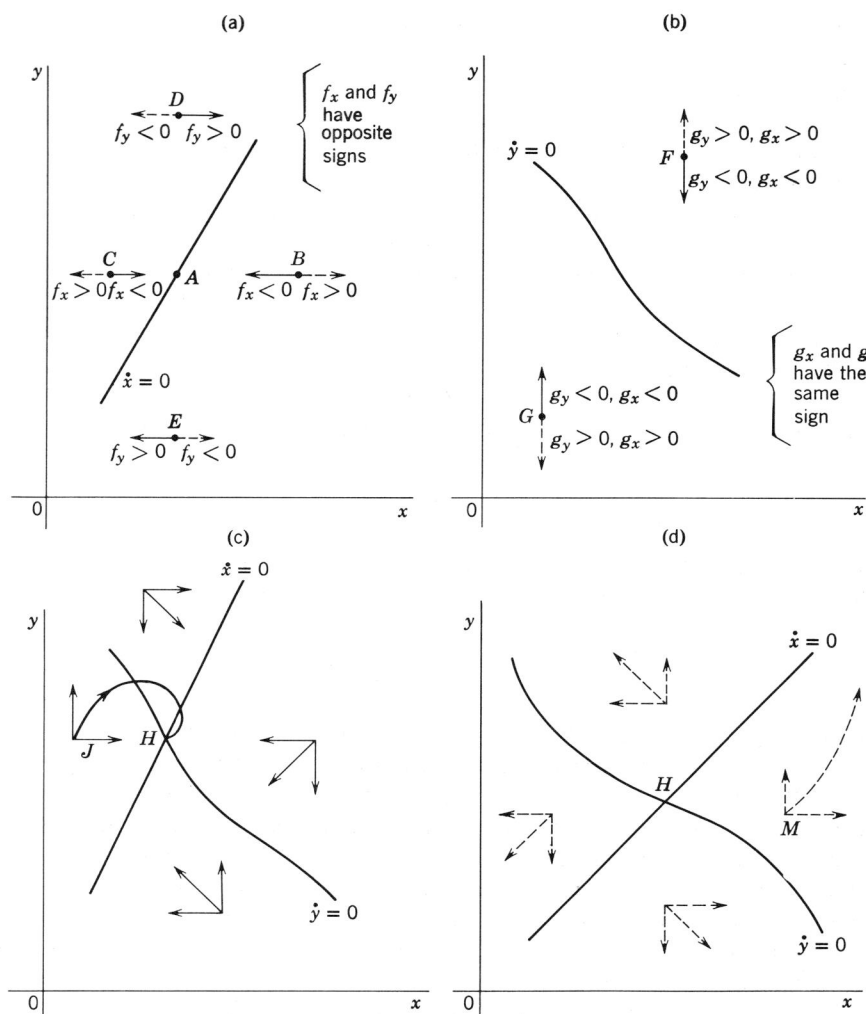

Figure 8.6 Systems of two simultaneous differential equations.

This relation appears in Figure 8.6a, and it has a positive slope. We could have inferred its slope from our recent conclusions. In this example,

$$f_x = -a$$

and

$$f_y = b$$

The partial derivatives have opposite signs, so we could have concluded directly that x and y are positively related when $\dot{x}$ equals zero.

The next step is to ask the *direction* in which x is moving when $0 = f(x, y)$ is *not* satisfied. Again, moving off the $0 = f(x, y)$ relation by increasing x ($dx > 0$) and holding y constant ($dy = 0$) means that $\dot{x}$ is positive if f_x is positive, or that $\dot{x}$ is negative if f_x is negative. Just the opposite happens when moving off the $0 = f(x, y)$ relation by decreasing x ($dx < 0$) and holding y constant ($dy = 0$): $\dot{x}$ becomes positive if f_x is negative, or $\dot{x}$ becomes negative if f_x is positive.

These results are illustrated in Figure 8.6a. Holding y constant, we move from A on $0 = f(x, y)$: first to B by increasing x ($dx > 0$); and then to C by decreasing x. The corresponding movement of x is denoted by the arrows at B and C. For example: at B, $\dot{x}$ is negative if f_x is negative, and this is indicated by the solid arrow, which shows that x is decreasing at point B; at C, $\dot{x}$ is positive if f_x is negative, and this is indicated by the solid arrow, which shows that x is increasing at point C.

By moving off the $0 = f(x, y)$ relation in the y direction, holding x constant, we can trace the effects of y on the movement of x in the same manner. For example, movement from A to E in Figure 8.6a illustrates a decrease in y ($dy < 0$), when x is held constant ($dx = 0$). As a consequence, x is decreasing ($\dot{x} < 0$) if f_y is greater than zero, or increasing ($\dot{x} > 0$) if f_y is less than zero. These movements of x are denoted by the solid and dotted arrows respectively.

Recall that the upward sloping $0 = f(x, y)$ relation is associated with f_x and f_y having opposite algebraic signs. As a consequence, the solid arrows at B, C, D, and E are associated with one another, and the dotted arrows at B, C, D, and E are associated with one another.

Put another way, the upward sloping $0 = f(x, y)$ relation divides the area in Figure 8.6a in two:

1. To the right of $0 = f(x, y)$, and below it, we have combinations of x and y for which x is increasing, if $f_x > 0$ (and $f_y < 0$) *or* combinations of x and y for which x is decreasing, if $f_x < 0$ (and $f_y > 0$).
2. To the left of $0 = f(x, y)$, and above it, we have combinations of x and y for which x is decreasing, if $f_x > 0$ (and $f_y < 0$) *or* combinations of x and y for which x is increasing, if $f_x < 0$ (and $f_y > 0$).

The case in which the partial derivatives of x and y have the same sign can be analyzed by similar reasoning. Then $0 = g(x, y)$ must have a negative slope and divide the area in Figure 8.6b in two:

1. To the right and above $0 = g(x, y)$, we have combinations of x and y for which y is increasing, if $g_y > 0$ (and $g_x > 0$) *or* combinations of x and y for which y is decreasing, if $g_y < 0$ (and $g_x < 0$).

2. To the left and below $0 = f(x, y)$, we have combinations of x and y for which y is decreasing, if $g_y > 0$ (and $g_x > 0$) *or* combinations of x and y for which y is increasing, if $g_y < 0$ (and $g_x < 0$).

The system of Equations (8.1a and 8.1b) can be plotted on the same graph, by showing combinations of x and y that satisfy $0 = f(x, y)$, plus combinations of x and y that satisfy $0 = g(x, y)$, and indicating the movements of x and y with arrows for combinations of x and y that do not satisfy $0 = f(x, y)$ and $0 = g(x, y)$.

This is illustrated in Figure 8.6c, where Figure 8.6a and 8.6b are superimposed and it is assumed that $f_x < 0$, $f_y > 0$, $g_x < 0$, and $g_y < 0$. Equilibrium values of x and y *exist* if both $0 = f(x, y)$ and $0 = g(x, y)$ are simultaneously satisfied. The equilibria are *stable* if the arrows indicate that x and y will return to their equilibrium values if displaced therefrom. For example, if x and y are displaced from their equilibrium values at H to disequilibrium values at J, forces are set in motion that cause x to "home in" on the equilibrium point, H. There is *unbalanced growth* throughout the "homing-in" period, but equilibrium is eventually established through a *convergent* dynamic process.

However, a dynamic process may be *divergent*, giving rise to inherent *unbalanced growth* and a movement away from equilibrium values. An example is illustrated in Figure 8.6d, where it is assumed that $f_x > 0$, $f_y < 0$, $g_x > 0$, and $g_y > 0$. If x and y are displaced from their equilibrium values at H, say to M, they will never return. Although an equilibrium *exists* at H, it is *unstable*.

Fortunately, there is a theorem proposed by C. Olech that permits direct determination of an important stability property of two equation systems.[4] The equilibrium solution for x and y in the system (8.1) is *globally stable* if

$$f_x + g_y < 0 \quad \text{everywhere}$$

and

$$f_x g_y - f_y g_x > 0 \quad \text{everywhere}$$

and either

$$f_x g_y \neq 0 \quad \text{everywhere}$$

or

$$f_y g_x \neq 0 \quad \text{everywhere}$$

[4] C. Olech, "On the Global Stability of an Autonomous System on the Plane," *Contributions to Differential Equations*, Vol. I, (1963), pp. 389–400.

Global stability[5] means that x and y will approach their equilibrium values at H from *any* point, like J or M in Figure 8.6c and 8.6d. In these examples, we can confirm that the equilibrium in Figure 8.6c is globally stable. In that case, $f_x < 0$ and $g_y < 0$, so the first Olech condition is satisfied; $f_x g_y$ is positive and $f_y g_x$ is negative, so the second Olech condition is satisfied; and none of the partial derivatives are zero, so the third Olech condition is also satisfied. The reader can confirm that the equilibrium in Figure 8.6d is not globally stable, because the first Olech condition is not satisfied.

Another important kind of stability is *saddle-point* stability, where the equilibrium is stable if the system is displaced in certain directions, but unstable if it is displaced in other directions. An example of saddle-point stability is examined in the next section.

A Model of Explosive Growth

There is no reason why we should constrain ourselves to thinking about models of economic growth that eventually converge toward balanced growth configurations. Many writers believe that essentially explosive, nonconvergent processes are responsible for economic growth and decline.[6] The terms "takeoff," "accelerating growth," and "cumulative decay" have become familiar buzz-words, not only to professional economists but also to the well-informed public. It is unfortunate that most of these writers do not specify with precision the relations that they believe give rise to these explosive movements. As a consequence, we are often asked to accept the assertion that a system of differential equations has an explosive solution when the equations have not been specified.[7] A model of explosive economic growth is specified in this section.[8] Like the models in other chapters, this model is highly aggregative. But it is unlike those other models in that technical change must be produced with scarce resources. Mathematically, it is different because its solution requires solving a system of two differential equations. We will specify production conditions, a capital accumulation function, and a condition for technological progress. Taken together, these

---

[5] The more common Routh-Hurwicz stability conditions ($f_x + g_y < 0$ and $f_x g_y - f_y g_x > 0$) are conditions for local stability. The stricter conditions for global stability are not important if we are concerned only with "small" deviations from the equilibrium position. The Routh-Hurwicz conditions for local stability are necessary and sufficient for global stability if the differential equations are linear. For a derivation of these conditions, see F. R. Gatmacher, *The Theory of Matrices* (New York: Chelsea, 1960).

[6] A popular source of this view is G. Myrdal, *Economic Theory and Underdeveloped Regions* (London: Methuen, 1957).

[7] An example is R. Nurske's interesting discussion of circular causation and the inducement to invest in poor countries. See his *Problems of Capital Formation in Underdeveloped Countries and Patterns of Trade and Development* (New York: Oxford University Press, 1967).

[8] The model is based on K. Shell, "Toward a Theory of Inventive Activity," *American Economic Review* (May 1966).

relations constitute a simple model of growth for a technologically progressive (or regressive) economy.

The economy produces three economic goods: a consumption good, a capital good, and improvements in technology. For simplicity, we shall assume that the production relations for the three sectors are identical. Thus, the three economic goods, "chocolates" (consumer goods), "machines" (capital goods), and "successful inventions" (technological change) are economically indistinguishable in production. Let us designate the gross output of this composite economic good as X and specify that it produced with constant returns to scale in capital and labor. Let A denote the technical efficiency of production. Then

$$X = A \cdot F(K, L)$$

expresses production conditions. If A increases, it is possible to produce more X with the *same* K and L.[9]

The gross output is used for

1. Consumption (X_c).
2. Net augmentation of the capital stock ($dK/dt = \dot{K}$).
3. Replacing worn-out capital. If we assume that a proportion, h, of the capital stock "evaporates" each period, then depreciation of capital is $h \cdot K$.
4. Increasing the technical efficiency of production. We have let A stand for the *level* of technical efficiency. Thus, its net *rate of change* is $dA/dt = \dot{A}$.
5. Replacing technical information that has gotten lost, and transmitting technical knowledge from one generation to the next. If we assume that the cost of these efforts is proportional to the level of technical efficiency, then $j \cdot A$ expresses its depreciation.

Taken together, these five uses of gross output totally exhaust it.

$$X = X_c + \dot{K} + h \cdot K + \dot{A} + j \cdot A$$

We need theories to explain how society allocates its output among the five uses. But lacking these theories, we assume that a constant proportion of gross output is allocated to gross capital accumulation (H) and another portion to gross increases in technical efficiency (J).[10]

$$\dot{K} + h \cdot K = H \cdot X$$
$$\dot{A} + j \cdot A = J \cdot X$$

---

[9] We thus assume that technical change is Hicks neutral and "disembodied." See Chapter Six.

[10] One theory might be that the returns on K and A are always equalized at the margin by competitive firms and individuals. The trouble is that A requires scientific research, development of practical technique, and the training of new workers. The benefits of doing this are largely externalized to the competitive firm, while the costs are chiefly borne internally. This suggests a "market failure" and a role for government.

The output that remains is consumed. Thus

$$X_c = (1 - H - J)X$$

is consumption and $H + J$ is interpreted as the gross saving ratio.

Finally, we assume for simplicity that the labor force does not grow. Thus, the production relation

$$X = A \cdot F(K, L)$$

can be rewritten by absorbing L into the function and writing

$$X = A \cdot f(K)$$

where, in addition,

$$f'(K) > 0$$

and

$$f''(K) < 0$$

Gathering together our equations, we have a compact, three-equation, three-variable model of a stylized economy where technological change is endogenous.

$$X = A \cdot f(K) \tag{8.2}$$

$$\dot{K} = H \cdot X - h \cdot K \tag{8.3}$$

$$\dot{A} = J \cdot X - j \cdot A \tag{8.4}$$

To discover the model's dynamic properties, we first note that the model can be reduced by substitution to two equations in K and A.

$$\dot{K} = H \cdot A \cdot f(K) - h \cdot K \tag{8.5}$$

$$\dot{A} = J \cdot A \cdot f(K) - j \cdot A \tag{8.6}$$

Taking the equations one at a time, we can solve first in (8.5) for combinations of K and A for which $\dot{K} = 0$.

$$A = \frac{h}{H} \cdot \frac{K}{f(K)} \tag{8.7}$$

This equation is plotted in Figure 8.7a. The capital stock is unchanging when it is satisfied.

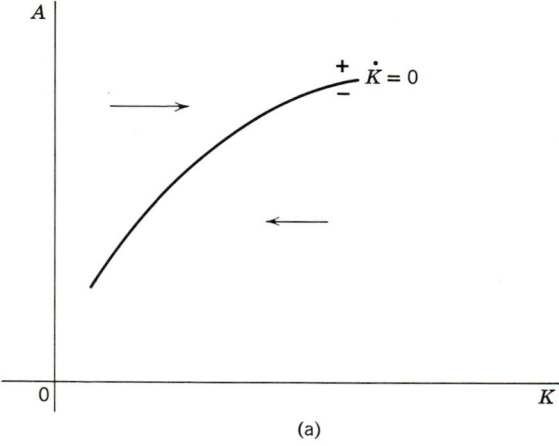

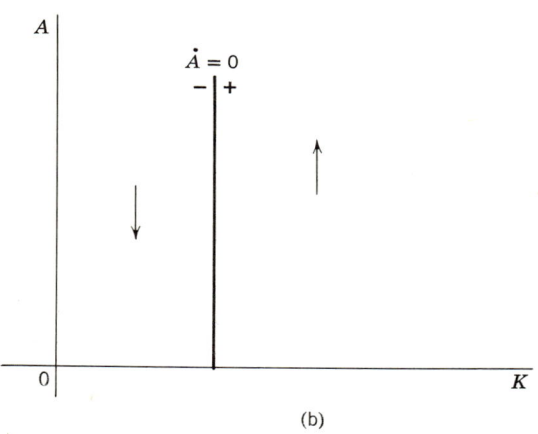

Figure 8.7 The growth of capital and technology.

An economic interpretation of these results begins with (8.7). Rewriting it,

$$H \cdot Af(K) = hK$$

or

$$H \cdot X = hK$$

The capital stock is stationary ($\dot{K} = 0$) when saving for replacement and accumulation ($H \cdot X$) just equals replacement (hK).

When is $\dot{K}$ increasing? That is, when is the inequality

$$H \cdot A \cdot f(K) - hK > 0$$

satisfied? Solving the inequality for A,

$$A > \frac{h}{H} \cdot \frac{K}{f(K)}$$

The capital stock is increasing for values of A that lie above the $\dot{K} = 0$ relation. This is indicated in Figure 8.7a by the arrow pointing east. In this case,

$$H \cdot X > hK$$

and saving for replacement and accumulation ($H \cdot X$) exceeds depreciation; the capital stock grows ($\dot{K} > 0$).

In the same way, we can show that K is decreasing for values of A that lie below the $\dot{K} = 0$ relation. This is shown by the arrow pointing west in Figure 8.7a.

Turning next to the equation of growth for A, (8.4), we can solve for combinations of K and A for which $\dot{A} = 0$.

$$f(K) = \frac{j}{J} \tag{8.8}$$

This equation is plotted in Figure 8.6b. It is satisfied when the depreciation of A just equals saving for its replacement and technological advance. Rewriting the condition,

$$J \cdot f(K) = j$$

or

$$J \cdot Af(K) = jA$$

or

$$J \cdot X = jA$$

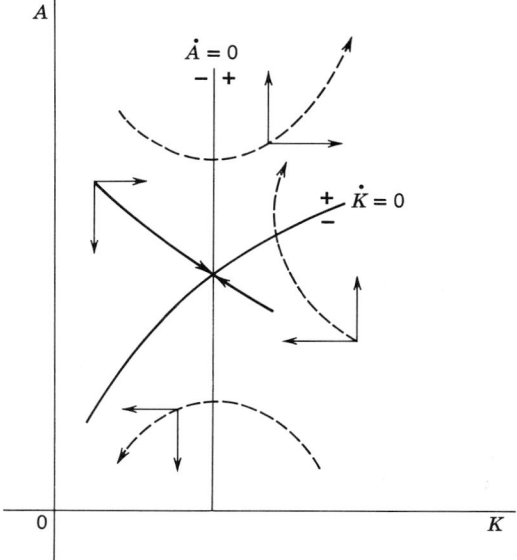

Figure 8.8 A model of explosive growth and decline.

It is evident from (8.8) that A is increasing to the right of the $\dot{A} = 0$ line and decreasing to the left of it. To the right of the $\dot{A} = 0$ line, K is greater and so is X as well; and more X is saved to replace A and to make net additions. Just the opposite occurs to the left of the $\dot{A} = 0$ line. These movements are indicated by the appropriate arrows in Figure 8.7b.

Figures 8.7a and 8.7b are superimposed in Figure 8.8. There is a dynamic equilibrium where the $\dot{K} = 0$ and $\dot{A} = 0$ relations intersect. Elsewhere, K and/or A are moving through time in directions indicated by the solid arrows that have been transferred from Figures 8.7a and 8.7b. Taking together the north-south and east-west components of motion at each point reveals the direction in which K and A are moving. Representative paths for K and A are denoted by the dotted arrows.

The equilibrium, however, is generally unstable. It is a *saddle point*. The slightest disturbance in almost any direction will eventually give rise to *cumulative* movement away from the equilibrium, with K and A changing at rates that differ from one another, and that also differ from the rate of change of population (which is zero in this case). Only if the economy gets on, and stays on, the paths indicated by the heavy arrows (called *stable arms*) will it converge toward balanced growth.

Capital-rich economies with efficient technologies may experience capital deepening and increasing efficiency. At the same time, capital-poor economies with inefficient production methods may experience capital shallowing and a deterioration of efficiency. "The rich get richer and the poor get poorer" in this model. Whether a country is affluent and growing, or poor and declining, depends on the country's willingness and ability to save out of gross income. If the replacement of capital and available technology is not accomplished, the resource base (K) and available technology (A) will wither away, and per capita income will decline as a consequence. But if capital is more than replaced as it wears out, and if technological advance is accomplished, ever more capital is combined with labor with increasing efficiency, and per capita income will grow and grow.

One should not push the analysis too far, however. There are probably upper and lower bounds to these explosive movements. Moreover, when countries are compared, international capital movements and diffusion of technical information among countries may not be negligible.

EXERCISES

1. Draw a diagram that simultaneously employs the variable saving function of Figure 8.3 and the variable population function of Figure 8.4. Indicate the possibility of multiple specific solutions and assess their stability properties.

2. If low-level traps are believed to exist in a country, what specific measures would you propose in order to escape them?

3. Consider the following system of linear differential equations:

$$\dot{x} = -2x + 3y$$
$$\dot{y} = -x - 2y + 4$$

(a) Solve for, and graph, the isokines for

$$\dot{x} = -1 \qquad \dot{y} = -1$$
$$\dot{x} = 0 \qquad \dot{y} = 0$$
$$\dot{x} = 1 \qquad \dot{y} = 1$$

(b) Find the (x, y) coordinates that correspond to

$$\dot{x} = -1, \qquad \dot{y} = -1$$
$$\dot{x} = 0, \qquad \dot{y} = -1$$
$$\dot{x} = 0, \qquad \dot{y} = 0$$

(c) Draw the appropriate arrows at these coordinates.
(d) Are the Olech conditions for global stability satisfied for this system?

REFERENCES AND SUGGESTIONS FOR FURTHER READING

1. Gatmacher, F. R., *The Theory of Matrices*. New York: Chelsea, 1960.
2. Myrdal, G., *Economic Theory and Underdeveloped Regions*. London: Methuen, 1957.
3. Nurske, R., *Problems of Capital Formation in Underdeveloped Countries and Patterns of Trade and Development*, New York: Oxford University Press, 1967.
4. Olech, C., "On the Global Stability of an Autonomous System on the Plane," *Contributions to Differential Equations*, Vol. I. 1963, pp. 389–400.
5. Pontryagin, L. S., *Ordinary Differential Equations*. Reading, Mass.: Addison-Wesley, 1962.
6. Shell, K., "Toward a Theory of Inventive Activity." *American Economic Review*, May 1966.

Chapter Nine

AN INTRODUCTION TO THE THEORY OF OPTIMAL ECONOMIC GROWTH

Optimum Points
Profit Maximizing
The Golden Rule
Optimum Paths
A Turnpike
Optimal Growth Paths—The Basic Model
The Euler Equation
Control Theory
Optimal Growth Paths—Extensions of the Basic Model
Exercises
References and Suggestions for Further Reading

OPTIMUM POINTS

Profit Maximizing

Many problems in economics are posed in such a way that a solution requires finding a maximum value for an appropriate variable. For example, one encounters near the beginning of his studies the problem of explaining the rate of production chosen by a monopoly firm. On the assumption that the firm maximizes profits (P_r), the problem becomes one of finding the production rate that maximizes the difference between total revenues (TR) and total costs (TC). The problem, and its solution, is illustrated in the left-hand panels of Figure 9.1. In Figure 9.1a, marginal costs of production (MC) are assumed to be constant and insensitive to the level of output (x), so that average costs equal marginal costs ($MC = AC$). With downward sloping demand, average revenue (AR) falls with output.

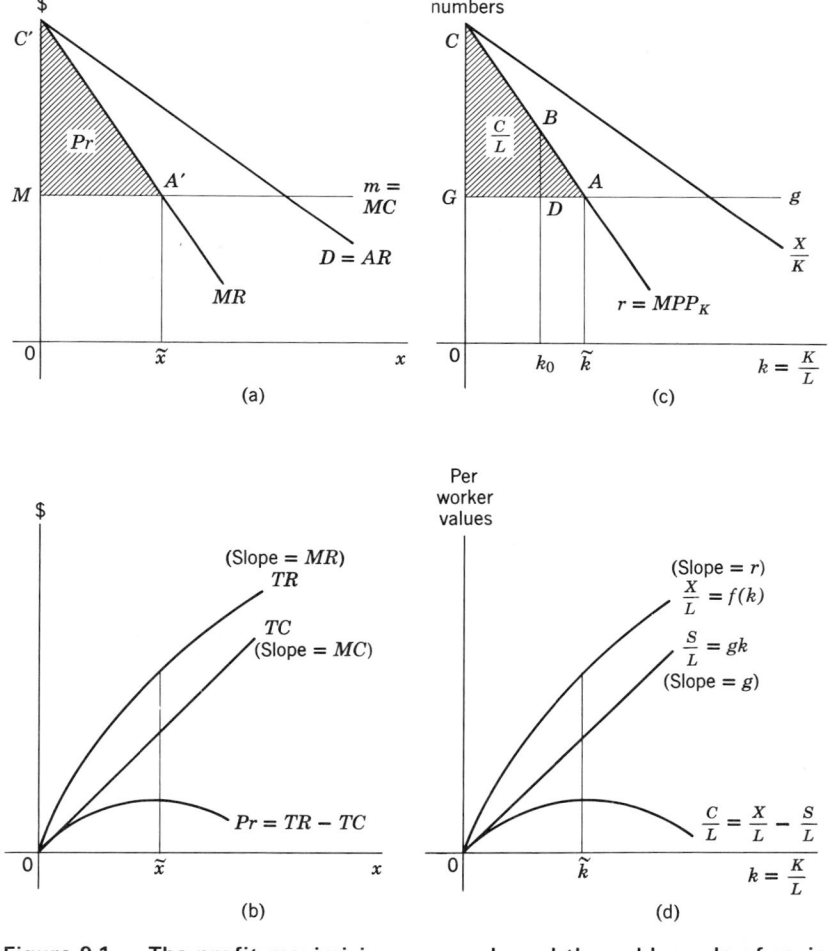

Figure 9.1 The profit-maximizing monopoly and the golden rule of saving.

These revenue and cost conditions give rise to the total-revenue (*TR*) and total-cost (*TC*) curves in Figure 9.1b. Total revenue is price times output, the area of the rectangle inscribed under the demand curve. Total cost is average costs times output, the area under the average-cost curve.

We assume that the firm chooses the *output* ($\tilde{x}$) that maximizes the *single* variable, *profit* (P_r). How then, does profit vary with output? Since

$$P_r = TR - TC = P_r(x)$$

it follows that as x is changed

$$\frac{dP_r}{dx} = \frac{dTR}{dx} - \frac{dTC}{dx}$$

$$dP_r = (MR - MC)\, dx$$

change in profit = [slope of *TR* curve − slope of *TC* curve] · change in output

When $MR = MC$, the first order (necessary) condition for maximum profit is satisfied and $x = \tilde{x}$. A glance at Figure 9.1b convinces us that the second order (sufficient) conditions are also satisfied. Profit is at a maximum (rather than at a minimum, or at neither a maximum nor a minimum) where $MC = MR$.

The profit-maximizing conditions are also illustrated in Figure 9.1a. Total revenue is the sum of marginal revenues, or the area under the *MR* curve.

$$TR = \sum MR\, \Delta x = 0\tilde{x}A'C'$$

Total cost is the sum of marginal costs, or the area under the *MR* curve.

$$TC = \sum MC\, \Delta x = 0\tilde{x}A'M$$

Profits

$$P_r = TR - TC = MA'C'$$

are a maximum when $MC = MR$.

We have solved a very simple maximizing problem. Profits (P_r) are a smooth function of output (x), rising at first and then falling. The profit-maximizing rate of output ($\tilde{x}$) is simply that x where P_r is the greatest.

The Golden Rule

The simple profit-maximizing problem in the last section is formally identical to that of choosing a consumption-maximizing capital-labor ratio, $\tilde{k}$, for an advanced economy moving along a balanced growth path.

The raison d'être of economic activity is, presumably, consumption. Moreover, in societies where individuals count, we may wish to think of maximizing per capita consumption as an appropriate goal.

Suppose, now, that society could choose *at will* among different balanced growth paths, each characterized by a different capital-labor ratio (k) and the associated saving ratio (s) required to maintain it. Which s (or which k) would it choose in order to maximize per capita consumption (C/L)? Or, since balanced growth paths are sometimes called *Golden Ages*, can we find a *Golden Rule* of Saving that would maximize per capita consumption?[1] For the moment, we shall confine ourselves to comparing different balanced growth (Golden Age) paths. This limits our problem at the outset, for it is possible that a nonbalanced growth path may be optimal.

Since any one Golden Age lasts forever, we are really asking "Which s (or which k) would society choose to maximize per capita consumption, providing the initial k could be chosen at will, and were subject to being maintained forever?" No society can really choose its initial k, so finding a Golden Rule is a mere *Gedanken-experiment*.

That such a Golden Rule of saving might exist is suggested by the following reasoning: Suppose society were to save virtually nothing. Then nearly all income could be consumed. But per capita income would be virtually nil since, if next to nothing is saved, k would be nearly zero. (Recall that $X/L = f(k), f'(k) > 0, k \equiv K/L$.) Thus, C/L would be quite small.

On the other hand, suppose society chose to save virtually all its income. Then k would be very great, as would X/L. But with nearly all income being invested, little is left over for consumption. Again, C/L would be quite small. There would seem to be a saving ratio (and an associated k) somewhere between these extremes where C/L is the greatest possible for a Golden Age.

It is easy to show that such a saving ratio exists. Let us first find the capital-labor ratio (k) that maximizes consumption per capita in a Golden Age, and then find the associated saving ratio (s) required to maintain that optimal $k = \tilde{k}$. We can write an expression for consumption per capita in terms of the capital-labor ratio and its rate of growth. Consumption is output minus investment.

$$c \equiv \frac{C}{L} = \frac{X}{L} - \frac{\dot{K}}{L}$$

---

[1] The Golden Rule of saving was independently discovered by several investigators. Of the early contributions, a most readable one is E. S. Phelps, "The Golden Rule of Accumulation: A Fable for Growthmen," *American Economic Review* (September 1961). Phelps has derived the Golden Rule in the context of a number of models. See E. S. Phelps, *Golden Rules of Economic Growth* (New York: Norton, 1966). The presentation here is derived from J. A. Hansen and P. A. Neher, "The Neoclassical Theorem Once Again," *American Economic Review* (September 1967) and A. L. Marty, "The Neoclassical Theorem," *American Economic Review* (December 1964).

or
$$c = \frac{X}{L} - \frac{\dot{K}}{K} \cdot \frac{K}{L}$$

Recalling that $X/L = f(k)$, $k \equiv K/L$, we have

$$c = f(k) - \frac{\dot{K}}{K} \cdot k$$

But our maximizing problem is with reference to Golden Ages (balanced growth paths) along which the capital-labor ratio is constant. If we assume that labor growth is a demographically determined constant, g, an unchanging k requires that capital grow at the rate g as well. That is,

$$\frac{\dot{K}}{K} = g = \frac{\dot{L}}{L}$$

for *any* Golden Age. Thus

$$c = f(k) - gk \qquad (9.1)$$

expresses

$$\frac{C}{L} = \frac{X}{L} - \frac{S}{L}$$

for *any* Golden Age. This relation, (9.1), is plotted in Figure 9.1d. Per capita consumption rises at first, and then falls as k gets larger. We wish to know that value for k when c is the greatest.

How does c vary with k? Differentiating (9.1) with respect to k,

$$\frac{dc}{dk} = f'(k) - g$$

Recalling from Chapter Five that

$$f'(k) = MPP_K = r$$

we can write

$$\frac{dc}{dk} = r - g \qquad (9.2)$$

or

$$dc = (r - g)\, dk$$

Referring to Figure 9.1d, the slope of the X/L curve is $f'(k)$ or r. The slope of the C/L curve is g. Thus, as k is changed,

$$\begin{matrix}\text{change in}\\ \text{consumption}\\ \text{per capita}\end{matrix} = \left[\begin{matrix}\text{slope of}\\ X/L\text{ curve}\end{matrix} - \begin{matrix}\text{slope of}\\ C/L\text{ curve}\end{matrix}\right] \cdot \begin{matrix}\text{change in}\\ \text{capital}\\ \text{per capita}\end{matrix}$$

Since $f'(k) = r$, the Golden Rule $\tilde{k}$ is given by $f'(\tilde{k}) = g$.

If the rate of return on capital (r) equals the growth of population and labor (g), the first-order (necessary) condition for a maximum is satisfied. A glance at Figure 9.1d convinces us that the second order (sufficient) conditions are also satisfied. Output per worker (X/L) rises with capital per worker (k) but at a decreasing rate, reflecting diminishing returns. Saving per worker (S/L) is a ray out of the origin with slope g, reflecting the necessity in a Golden Age of equipping new workers with the same amount of capital as their fathers (maintenance investment). Subtracting S/L from X/L yields C/L, which rises at first with k, but then falls. Consumption per worker is a maximum ($c = \tilde{c}$) at $k = \tilde{k}$, where the slopes of X/L and S/L are equal (where r equals g).

What saving ratio ($s = \tilde{s}$) is associated with the capital-labor ratio ($k = \tilde{k}$) where $r = g$? We begin with the definition of the saving ratio

$$s \equiv \frac{S}{X} = \frac{\dot{K}}{X} = \frac{\dot{K}}{K} \cdot \frac{K}{X}$$

But in a Golden Age, and observing the Golden Rule,

$$\frac{\dot{K}}{K} = g = r$$

Thus

$$\tilde{s} = \frac{rK}{X}$$

Now, rK is nothing but the output imputed to capital on the basis of its marginal productivity. Consequently, rK/X is nothing but the proportion of output imputed to capital, or what we have been calling $(1 - a)$. Thus, the *Golden Rule of Saving* is to save a proportion of output (s) equal to the proportion of output imputed to capital $(1 - a)$. In symbols,

$$\tilde{s} = (1 - a) \tag{9.3}$$

or

$$S = \tilde{s} \cdot X = (1 - a)X$$

Optimum Points   213

Note that the Rule does not require capitalists to save all their income and workers to consume all theirs in a competitive economy. All that is required is for saving, no matter what its source, to equal capital's share of output.

The geometry of the $s = 1 - a$ or $r = g$ rule of saving is illustrated in Figure 9.1c. We wish to maximize the triangle GAC by choosing the optimal k (and the associated s to maintain it). The triangle GAC equals c because output per capita is the sum of capital's marginal products, or the area under the r curve.

$$\frac{X}{L} = \int r \, dk = \int f'(k) \, dk = 0kAC$$

Saving per capita is the area under the growth-of-labor curve

$$\frac{S}{L} = \frac{\dot{K}}{K} \cdot k = gk = 0kAG$$

Consumption per capita,

$$c \equiv \frac{C}{L} = \frac{X}{L} - \frac{S}{L} = GAC$$

is a maximum when $g = r$ and when $k = \tilde{k}$. For instance, suppose that $k \neq \tilde{k}$. As an example, let k equal $k_0 < \tilde{k}$. Then c could be increased by selecting a higher k (and saving more). Increasing k by a little bit would add k_0B to X/L and add k_0D to S/L. Thus, C/L would rise by BD.

Selecting a higher k yields a payoff by increasing per capita income by the marginal product of capital.

$$d\left(\frac{X}{L}\right) = f'(k) \, dk = r \, dk$$

Offsetting this effect is a penalty in the form of the obligation to save more, in order to maintain the higher k.

$$d\left(\frac{S}{L}\right) = g \, dk$$

Only when the payoff (r) no longer exceeds the penalty (g) should k be increased no further.

The Golden Rule, therefore, is a rule for selecting the Golden Age where $c \equiv C/L$ is the greatest. Put another way, the *Golden Rule is a rule for*

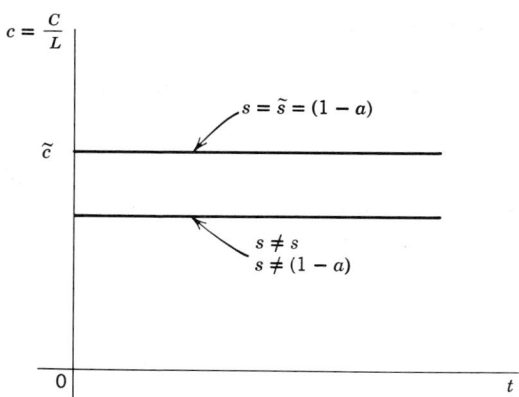

Figure 9.2 Golden age growth paths of per capita consumption.

selecting the highest of sustainable paths of per capita consumption. If there is no technological change, as we have assumed, this growth path is horizontal. Per capita consumption is not growing, but it is the highest possible. This property is illustrated in Figure 9.2, where two parallel Golden Age growth paths are plotted. The higher one is the Golden Rule path. The lower one represents any other Golden Age path where the Golden Rule is not being observed, either because the economy is saving "too much" ($s > 1 - a$) or "too little" ($s < 1 - a$).

If an economy were already on a Golden Rule path, there might be an argument for staying on it. With no technological change, each generation can say, "We are saving as much for future generations as we would have had past generations save for us." Each generation is as well off as it can possibly be without making other generations worse off. But, if we are willing to assert that a society should *stay on* a Golden Age path obeying the Golden Rule, what should we say to a society that is not already in a balanced-growth, Golden Rule configuration? Western economies generally save less than capital's share, and their interest rates exceed the rate of growth of their populations. Should these societies try to raise their saving ratios? Should they even try to get on Golden Rule paths?

The problem is illustrated in Figure 9.3. Suppose the initial equilibrium growth path of c is the one labeled c_0 and associated with a $k = k_0 < \tilde{k}$, $r > g$ and $s < 1 - a$. Lying above the c_0 path is the Golden Rule path marked $\tilde{c}$ and associated with $k = \tilde{k} > k_0$, $r = g$, and $s = 1 - a$. Since the capital required to raise k to $\tilde{k}$ is not free, the saving ratio must be raised and capital deepening accomplished to move from c_0 to $\tilde{c}$. One strategy might be to raise s from its current value of less than the current $1 - a$ to an $s \geq 1 - a$.

If this is done at $t = 0$, c falls initially (the dotted line in Figure 9.3) when the saving ratio is increased to its new and higher level. But now capital deepening begins and per capita income begins to rise. With the constant (but higher) saving ratio, per capita consumption also begins to rise. After a time, the initial per capita consumption levels are reached and even greater consumption is attained later on.

This strategy seems to call for discriminating against "near future" generations in order to make "far future" generations better off than they would have been if the saving program had not been undertaken.

An alternative strategy might be to raise the saving ratio rather little at first while c is relatively low, and then increase it further as c rises toward its Golden Rule level. This strategy is illustrated by the solid line in Figure 9.3.

The question is, of all the feasible programs (possible ones), which one is *best* (optimal in some sense)? Put another way, what is the optimal (in some sense) *time path* for the capital-labor ratio to take? Symbolically, we want to find a *function*.

$$k = k(t)$$

that is optimal in some sense. This is an entirely different, but related, problem from that of finding, for example, the *number* representing the quantity of goods produced by a monopolist,

$$x = \tilde{x}$$

which is optimal output because it maximizes profits.

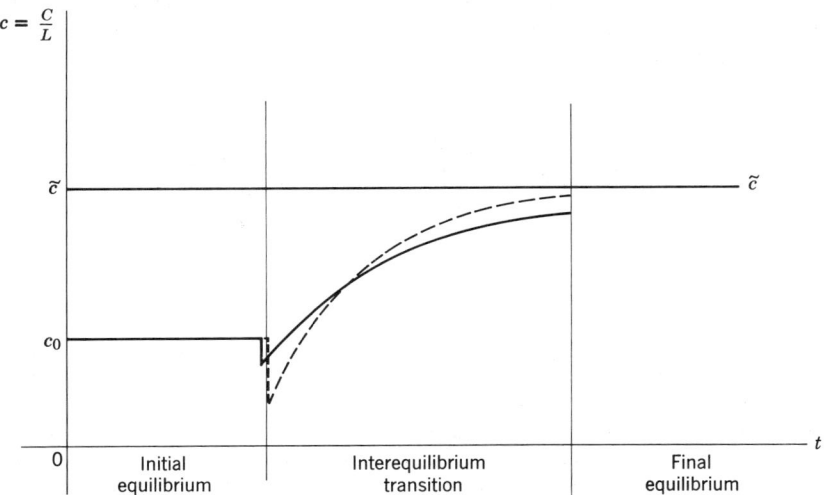

Figure 9.3   Alternate accumulation programs.

It would be sufficient, of course, if we could solve for the optimal *number* for k *at every point in time* throughout the program. That is, if we could find the optimal sequence of k's,

$$k_1 = k(1)$$
$$k_2 = k(2)$$
$$k_3 = k(3)$$
$$\vdots$$
$$k_n = k(n)$$

we would have defined the optimal program. But better still, why not try to express the optimal time sequence of k's as a function of time, $k = k(t)$? This is a problem in the calculus of variations and/or optimal control theory to which we now turn.

OPTIMUM PATHS

A Turnpike

Figure 9.4 illustrates a simple problem in the calculus of variations.[2] Points A and B lie in the xy plane. An automobile starts out from A on a journey to B. The driver wishes to minimize his transit time, but he must obey the following rule: the closer his automobile is to the x-axis, the greater its forward velocity can be. Specifically, the rule is:

$$\text{velocity} \equiv \text{the rate of change of distance} = \frac{\text{inversely proportional to the vertical distance from the } x\text{-axis}}{}$$

$$v \equiv \frac{ds}{dt} = \frac{1}{y}$$

---

[2] It is difficult to find elementary treatments of the classical calculus of variations. A short introduction is found in R. D. G. Allen, *Mathematical Analysis for Economists* (London: Macmillan, 1960), Chapter XX. An alternative to Allen is R. Courant, *Differential and Integral Calculus*, Volume II (New York: Interscience, 1936), Chapter VII. A more extended exposition is I. M. Gelfand and S. V. Fomin, *Calculus of Variations* (Englewood Cliffs: Prentice-Hall, 1963). Modern variational problems often are solved using Pontryagin's "maximum principle," in L. S. Pontryagin et al., *The Mathematical Theory of Optimal Processes* (New York: Interscience, 1962).

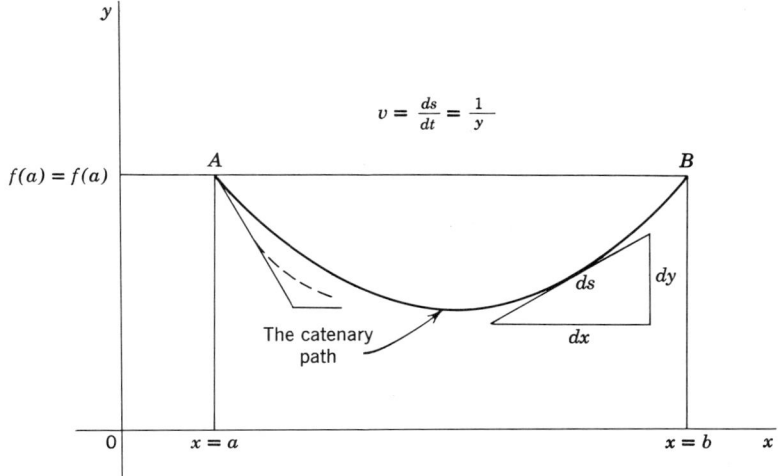

Figure 9.4   A turnpike problem.

We can think of the x-axis as the *turnpike*, because the automobile's forward velocity is the greatest possible while traveling along it. The problem is to choose the optimal (least-time) path between A and B. That is, we search for a *function*

$$y = f(x)$$

such that transit time is a minimum.[3]

Our intuition tells us that certain paths between A and B can be ruled out as nonoptimal. The driver should never start out in a northeast direction, because he would not only be going out of his way (making s greater), but he would also be reducing his velocity (making $v = ds/dt$ lower). On the other hand, he might start out in a southerly direction, hoping to pick up speed, then turning a sharp corner and heading east. But his intuition should tell him that it might pay to cut the proposed corner (the dotted route).

After a little thought, we might suspect that the optimal path will curve downwards, and then upwards in a symmetrical way. Moreover, if A and B are quite far apart, the optimal path might spend more time nearer the turnpike than if A and B were quite close together. The further one has to go, we suspect, the more it pays to go out of the way to take (get closer to) the turnpike.

[3] A least-time path is called a brachistochrone, meaning "least time."

218   An Introduction to the Theory of Optimal Economic Growth

The problem can be formalized as follows: Any change in distance (ds) in the xy plane can be resolved into (dx) and (dy) components by evoking a familiar theorem of Pythagoras.

$$(ds)^2 = (dx)^2 + (dy)^2$$

or

$$ds = [(dx)^2 + (dy)^2]^{1/2}$$

or

$$ds = \left[1 + \left(\frac{dy}{dx}\right)^2\right]^{1/2} dx$$

or

$$ds = (1 + y'^2)^{1/2} dx$$

We wish to minimize the transit time. But transit time is nothing but the sum of time spent at points along the route. We want to

$$\text{MIN } t = \int_{x=a}^{x=b} dt$$

But from

$$v = \frac{ds}{dt}$$

we have that

$$dt = \frac{1}{v} \cdot ds$$

or

$$dt = \frac{1}{v}(1 + y'^2)^{1/2} dx$$

The rule for forward velocity was that

$$v = \frac{1}{y}$$

Substituting

$$dt = y(1 + y'^2)^{1/2} dx$$

Finally, the problem becomes one of minimizing

$$J(y) = t = \int_a^b F\, dx, \qquad F = y(1 + y'^2)^{1/2} \qquad (9.4)$$

By doing so, we hope to obtain a route

$$y = f(x)$$

that passes through the points A and B, and for which the transit time is the smallest possible.

The integral $J(y)$ is called a *functional*. Equation 9.4 is satisfied by a number of functions (routes), $y = f(x)$, that connect A and B. The particular *function* (route), $y = f(x)$, that yields the least time is called an *extremal* to the functional.

Compare this problem with the more familiar point maximum (or minimum) problem that begins with a *function*—for example, $P_r = P_r(x)$. It is satisfied by a number of values for the independent variable (x). The particular *value* of $x(\tilde{x})$ that maximizes (or minimizes) the function is called an *extreme* value of the function. By analogy, then, an extremal (function) is to a functional as an extreme (point) is to a function.

A large number of problems like the one represented by (9.4) can be solved with a very simple formula developed by Euler. If

$$J(y) = \int_a^b F\, dx, \qquad F = y(1 + y'^2)^{1/2}$$

then a necessary condition[4] for a $y = f(x)$ to be an extremal is that $y = f(x)$ satisfy *Euler's equation*.

$$F_y - \frac{d}{dx} F_{y'} = 0 \qquad (9.5)$$

Here, F_y = the partial derivative of F with respect to y and $F_{y'}$ = the partial derivative of F with respect to $y' = dy/dx$. Equation 9.5, Euler's equation, is usually an ordinary second-order differential equation that can sometimes be solved for $y = f(x)$ by methods introduced in the first calculus course. We shall find the Euler equation here and indicate the nature of its solution.

---

[4] F must have continuous first and second partial derivatives, which the F has in this example. For a derivation of Euler's equation, see I. M. Gelfand and S. V. Fomin, *op. cit.*, pp. 14–15.

We begin by finding the relevant partial derivatives of $F = y(1 + y'^2)^{1/2}$. First, find F_y, treating y' as a constant. Then, find $F_{y'}$, treating y as a constant.

$$F_y = (1 + y'^2)^{1/2}$$
$$F_{y'} = y \cdot \tfrac{1}{2}(1 + y'^2)^{-1/2} \cdot 2y'$$
$$F_{y'} = y(1 + y'^2)^{-1/2} y'$$

Next we must differentiate $F_{y'}$ with respect to x, remembering that y and y' are functions of x.

$$\begin{aligned}\frac{d}{dx} F_{y'} = &\; y(1 + y'^2)^{-1/2} y'' \\ &+ y \cdot y'(-\tfrac{1}{2})(1 + y'^2)^{-3/2} 2y' \cdot y'' \\ &+ (1 + y'^2)^{-1/2} y' \cdot y'\end{aligned}$$

Substituting these results into (9.5), we have

$$\begin{aligned}&(1 + y'^2)^{1/2} \\ &- y(1 + y'^2)^{-1/2} y'' \\ &+ y(1 + y'^2)^{-3/2} y'^2 y'' \\ &- (1 + y'^2)^{-1/2} y'^2 = 0\end{aligned}$$

Multiplying by $(1 + y'^2)^{1/2}$,

$$\begin{aligned}&(1 + y'^2) \\ &- yy'' \\ &+ y(1 + y'^2)^{-1} y'^2 y'' \\ &- y'^2 = 0\end{aligned}$$

Simplifying,

$$1 - yy'' + \frac{yy'^2 y''}{1 + y'^2} = 0$$
$$1 + y'^2 - yy'' = 0$$

or

$$y''y - y'^2 - 1 = 0 \qquad (9.6)$$

This is a second order, nonlinear, nonhomogeneous differential equation. It can be solved to yield a catenary[5] as illustrated in Figure 9.4. A catenary can be expressed in the form[6]

$$y = f(x) = \frac{a}{2}(e^{x/a} + e^{-x/a})$$

where the constant a is so chosen that the path passes through prescribed start and finish positions such as A and B in Figure 9.4.[7]

In the present problem, note that F contains only y and $y' = dy/dx$. The variable x does not appear explicitly. Euler's equation (9.5) is generally applicable to problems where x *does* appear explicitly. In general, if

$$J(y) = \int F \, dx; \qquad F = F(x, y, y')$$

then Euler's equation

$$F_y - \frac{d}{dx} F_{y'} = 0 \qquad (9.5)$$

must be satisfied for $y = f(x)$ to be an extremal. For example, we could apply (9.5) to a case where

$$F = \frac{y}{x}(1 + y'^2)^{1/2}$$

But we can often get closer to finding an extremal, $y = f(x)$, by direct methods if F contains only y and its derivative, y'. It can be shown in this case that (9.5) has the *first integral*[8]

$$F - y'F_{y'} = C \qquad (9.9)$$

where C is a constant of integration.

---

[5] A string, suspended between two points, hangs in the form of a catenary, thereby minimizing its center of gravity. Catenaries are commonly encountered in classical mechanics.

[6] As a check to see if (9.7) satisfies the differential equation (9.6), we note that from (9.7), $y' = \frac{1}{2}(e^{x/a} e^{-x/a})$, $y'^2 = y^2/a^2 - 1$, and $y'' = y/a^2$. These values satisfy (9.6). A more general form of the catenary is

$$y = \frac{a}{2}(e^{x-b/a} + e^{-x-b/a})$$

[7] For example, suppose at $A: x = -1$, $y = (1 + e)/e^{1/2}$; and at $B: x = 1, y = (1 + e)/e^{1/2}$. Then $a = 2$.

[8] See, for example, I. M. Gelfand and S. V. Fomin, *op. cit.*, p. 18–19 for the proof. As a check, we can differentiate (9.9) with respect to x and get (9.5). $F = F(y, y')$, $dF/dx = F_y \cdot y' + F_{y'} \cdot y''$, $d/dx(y'F_{y'}) = y' \cdot d/dx(F_{y'}) + F_{y'} \cdot y''$. By substitution,

$$d/dx(F - y' \cdot F_{y'} - C) = F_y - d/dx(F_{y'}) = 0$$

Applied to our least-time problem,

$$J(y) = \int_a^b F(y, y') \, dx = \int_a^b y(1 + y'^2)^{1/2} \, dx$$

we have for the first integral of Euler's equation

$$y(1 + y'^2)^{1/2} - y' \cdot y(1 + y'^2)^{-1/2} y' = C$$

or

$$y(1 + y'^2) - y \cdot y'^2 = C(1 + y'^2)^{1/2}$$

or

$$y = C(1 + y'^2)^{1/2}$$

or

$$y' = \left(\frac{y^2 - C^2}{C^2}\right)^{1/2}$$

a first-order differential equation. Recall that the direct application of Euler's equation led to

$$y''y - y'^2 - 1 = 0$$

a second-order differential equation. Both these equations, when solved, yield the catenary. The former is of a lower order than the latter, and thus one step closer to the desired extremal $y = f(x)$.

Optimal Growth Paths—The Basic Model

The Euler Equation. We turn now to the problem of finding an optimal growth path for an economy that must begin with a historically given stock of capital. The basic model is explored in this section, where in addition to the usual simplifying assumptions we shall take it that:

1. There is no technological change.
2. The utility yielded by consumption today counts as much as utility yielded by consumption tomorrow. Myopia is ruled out. The future is not discounted.

In addition, let us suppose that the link between consumption and utility is always given by

$$u = u(c); \qquad u(c) = u > 0$$
$$\mu = u'(c); \qquad \mu(c) = \mu < 0$$

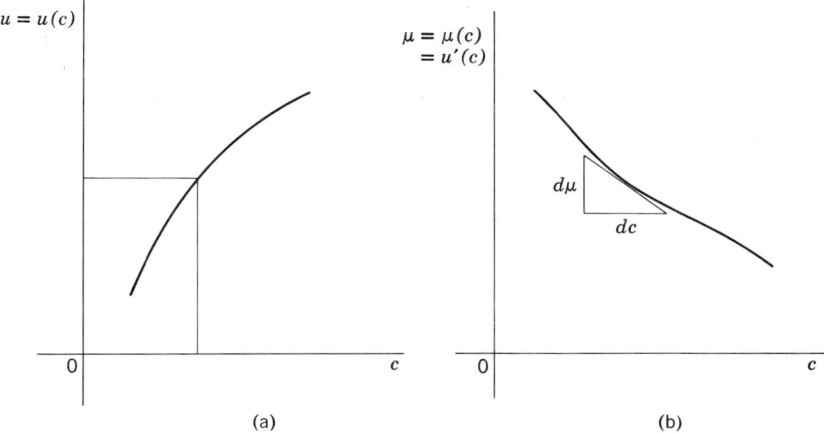

Figure 9.5 A utility function.

where u is per capita utility and c is per capita consumption. More consumption yields more utility but at a decreasing rate. Marginal utility $[\mu = u'(c)]$ is positive but declining. A function consistent with the one just specified is illustrated in Figure 9.5.

We take the point of view of a central planner who can control the amount of consumption enjoyed by society at each point in time. He is subject to certain constraints that are made explicit below. But first, we should specify an *objective function*.

If a $u(c)$ is to count equally, whenever enjoyed, then our objective is simply to maximize the sum of all per capita utilities from the beginning of the capital accumulation program ($t = 0$) to its end ($t = T$).[9] That is, we want to

$$\text{MAX } J(k) = \sum_{t=0}^{t=T} u[c(t)]\,\Delta t$$

by choosing a feasible time path for capital accumulation. The program begins at $t = 0$ and ends at $t = T$. Consumption will normally vary over time, so we should denote the consumption flow at a point in time by $c(t)$. But for notational convenience, we shall denote $c(t)$ simply by c. In that notation, we want to

$$\text{MAX } J(k) = \sum_{t=0}^{t=T} u(c)\,\Delta t$$

This will be approximated by an integral below.

---

[9] We thus rule out possible complementarities of consumption enjoyed at different times.

It is better to have more per capita consumption throughout the program. But consumption at any point of time is at the expense of capital accumulation and maintenance investment (holding capital per worker constant in the face of labor-force growth). We need an expression for per capita consumption. Begin with

$$C = X - \dot{K}, \qquad \dot{K} \equiv \frac{dK}{dt}$$

In per capita terms,

$$\frac{C}{L} \equiv c = \frac{X}{L} - \frac{\dot{K}}{L}$$

The production function relates the capital-labor ratio to per capita income.

$$\frac{X}{L} = f(k), \qquad k \equiv \frac{K}{L}, \qquad f'(k) > 0, \qquad f''(k) < 0$$

Thus

$$c = f(k) - \frac{\dot{K}}{L}$$

or

$$c = f(k) - \frac{\dot{K}}{K} \cdot \frac{K}{L}$$

or

$$c = f(k) - \frac{\dot{K}}{K} \cdot k$$

Moreover,

$$\dot{k} = \frac{L \cdot \dot{K} - K \cdot \dot{L}}{L^2}$$

$$\dot{k} = \frac{1}{L}\dot{K} - \frac{K}{L} \cdot \frac{\dot{L}}{L}$$

or

$$\frac{\dot{k}}{k} = \frac{\dot{K}}{K} - \frac{\dot{L}}{L} = \frac{\dot{K}}{K} - g$$

Now we can write

$$c = f(k) - \left(\frac{\dot{k}}{k} + g\right)k$$

or

$$c = f(k) - \dot{k} - gk \tag{9.10}$$

Consumption per capita is equal to per capita income, $f(k)$, minus increases in capital per capita ($\dot{k}$), minus additions to the capital stock necessary to maintain a constant k in the face of rising population (gk). Put another way, (9.10) can be written

$$c + \dot{k} = f(k) - gk$$

Per capita product, $f(k)$, which is not used to maintain the capital-labor ratio (gk), is available for consumption (c) and for increasing the capital-labor ratio ($\dot{k}$).

Now we have all but one component of the problem. We have a beginning capital endowment and a beginning labor force, so we have the initial capital-labor ratio $[k(0) = k_0]$. We know the objective: to maximize the sum of per capita utilities. And now we know how consumption is related to capital and investment at each point of time $0 \leq t \leq T$. But where is the program headed? How should it terminate? For now, let us specify that the program must end at time T with a certain amount of capital on hand per worker $[k(T) = k_T]$.

Now the problem can be stated formally. Writing the objective function in continuous terms:

$$\text{MAX } J(k) = \int_{t=0}^{t=T} u(c)\, dt \tag{9.11}$$

where

$$c = f(k) - \dot{k} - gk \tag{9.10}$$

subject to:

$$k(0) = k_0 \tag{9.12}$$

and

$$k(T) = k_T \tag{9.13}$$

The end-point conditions are called *boundary conditions* because they put bounds on the permissible values of k at the boundaries of the interval considered. Since they apply to the end points, they are also called *transversality conditions*. They show how the program links up, or tranverses, from the past and into the future.

We search for an extremal, $k = $ a function of time $= k(t)$, to the functional, $J(k)$. As before, a necessary condition for an extremal is that it satisfy the Euler equation. In the automobile problem, we had

$$\text{MAX } J(y) = \int_a^b F \, dx, \qquad F = F(x, y, y')$$

and the Euler equation was

$$F_y - \frac{d}{dx} F_{y'} = 0$$

Or, if x did not appear explicitly in F,

$$\text{MAX } J(y) = \int_a^b F \, dx, \qquad F = F(y, y')$$

we could use the first integral of the Euler equation

$$F - y' F_{y'} = C$$

Here, substitute t (time) for x, k for y, and $\dot{k} = dk/dt$ for $y' = dy/dx$.

$$\text{MAX } J(k) = \int_{t=0}^{t=T} F \, dt, \qquad F = u(c) \qquad (9.14)$$

where

$$c = f(k) - \dot{k} - gk$$

We note that F does not contain t explicitly: $F = F(k, \dot{k})$, not $F = F(t, k, \dot{k})$. The system is said to be *autonomous* (of time), so we can use either the Euler equation

$$F_k - \frac{d}{dt} F_{\dot{k}} = 0 \qquad (9.15)$$

or its first integral

$$F - \dot{k}F_{\dot{k}} = C \tag{9.16}$$

Let us first employ the Euler equation (9.14). From that equation,

$$F = u[f(k) - \dot{k} - gk].$$

Thus, letting μ equal the marginal utility of consumption

$$\mu = u'(c) = du/dc$$
$$F_k = \mu[f'(k) - g]$$
$$F_{\dot{k}} = \mu[-1] = -\mu$$
$$\frac{d}{dt}F_{\dot{k}} = -\dot{\mu}$$

and Euler's equation is

$$\mu[f'(k) - g] + \dot{\mu} = 0$$
$$\frac{\dot{\mu}}{\mu} = -[f'(k) - g]$$

Recalling that $f'(k)$ is the marginal physical product of capital (the interest rate, r),

$$\frac{\dot{\mu}}{\mu} = \mu^* = -(r - g) \tag{9.17}$$

A necessary condition for an optimal growth path is that capital accumulation and consumption be continuously adjusted so that the marginal utility of consumption falls at a proportional rate equal to the difference between the interest rate and the growth rate of the population. As a numerical example, if at a moment of time $r = 0.10 = 10$ percent and $g = 0.02 = 2$ percent, then the marginal utility of consumption should be falling at the instantaneous rate of 0.08 or 8 percent. If, in addition, it requires a 1 percent rise in consumption to lower its marginal utility by 2 percent, then consumption should be rising at the momentary rate of 4 percent.

Optimal programs are often conveniently portrayed on phase diagrams of the kind introduced in the last chapter. Taken together, (9.10) and (9.17) are a system of two differential equations in k and μ.

$$\dot{k} = f(k) - gk - c(\mu) \tag{9.10}$$
$$\dot{\mu} = -\mu[f'(k) - g] \tag{9.17}$$

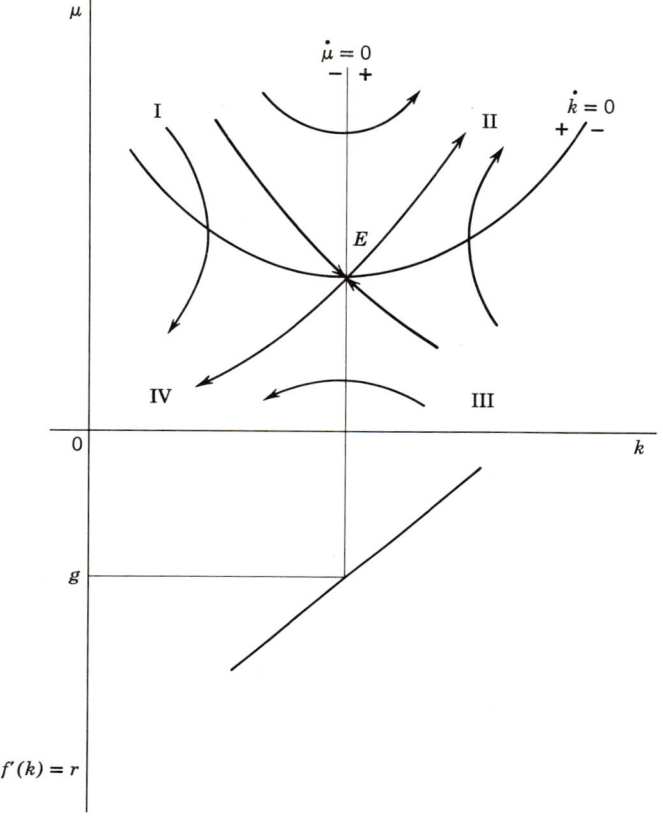

Figure 9.6 Optimal growth paths of the capital-labor ratio and of the marginal utility of consumption.

Note that c has been replaced by $c(\mu)$ in (9.10). If $\mu = u'(c)$, then $\mu = \mu(c)$ as in Figure 9.5b and we now recognize the inverse relation: consumption is related to its marginal utility by $c = c(\mu)$, $\quad c'(\mu) < 0$.

Equations 9.10 and 9.17 are plotted in Figure 9.6. The general shape of the $\dot{k}$ isokines are revealed by differentiating (9.10) totally and setting $d\dot{k} = 0$.

$$d\dot{k} = f'(k)\, dk - g\, dk - c'(\mu)\, d\mu = 0 \qquad (9.18)$$

$$[f'(k) - g]\, dk - c'(\mu)\, d\mu = 0$$

or

$$\frac{d\mu}{dk} = \frac{f'(k) - g}{c'(\mu)}$$

Recall that $c'(\mu)$ is negative. Thus the $\dot{k}$ isokines slope downward if k is so small that $f'(k) = r$ exceeds g. The $\dot{k}$ isokines slope upward if k is so large that $f'(k) = r$ falls short of g. The $\dot{k}$ isokines are "U"-shaped, with the lowest point where k is such that $r = g$.

Focusing attention on the $\dot{k} = 0$ isokine and (9.18), we note that if μ is increased ($d\mu > 0$), then $\dot{k}$ increases ($d\dot{k} > 0$), since $c'(\mu)$ is negative. Thus, everywhere above the $\dot{k} = 0$ isokine, $\dot{k}$ is positive; everywhere below the $\dot{k} = 0$ isokine, $\dot{k}$ is negative. These results are shown in Figure 9.6 by the $+$ and $-$ signs next to the $\dot{k} = 0$ notation, instead of the arrows used in the last chapter.

The $\dot{\mu} = 0$ isokine is easily discovered by inspection of (9.17). The marginal utility of consumption is stationary ($\dot{\mu} = 0$) if k is such that $f'(k) = g$. The $\dot{\mu} = 0$ isokine is a vertical straight line at the corresponding value of k. For larger values of k, $f'(k)$ is smaller than g, the term in square brackets is negative, so $\dot{\mu}$ is positive. For smaller values of k, $f'(k)$ is less than g, so $\dot{\mu}$ is negative. These results are shown in Figure 9.6 next to the $\dot{\mu} = 0$ notation.

The $\dot{k} = 0$ and $\dot{\mu} = 0$ isokines divide the phase diagram into four "quadrants" labeled with Roman numerals. Both μ and k are decreasing (increasing) in IV (II). In I and II, μ and k are moving in opposite directions. Clearly, the equilibrium at E is a saddle-point equilibrium. Only if μ and k move along the paths indicated by the heavy arrows (the stable arms) in I and III will the economy eventually end up at point E.[10] Otherwise, for sufficiently long programs, the economy eventually explodes upward (quadrant II) or downward (quadrant IV).

Figure 9.6 could be used to display an indefinitely large number of growth paths which satisfy the Euler equation (9.15). It is a necessary condition for optimality that the economy grow (or decline) along *one* of these paths. Next, we must choose *the* path that satisfies the transversality conditions (9.12) and (9.13), that the economy start out at k_0 and end up after T years at k_T.

It is perhaps more revealing at this point to convert the system of Equations 9.10 and 9.17 into a system that focuses on consumption instead of its marginal utility. Recall that the marginal utility of consumption depends upon consumption.

$$\mu = \mu(c), \qquad \mu'(c) \equiv \frac{du}{dc} < 0$$

Differentiating with respect to time,

$$\dot{\mu} = \mu'(c) \cdot \dot{c}$$

[10] Point E represents a Golden Rule Golden Age. The significance of this is discussed below.

230 An Introduction to the Theory of Optimal Economic Growth

Let us denote by ϵ (a positive number) the elasticity of marginal utility with respect to consumption.

$$\epsilon \equiv -\frac{du}{dc} \cdot \frac{c}{\mu} = -\frac{\mu'(c) \cdot c}{\mu}$$

Then

$$\mu'(c) \equiv -\epsilon \cdot \frac{\mu}{c}$$

and

$$\dot{\mu} \equiv -\epsilon \cdot \mu \cdot \frac{\dot{c}}{c}$$

or

$$\mu^* \equiv -\epsilon \cdot c^*$$

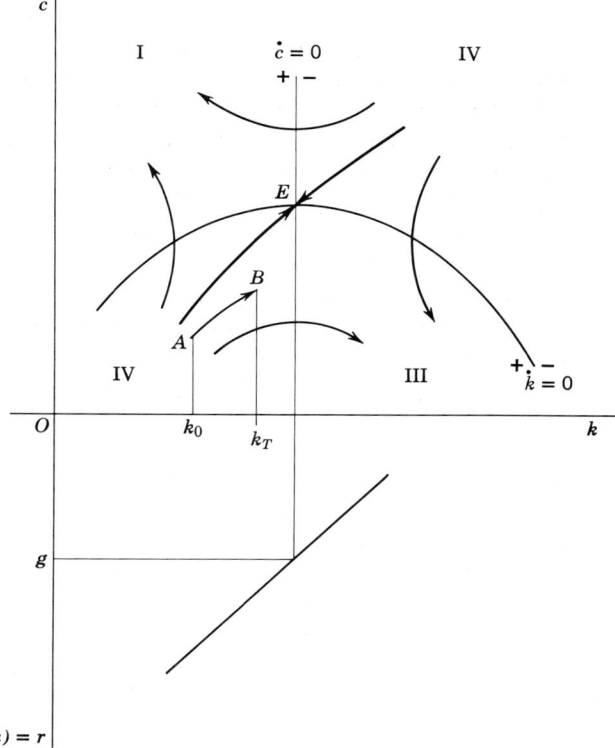

Figure 9.7 Optimal growth paths of the capital-labor ratio and of consumption.

The proportional fall in the marginal utility of consumption is linked to the rise in consumption by the (not necessarily constant) elasticity ϵ.

Substituting back into (9.17), we obtain

$$\dot{c} = \frac{c}{\epsilon}[f'(k) - g] \tag{9.17'}$$

which along with

$$\dot{k} = f(k) - gk - c \tag{9.10'}$$

is a system of differential equations in k and c. [Note that $c(\mu)$ in (9.10) has been replaced by c.] Now we interpret (9.17') as requiring that consumption rise along an optimal growth path at a proportional rate that depends upon the excess of the interest rate over the growth rate and upon ϵ. Suppose, for example, that at a moment of time $r = 0.10 = 10$ percent, $g = 0.02 = 2$ percent and $\epsilon = 2$; then consumption should be rising at the momentary rate of 4 percent.

The new system (9.17') and (9.10') is portrayed in Figure 9.7. The reader should confirm that the shapes of the $\dot{k} = 0$ and $\dot{c} = 0$ isokines are correctly drawn and that the direction of movement of k and c in the four "quadrants" is properly indicated. Again there is a saddle-point equilibrium at E, where $f'(k) = r = g$.

An optimal capital-accumulation path satisfying the transversality conditions is found in Figure 9.8, which "blows up" the left hand portion of Figure 9.7. Our problem now is to select the initial level of consumption which, given k_0, will get the economy moving along a path (arrow) that just reaches the required k_T after exactly T years. In Figure 9.8, we must choose one of an indefinitely large number of paths (all of which satisfy the Euler equation). The path must originate on the vertical $k = k_0$ line (satisfying the left-hand transversality condition) and terminate on the vertical $k = k_T$ line (satisfying the right-hand transversality condition). Finally, the program must last exactly T years.

A number of T-year programs are illustrated in Figure 9.8. Each of them originates on the $k = k_0$ line. The higher the initial saving ratio, the lower is initial consumption, and the higher is initial capital accumulation. This is shown graphically by the relatively "shallower" paths lying further down from the $\dot{k} = 0$ isokine on the $k = k_0$ line. Throughout, the lower consumption- faster accumulation paths lie further below the $\dot{k} = 0$ isokine. Note that capital decumulation is possible in per capita terms. Society "eats up" its capital above the $\dot{k} = 0$ isokine.

Below the $\dot{k} = 0$ isokine, the lower the path, the further it travels in the plus-k direction during the T years. The Tth-year terminal point is indicated for each path by an arrowhead. If the arrowheads of all possible paths are

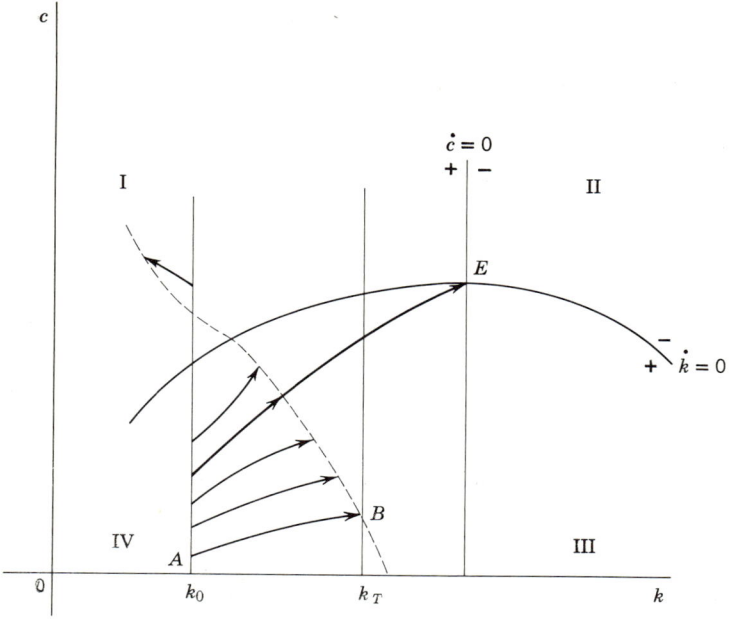

Figure 9.8   An isochrone.

connected, we have a locus of Tth-year terminal points. This locus is denoted by the dotted line in the figure. It could be called an *isochrone* (equal-time) line.[11] Everywhere along it:

1. The initial transversality condition is satisfied, $k(0) = k_0$.
2. The Euler equation is satisfied.
3. The program terminates after exactly T years.

Only where the dotted isochrone crosses the k_T line is the terminal transversality condition also satisfied. This occurs at point B in the figure. The optimal path we seek begins at point A and terminates at point B. That path maximizes the sum of (undiscounted) utilities during the planning period and the constraints are satisfied.

So far we have taken the planning period (T years) to be given as well as the terminal capital-labor ratio (k_T). It is natural to think of the planner as being bound by the state of the world as it is passed on to him (k_0). But the selection of k_T seems rather arbitrary, since a specification of $k_T > 0$ implies that *some* weight is being given to the future in the current plan. But *how much* consideration should be given to the future; *how large* should k_T be?

[11] It is commonly called a *wavefront* in noneconomic problems.

A natural way to solve the problem for the current T-year plan is to absorb the next T-year plan into the current one. But then, how does one determine k_{2T}?

The selection of the terminal k and the selection of T itself can be related problems. But for now, let us examine separately:

1. The consequences of selecting different terminal k's, taking T as given.
2. The consequences of selecting different T's, taking the terminal k as given.

Figure 9.9 illustrates the consequences of having different k_T's specified. All three programs (A, B, and C) satisfy the Euler equation and can be completed in T years. The phase diagram in 9.9a is the usual one in c and k. The corresponding time paths of c and k are shown in 9.9b and 9.9c. Figure 9.9d is derived from 9.9c and shows phase relations for k. (An analogue of 9.9d for c is easily derived but not shown.)

Path A represents a "spendthrift" program. Society eventually ends up with less capital per worker by "eating up" the inventory, or by failing to replace capital equipment as it wears out, or by simply failing to increase the capital stock in the face of the rising population. In any case, we assume that the required rate of decumulation along path A can be achieved, even if it means unbolting lathes from their foundations and eating them. Note that the path arches up toward E for an accumulation phase with consumption rising too. Then as the path crosses the $\dot{k} = 0$ isokine, consumption accelerates at the expense of accumulation, and the program ends on an upbeat of consumption. Little capital is left to the future. Clearly, a "spendthrift" path makes sense if the world were known with certainty to literally end at some time greater than T. For then we would plan to swallow the last morsel of capital at the sound of the last trumpet (follow the dotted line).

Path B represents a "thrift" program. Both consumption and capital rise for a while as the path arches up toward E. But after the path crosses the $\dot{c} = 0$ isokine (where $r = g$), consumption is forgone in order to provide the future with even more capital. If the program were of even longer duration, consumption would eventually go to zero (follow the dotted line).

Path C permits both more consumption and more capital throughout the program. It would eventually take the economy along the *stable arm* to point E if the planning period were extended indefinitely. Note that path C is shorter than paths A or B because both $\dot{c}$ and $\dot{k}$ are decreasing along it. The path moves closer and closer to the $\dot{c} = 0$ and $\dot{k} = 0$ isokines. It moves more and more slowly as a consequence.

The next step is to see what happens if k_0 and k_T are held constant, but the length of the program (T) is increased. It is evident in Figure 9.10 that longer and longer programs must arch closer and closer to point E in order to slow

234 An Introduction to the Theory of Optimal Economic Growth

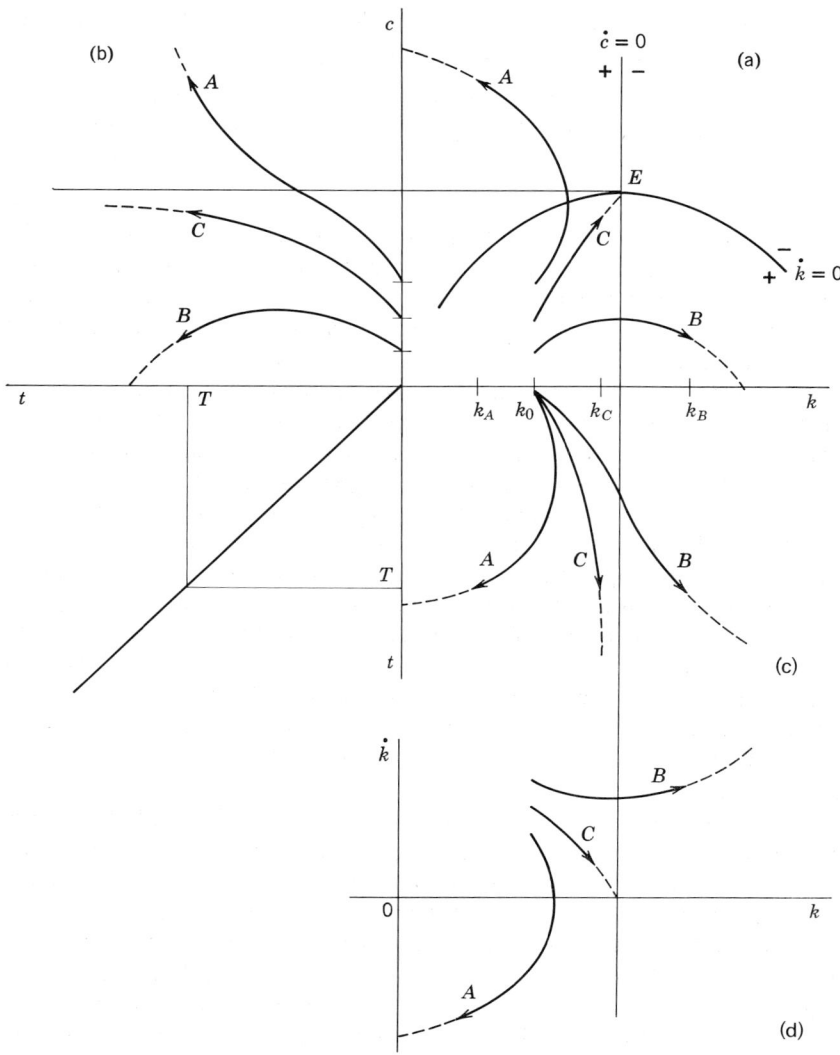

Figure 9.9 Optimal T-year programs with different terminal capital-labor ratios.

Optimum Paths 235

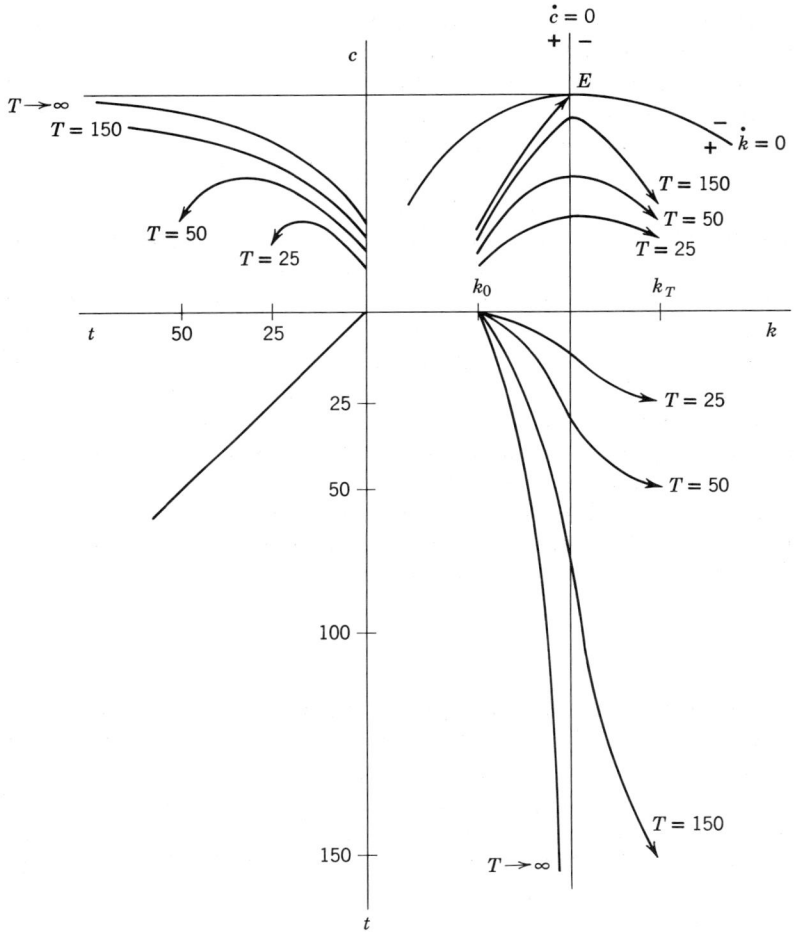

Figure 9.10 Optimal programs for different periods of time, with initial and terminal capital-labor ratios the same for each program.

down movement in the plus-k direction. The longer the program, the longer it must spend in the neighborhood of point E. A glance back to Figure 9.7 reminds us that point E is associated with $f'(k) = g$, the Golden Rule rate of interest. We can think of the Golden Rule path as a *consumption turnpike*, and state that an optimal program [extremal to the functional (9.1)] "will as T becomes sufficiently large, spend an arbitrarily large portion of the time arbitrarily near the turnpike."[12]

---

[12] P. A. Samuelson, "A Catenary Turnpike Theorem Involving Consumption and the Golden Rule," *American Economic Review* (June 1965), p. 491.

It was suggested before that there seemed to be no compelling reason why any particular terminal capital-labor ratio (k_T) should be chosen in formulating the plan. As long as some $k_T > 0$ is chosen, there is an implied consideration in the present T-year plan for the postplan period. So why not absorb the second T year plan into the present one and just plan for twice T years? But that just postpones the problem. We still must select k_{2T}. So why not plan for $3T$ years? But then, ..., and so on. We seem forced to think about plans that are indefinitely long. A review of Figure 9.9 should convince us that if $T = \infty$, there is only one interesting plan: plan C, along the stable arm. This plan approaches point E, the Golden Rule point. All other infinite programs veer away from E and eventually yield zero c or zero k. If capital is indispensable in production, zero k means zero output and zero c as well. Zero c just will not do in an infinite horizon plan. We should plan to approach the Golden Rule configuration at E. There, in the limit, the economy achieves balanced growth, a Golden Age. Net capital formation is just sufficient to maintain the capital-labor ratio as the labor force grows ($\dot{k} = 0$). With $f'(k) = g$ along this Golden Age path, our previous analysis tells us that the Golden Rule of Saving is being observed. The output imputed to capital is being returned as net investment:

$$I = \dot{K} = S = f'(k)K; \qquad s = (1 - a)$$

We have shown that we want to approach the Golden Rule path if we have an infinite program. And, as noted above, we seem forced to think about infinite programs because there are no compelling grounds for specifying a terminal k. However, the properties of infinite programs may not be of much practical interest, since economies are always observed in finite time. The approach to the Golden Rule path is therefore completed after we cease to observe the economy. The asymptotic result is interesting but of rather limited usefulness.

Let us, however, use this asymptotic result, along with the first integral of the Euler equation. Now, we want to maximize the integral (sum) of per capita utilities from $t = 0$ to $T =$ infinity.

$$\text{MAX } J(k) = \int_{t=0}^{t=\infty} u(c) \, dt$$

The program lasts forever. There may be no upper limit on the integral. As a consequence, we may not be able to say that one capital-accumulation program is "better" than another because neither is associated with a convergent integral of per capita utilities.

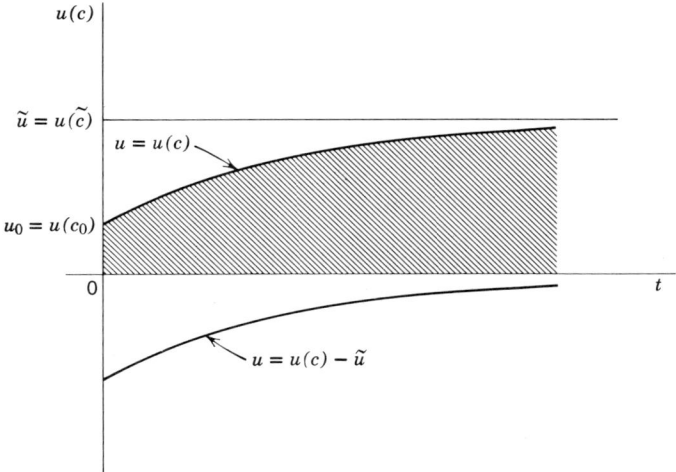

Figure 9.11 The integral of per capita utilities.

The problem is illustrated in Figure 9.11. The initial level of utilities derived from the initial consumption level is $u(c_0)$, while $\tilde{u} = u(\tilde{c})$ is the Golden Rule level of utility associated with Golden Rule consumption. The problem is to find the (feasible) time path for $u(\tilde{c})$, originating at $u(c_0)$ and approaching $u(c)$, which maximizes the shaded area ▨ under the curve from its origin, on into the indefinite future. The trouble is that *any* time path we choose of the kind illustrated in Figure 9.11 will appear equally desirable because *all* will have indefinitely large areas underneath them. Their integrals will not converge, and nonconvergent integrals are not easily compared.

The nonconvergence problem can be averted, however, if we subtract Golden Rule utility $\tilde{u} = u(\tilde{c})$ from $u = u(c)$ at every point in time from the beginning of the program on into the indefinite future.[13] The resulting integral is negative but it will converge, even if the time path of $u = u(c) - \tilde{u}$ approaches zero only asymptotically. With convergent integrals, we can say, for example, that a program of capital accumulation yielding -16 units of utility is "better" than one that yields -17 units.

With maximum possible utility shifted from $\tilde{u} = u(\tilde{c})$ to zero, we seek to

$$\text{MAX } J(k) = \int_{t=0}^{t=\infty} F \, dt \tag{9.19}$$

---

[13] In Figure 9.11, we shift the utility curve downward by $\tilde{u}$. Since the choice of measurement units is arbitrary, we are free to choose the origin for analytic convenience.

where
$$F = u(c) - \tilde{u}$$
Subject to
$$c = f(k) - \dot{k} - gk$$
$$k(0) = k_0$$

This time we employ the first integral of the Euler equation. A necessary condition for a maximum is that the time path of k satisfy

$$F - \dot{k} \cdot F_{\dot{k}} = C \qquad (9.16)$$

where C is the constant of integration. Proceeding,

$$F_{\dot{k}} = -u'(c) = -\mu$$

and we have

$$[u(c) - \tilde{u}] + \dot{k} \cdot u'(c) = C$$

Evaluating the constant of integration, we reason that capital deepening should halt ($\dot{k} = 0$) when per capita utility $u(c)$ finally reaches its maximum value, $\tilde{u}$. Thus, C equals zero and

$$\dot{k} = \frac{\tilde{u} - u(c)}{u'(c)}$$

or

$$\dot{k} = \frac{\tilde{u} - u}{\mu} \quad \text{for short}^{14} \qquad (9.20)$$

Current capital deepening ($\dot{k}$) should proceed more rapidly, the greater the shortfall of current per capita utility (u) from its maximum, Golden Rule value ($\tilde{u}$). However, this effect should be attenuated by the current value of the marginal utility of per capita consumption (μ).

Rewriting (9.20) as

$$u'(c) \, dk = [\tilde{u} - u(c)] \, dt$$

we can interpret the result intuitively. Giving up per capita consumption at a point in time ($-dc$) permits us to increase the capital-labor ratio (dk).

---

[14] This is a classic result. F. P. Ramsey, "A Mathematical Theory of Saving," *Economic Journal* (December, 1928).

The utility loss is $u'(c)\,dk$. Against this loss must be balanced the concomitant gain of progressing through time (dt) toward the maximum possible utility, $\tilde{u}$. Progress means that $\tilde{u}$ will be enjoyed sooner by dt. On the other hand, we lose our enjoyment of today's consumption, $u(c)$, for a period dt as we move on. Thus, the "net" payoff of progress is $[\tilde{u}\,dt - u(c)]\,dt$. For example, if $\tilde{u} = 100$ and we accumulate sufficient capital per capita to advance one "day" faster through the program, then we will be able to enjoy $\tilde{u} = 100$ one "day" sooner. But when we move up the program by one day, we lose, say, $u(c) = 80$, which we would have enjoyed if we had not proceeded through the program more quickly. The "net" gain is 20.

Balancing gains of utility against losses per capita,

$$u'(c)\,dk = [\tilde{u} - u(c)]\,dt$$

or

$$u'(c)\frac{dk}{dt} = \tilde{u} - u(c)$$

A related interpretation of (9.20) focuses on the concept of a national product (H) evaluated in terms of per capita utility.

$$H = u(c) + P \cdot \dot{k} \tag{9.21}$$

The consumption component is $u(c)$. The investment component is $P \cdot \dot{k}$, physical investment times its price. The price of investment goods (P) is the opportunity cost of investing (not consuming). If k is increasing, the opportunity cost is the utility that was forgone. The forgone utility is nothing but the marginal utility of consumption (μ). Thus,

$$H = u(c) + \mu\dot{k}$$

Since per capita utility is assessed with equal weight throughout the program, we might suspect that national product in terms of per capita utility is a constant throughout the program. No generation should "get a break" at the expense of others, which would mean that H *should be a constant even though $u(c)$, μ, and $\dot{k}$ are generally changing all the time.* Equation 9.21 confirms the suspicion. Rewriting it as

$$\tilde{u} = u(c) + \mu \cdot \dot{k} \tag{9.20'}$$

we see that national product (H) is in fact constant throughout the program. Moreover, it is always equal to per capita utility associated with the Golden

Age path. But only as accumulation eventually dies away ($\dot{k} \to 0$), will realized utility approach its maximum possible (Golden Rule) value ($\tilde{u}$).

Control Theory. Modern control theory[15] has become a popular method for solving time optimal problems of the kind we have been considering. In part, this is because it can handle cases where there are effective lower and/or upper limits on control variables (consumption, the saving ratio, and the like). We note this in passing and shall emphasize the heuristic value of the control theory approach.

In control theory, we think of an (economic) system as being described at a point of time by a set of *state* variables that are subject to dynamic constraints, and they describe "how the system works." In addition, there are *control variables*. These are instruments, subject to choice, that influence the state variables in the following way. Let k represent the state variable(s) and c represent the control variable(s). Both are generally functions of time. Then the *rate of change* of the state variable(s) ($\dot{k}$) depends upon the *value* of the state variable(s) (k) *and* upon the *value* of the control(s), (c), being applied.

$$\dot{k} = h(k, c), \qquad k = k(t)$$
$$c = c(t) \tag{9.22}$$

where c is chosen from a set of admissible values. But we shall assume here that there are no effective limits on c. For example, if there are two state variables and two control variables,

$$\dot{k}_1 = h_1(k_1, k_2, c_1, c_2)$$
$$\dot{k}_2 = h_2(k_1, k_2, c_1, c_2)$$

where c_1 and c_2 can be freely chosen.

If we assign initial values for k_1 and k_2, a time interval $t = 0$ to $t = T$, and time paths for c_1 and c_2, we have a *control process* that translates the system from its initial configuration $[k_1(0), k_2(0)]$ to its final configuration $[k_1(T), k_2(T)]$. For every control process, there is a corresponding number, J, where

$$J = \int_{t=0}^{t=T} F(k, c)\, dt \tag{9.23}$$

[15] The basic reference is by L. S. Pontryagin *et al.*, *The Mathematical Theory of Optimal Processes* (New York: Interscience, 1962).

In the case of two state and two control variables,

$$J = \int_{t=0}^{t=T} F(k_1, k_2, c_1, c_2)\, dt$$

J is a functional that is satisfied by any number of control processes. The problem is to pick the particular control process that maximizes J. The control process that does this is called the *optimal control process*.

To illustrate, consider our simple capital-accumulation model. We search for a control process with c as the control variable such that the integral (sum) of $u(c)$'s is maximized.

$$J = \int_{t=0}^{t=T} F(k, c)\, dt, \qquad F = u(c) \tag{9.24}$$

In this case, F does not contain t explicitly. The system is *autonomous*.[16] In addition, it happens that the state variable, k, does not appear in F. However, k is subject to the dynamic constraint that

$$\dot{k} = h(k, c) = f(k) - gk - c \tag{9.25}$$

We now form the *Hamiltonian* expression

$$H(P, k, c) = F(k, c) + P \cdot h(k, c) \tag{9.26}$$

or

$$H(P, k, c) = F(k, c) + P \cdot \dot{k}$$

For example,

$$H(P, k, c) = F(k_1, k_2, c_1, c_2) + P_1 \cdot h_1(k_1, k_2, c_1, c_2) + P_2 \cdot h_2(k_1, k_2, c_1, c_2)$$

or

$$H(P, k, c) = F(k_1, k_2, c_1, c_2) + P_1 \cdot \dot{k}_1 + P_2 \cdot \dot{k}_2$$

To illustrate,

$$H(P, k, c) = u(c) + P \cdot [f(k) - gk - c] \tag{9.27}$$

---

[16] Nonautonomous systems can be handled by appropriate transformations. See Pontryagin et al., ibid., pp. 58–66.

or
$$H(P, k, c) = u(c) + P \cdot \dot{k}$$

We have introduced new variables, P, one for each state variable. They are called *dynamic multipliers* because they generally take on different values in the course of the program. The dynamic multipliers here are analogous to Lagrange multipliers in static maximizing problems.

In our illustration, the Hamiltonian is interpreted as national product, evaluated in terms of per capita utility. The dynamic multiplier, we shall find, is simply the marginal utility of consumption: the utility price (opportunity cost) of investment (not consuming). We know this from comparing the above expression with (9.21). The price (P) of ($\dot{k}$) is the corresponding loss of utility $[\mu = u'(c)]$.

We now state the *maximum principle*. Necessary conditions for a control process to be optimal are that:

1. At every point in the program, the control variable(s), c, maximize the value of the Hamiltonian. If H first increases and then decreases smoothly as each c is increased, then we have a smooth interior maximum and the requirement is

$$\frac{\partial H}{\partial c} = 0 \tag{9.28}$$

for each control variable. To illustrate,

$$\frac{\partial H}{\partial c} = u'(c) - P = 0$$

or

$$P = u'(c) \tag{9.29}$$

2. The dynamic multiplier(s), P, satisfy the differential equation(s)

$$\dot{P} = -\frac{\partial H}{\partial k} \tag{9.30}$$

To illustrate,

$$\dot{P} = -P[f'(k) - g] \tag{9.31}$$

Equation(s) 9.30, along with the dynamic constraint(s) (9.22), form the *Hamiltonian system*:

$$\dot{k} = \frac{\partial H}{\partial P} = g(k, c) \tag{9.22}$$

$$\dot{P} = -\frac{\partial H}{\partial k} \tag{9.30}$$

For the simple growth model, the Hamiltonian system is:

$$\dot{k} = f(k) - gk - c \qquad (9.25)$$
$$\dot{P} = -P[f'(k) - g] \qquad (9.31)$$

These equations will be recognized as the dynamic system we obtained before by using the Euler equation. It is illustrated in Figure 9.6 ($P = \mu$).

If the Hamiltonian system (9.25) holds, then the Hamiltonian is a constant throughout the program. We had this result before (9.20') for the special case where $T = \infty$. Now we show that it is true in general. National product is constant throughout an optimal program of any duration.

$$H = u(c) + P \cdot \dot{k}$$

Differentiating with respect to time,

$$\dot{H} = u'(c)\dot{c} + P \cdot \ddot{k} + \dot{k} \cdot \dot{P}$$

Using (9.31),

$$\dot{H} = u'(c)\dot{c} + P \cdot \ddot{k} - \dot{k} \cdot P[f'(k) - g]$$

Using (9.29),

$$\dot{H} = P[\dot{c} + \ddot{k} - \dot{k}f'(k) + \dot{k}g]$$

Differentiating (9.25),

$$\dot{c} + \ddot{k} = \dot{k}f'(k) - \dot{k}g$$

Substituting,

$$\dot{H} = 0$$

Optimal Growth Paths—Extensions of the Basic Model

Up to this point we have assumed constant technology and no discounting of the future. Both these assumptions are dropped in this section.

We assume that technological change is labor-augmenting. Writing "augmented" or "efficiency" labor as $\hat{L}$, output is given by

$$X = F(K, \hat{L})$$

where

$$\hat{L} = Le^{mt}$$

and $F(\ )$ is assumed to possess the usual properties, including constant returns to scale in K and $\hat{L}$. By virtue of that property, we can define a new function.

$$\frac{X}{\hat{L}} = f(\hat{k}), \qquad \hat{k} = \frac{\hat{K}}{\hat{L}}$$

or

$$\frac{X}{L} = f(\hat{k})e^{mt}$$

Note that per capita income rises at the proportional rate m if capital per efficiency worker is a constant. (Recall from Chapter Seven that $\hat{k}$ is constant in a Golden Age).

We will be concerned with per capita consumption, $c = C/L$.

$$c = \frac{X}{L} - \frac{\dot{K}}{L}$$

$$c = f(\hat{k})e^{mt} - \frac{\dot{K}}{K} \cdot k$$

$$c = f(\hat{k})e^{mt} - K^* \cdot k$$

Since

$$K = \hat{k} \cdot \hat{L}$$

logarithmic differentiation yields

$$K^* = \hat{k}^* + \hat{L}^*$$

so that

$$c = f(\hat{k})e^{mt} - (\hat{k}^* + \hat{L}^*)\hat{k}e^{mt}$$

With natural labor growing at the rate g, and its efficiency growing at the rate m, efficiency labor grows at the rate $g + m$.

$$c = f(\hat{k})e^{mt} - [\hat{k}^* + (g + m)]\hat{k}e^{mt}$$

or

$$c = e^{mt}[f(\hat{k}) - \hat{k} - (g + m)\hat{k}] \qquad (9.32)$$

The next step is to define the appropriate objective functional. If we wish utilities enjoyed in the future to count less than utilities enjoyed now, we discount the future at a positive rate. In a two-period model,

$$u(c)_1 = (1 + \rho)u(c)_0$$

where ρ is the *discount rate*. If $\rho = 1$, then 100 units of utility next year is equivalent to 50 units this year. If we write

$$u(c)_0 = \frac{1}{(1 + \rho)} u(c)_1$$

$1/(1 + \rho)$ is the *discount factor*. Comparing a second period with the initial one,

$$u(c)_0 = \frac{1}{(1 + \rho)^2} u(c)_2$$

In general, for any period of time, 0 to t

$$u(c)_0 = \frac{1}{(1 + \rho)^t} u(c)_t$$

or

$$u(c)_t = (1 + \rho)^t u(c)_0$$

In a continuous-time model, we must discount continuously. Let j be the number of "compoundings" per period

$$u(c)_t = \left(1 + \frac{\rho}{j}\right)^{jt} u(c)_0$$

As pointed out in Chapter Two,

$$\lim_{j \to \infty} \left(1 + \frac{\rho}{j}\right)^j = e^\rho$$

Thus

$$u(c)_t = e^{\rho t} \cdot u(c)_0$$

or

$$u(c)_0 = u(c)_t e^{-\rho t}$$

246   An Introduction to the Theory of Optimal Economic Growth

where $u(c)_0$ can be thought of as the *present value* of utility enjoyed at time t and discounted at the rate ρ. The sum of discounted utilities is the sum of the present values of utilities to be enjoyed in the future.

$$\begin{aligned}
\text{THE SUM OF DISCOUNTED UTILITIES,} &= u(c)_0 + u(c)_1 e^{-\rho} + u(c)_2 e^{-2\rho} \cdots \\
t = 0 \text{ to } t = T & \\
&= \int_{t=0}^{t=T} u(c) e^{-\rho t}\, dt, \qquad u(c) = u(c)_t
\end{aligned}$$

If we accept this integral as our objective functional, we are asserting: "Only the utility of per capita consumption (appropriately discounted) matters. Nothing else counts." But suppose more people could enjoy the same per capita utility. Would not society be better off? Should not the quantity of life, as well as its quality, count too? In that case, we should weight the per capita utility enjoyed at each t with the number of people who enjoy it. Let us set the initial population equal to one by an appropriate choice of measurement units. Then,

$$L_t = e^{gt}$$

and we have:

$$\begin{aligned}
\text{THE WEIGHTED SUM OF DISCOUNTED UTILITIES} &= \begin{array}{l} u(c)_0 + u(c)_1 e^{-\rho} \cdot e^g + u(c)_2 e^{-\rho 2} \cdot e^{g2} \cdots \\[4pt] u(c)_0 + u(c)_1 e^{-(\rho - g)} + u(c)_2 e^{-(\rho - g)2} \cdots \end{array}
\end{aligned}$$

$$J(\hat{k}) = \int_{t=0}^{t=T} u(c) e^{-(\rho - g)t}\, dt, \qquad u(c) = u(c)_t \tag{9.33}$$

This is the objective functional we shall work with. Note that if g is "too large," the functional is an *improper integral*. It will not converge and it is difficult to compare nonconvergent integrals. Keeping that in mind, let us go ahead and find an extremal to the functional (9.33): The time path of $\hat{k}$ that maximizes (9.33).

This time, the integrand does contain t explicitly. The functional is of the form

$$J(y) = \int_{x=a}^{x=b} F\, dx, \qquad F = F(x, y, y')$$

because in this case,
$$F = F(t, \hat{k}, \dot{\hat{k}})$$

$$J(\hat{k}) = \int_{t=0}^{t=T} F\, dt, \qquad F = u(c)e^{-(\rho - g)t}$$

$$c = e^{mt}[f(\hat{k}) - \dot{\hat{k}} - (g + m)\hat{k}]$$

We cannot use the first integral of the Euler equation. The time path of $\hat{k}$ must satisfy the Euler equation itself.

$$F_{\hat{k}} - \frac{d}{dt} F_{\dot{\hat{k}}} = 0$$

Letting $\mu = u'(c)$, the marginal utility of consumption,

$$F_{\hat{k}} = \mu[f'(\hat{k}) - (g + m)]e^{-(\rho - g - m)t}$$

$$F_{\dot{\hat{k}}} = -\mu e^{(g - \rho + m)t}$$

$$\frac{d}{dt} F_{\dot{\hat{k}}} = -[\mu(g - \rho + m) + \dot{\mu}]e^{-(\rho - g - m)t}$$

Substituting into the Euler equation,

$$\mu[f'(\hat{k}) - (g + m)] - \mu(\rho - g + m) + \dot{\mu} = 0$$

or

$$\dot{\mu} = -\mu[f'(\hat{k}) - (g + m) + m - (\rho - g)]$$

Recall from Chapter Six that $f'(\hat{k})$ is the "rate of interest," the marginal productivity of capital. Thus

$$\dot{\mu} = -\mu[r - (g + m) + m - (\rho - g)] \tag{9.34}$$

where

$r =$ the rate of interest

$(g + m) =$ the "natural rate of growth" of the economy (the rate at which K, X, and $\hat{L}$ grow in a Golden Age)

$m =$ the rate of growth of labor efficiency; since X grows at the rate of $(g + m)$ in a Golden Age, m is the rate of growth of per capita income (X/L) in a Golden Age

$(\rho - g) =$ the "generalized" discount rate; it discounts future utilities by ρ, but weights these discounted utilities with ever-larger populations

$\mu =$ the utility price of capital

248   An Introduction to the Theory of Optimal Economic Growth

We can "account for" the interest rate in this model by rewriting (9.34).

$$r = (\rho - g) + g - \mu^*, \qquad \mu^* = \frac{\dot{\mu}}{\mu} \tag{9.35}$$

The interest rate is higher:

1. The greater is the generalized discount rate on the future. On one hand, impatience means more consumption and less capital. On the other hand, the faster population grows, the more capital must be put aside to provide for the utility of ever more people in the future.
2. The greater is the rate of growth of labor.
3. The less are the "capital gains" to be made by investing. If the utility price of capital is falling, there is less incentive to invest, and the interest rate is higher.

Equation 9.34 can be converted to a relation that shows how consumption per efficiency worker depends upon capital per efficiency worker and the constants of the system. Recall that if

$$\mu = \mu(c)$$

we can write

$$c^* = -\frac{1}{\epsilon} \cdot \mu^*, \qquad c^* = \frac{\dot{c}}{c}, \qquad \mu^* = \frac{\dot{\mu}}{\mu}$$

where ϵ is the (positive but not necessarily constant) elasticity of the marginal utility of consumption curve. Using this relation along with (9.34) yields

$$c^* = \frac{1}{\epsilon}[r - (g + m) + m - (\rho - g)]$$

Consumption per efficiency worker is

$$\hat{c} = \frac{C}{\hat{L}} = \frac{C}{L} e^{mt} = c e^{-mt}$$

so that

$$\hat{c}^* = c^* - m$$

and

$$\hat{c}^* = \frac{1}{\epsilon}[r - (g + m) + m - (\rho - g)] - m$$

or

$$\hat{c}^* = \frac{1}{\epsilon}[r - (g + m) + (1 - \epsilon)m - (\rho - g)]$$

or

$$\hat{c}^* = \frac{1}{\epsilon}[f'(\hat{k}) - (g + m) + (1 - \epsilon)m - (\rho - g)]$$

or

$$\dot{\hat{c}} = \frac{c}{\epsilon}[f'(\hat{k}) - (g + m) + (1 - \epsilon)m - (\rho - g)] \qquad (9.36)$$

Next, we need an expression for the growth of $\hat{k}$. Rewriting (9.32)

$$\hat{c} = f(\hat{k}) - \dot{\hat{k}} - (g + m)\hat{k}$$

we have

$$\dot{\hat{k}} = f(\hat{k}) - (g + m)\hat{k} - \hat{c} \qquad (9.37)$$

Equations 9.36 and 9.37 form a system of differential equations in $\hat{c}$ and $\hat{k}$, and we can graph them in the usual way. Let us first look at the special case where there is no technological change ($m = 0$, $\hat{k} = k$, $\hat{c} = c$), but where there is possible generalized discounting of the future ($\rho \neq g$). Equations 9.36 and 9.37 reduce to:

$$\dot{c} = \frac{c}{\epsilon}[f'(k) - g - (\rho - g)] \qquad (9.36')$$

$$\dot{k} = f(k) - gk - c \qquad (9.37')$$

The $\dot{\hat{c}} = \dot{c} = 0$ and $\dot{\hat{k}} = \dot{k} = 0$ isokines are plotted in Figure 9.12. Three possible generalized discount rates are illustrated. At E it is zero ($g = \rho$), at E' it is positive ($g < \rho$), and E'' it is negative ($g > \rho$). We have argued before that points like E', E'', and E''' are the only sensible terminal points for infinite programs. It is now possible to argue that if g exceeds ρ (positive discounting), an infinite program is *dynamically inefficient*.[17] For suppose a program should head for E'' ($g > \rho$), so that a Golden Age is eventually established where $f'(k) = r < g$. Clearly, that Golden Age is inferior to any other Golden Age lying between E'' and E. Not only would consumption be forever greater in the latter Golden Age, but some capital could also be

---

[17] E. S. Phelps, "Second Essay on the Golden Rule of Accumulation," *American Economic Review* (September, 1965).

250 An Introduction to the Theory of Optimal Economic Growth

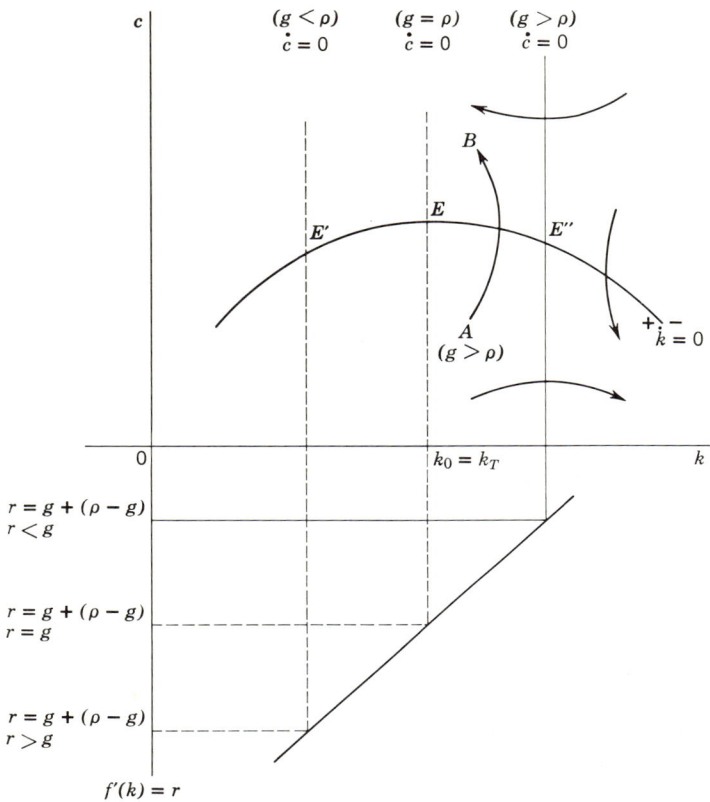

Figure 9.12 Optimal growth paths of k and c. The future is discounted; there is no technological change.

"eaten" as well. This statement could not be made for infinite programs in which ρ exceeds g. In that case, E' lies to the left of E where consumption gains are possible, but only if accumulation is undertaken. Thus, the "r equals g" Golden Age at E separates dynamically efficient and dynamically inefficient infinite programs. Since "r equals g" is the Golden Rule, we can say that the Golden Rule serves as a *separatrix* for efficient and inefficient programs.

To illustrate, suppose the planning authority is farsighted and therefore decides to pursue a plan that has no definite end ($T = \infty$). Moreover, it sees no reason why utilities tomorrow should not count as much as utilities today ($\rho = 0$). Would it want to specify a plan in which the quantity of life counts as well as its quality? That is, should it weight per capita utility by the number of people who enjoy it, when formulating the objective function?

Perhaps not, because by doing so, it plans for an eventual Golden Age in which per capita consumption and utility is less than it could be.[18]

Of course, *finite* time programs make sense if there is negative discounting of the future, although it is still not clear how one can seriously assign a terminal capital-labor ratio. But a trip from, say, A to B in Figure 9.12 is not dynamically inefficient, even if g exceeds ρ. (Note: k_T happens to be equal to k_0).

We return now to the more general case where there is technological progress. Finite time programs are inferred in the usual way. Necessary conditions for optimality are given by (9.36) and (9.37), and they are plotted in Figure 9.13. The $\dot{c} = 0$ isokine is vertical at the $\hat{k}$, for which

$$r = (g + m) - (1 - \epsilon)m + (\rho - g)$$
$$r = \rho + \epsilon \cdot m$$

The $\dot{k} = 0$ isokine rises and then falls. Its maximum occurs at the $\hat{k}$, for which

$$r = g + m$$

Figure 9.13 is drawn for the case where

$$g + m > \rho + \epsilon m$$

A program is illustrated that begins at A and ends at B after T years. Note that the program arches up toward E', a Golden Age where $\dot{k} = \dot{c} = 0$. Longer and longer programs would have to arch closer and closer to point E' in order to slow down motion in the plus $\hat{k}$ direction. As they arch closer and closer, they take longer and longer in the neighborhood of E'. Again, we can think of E' as the turnpike, and *on the turnpike* $r = \rho + \epsilon m$.

We saw before that $g + m$ was the "natural rate of growth" of the economy—the rate of growth of capital, output, and efficiency labor in a Golden Age. Now we can label $\rho + \epsilon m$ the "natural rate of interest." It has two components:

ρ = the rate of discount on future utilities

ϵm = the rate of growth of per capita consumption weighted by the elasticity of its marginal utility

---

[18] For a discussion of this point, see T. C. Koopmans, "On the Concept of Optimal Economic Growth," in *Semaine d'Etude sur le Rôle de l'Analyse Econométrique dans las Formulation de Plans de Développement* (Vatican City: Pontifical Academy of Sciences, 1965).

252 An Introduction to the Theory of Optimal Economic Growth

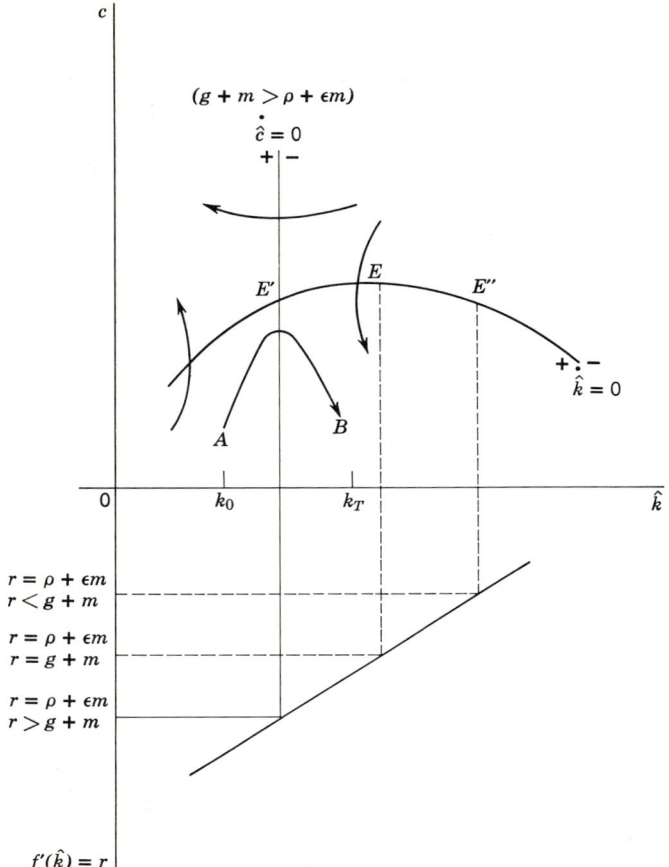

Figure 9.13 Optimal growth paths of k and c. The future is discounted; there is technological change.

Thus, the natural rate of interest arises out of a systematic undervaluation of future utilities and the expectation of "better days ahead" due to improving technology.

We saw before, with stationary technology, that any infinite plan that called for driving the Golden Age rate of interest below the growth rate of labor was dynamically inefficient. Now we shall argue that with improving technology, any infinite plan that calls for driving the Golden Age natural rate of interest ($\rho + \epsilon m$) below the natural rate of growth ($g + m$) is dynamically inefficient.

The simplest argument begins with the recognition that consumption per efficiency worker ($\hat{c}$) reaches a maximum Golden Age value on the

$\dot{k} = 0$ isokine, where the natural rate of interest equals the natural rate of growth ($r = \rho + \epsilon m = g + m$ at E). If capital deepening past that point were called for ($r = \rho + \epsilon m < g + m$) by the plan, the planner might sense that something is wrong, that the plan really is not as "optimal" as the Euler equation alone would suggest. For he would note that by increasing the rate at which future utilities are discounted (ρ), he would increase the Golden Age natural rate of interest ($\rho + \epsilon m$), raise Golden Age consumption per efficiency worker, and avoid some capital deepening in the bargain (that is, have some extra consumption along the way). The $r < g + m$ plan is *dynamically inefficient* in terms of efficiency labor. Moreover, the ratio of *natural* labor to efficiency labor is exogenously given, and therefore beyond his control. A plan that is dynamically inefficient in terms of efficiency labor is therefore dynamically inefficient in terms of natural labor. This time, the modified Golden Rule ($r = g + m$) serves as a separatrix for efficient and inefficient programs.[19] If the rate of interest (r) is driven below the natural rate of growth ($g + m$), the capital-labor ratio is permanently above its (modified) Golden Rule value, and Golden Age consumption is permanently below attainable values.

EXERCISES

1. Use the Euler equation or its first integral to show that a straight line is the least distance path between two points. [Hint: you should find that $F = (1 + y'^2)^{1/2}$.] Why is it possible to use the first integral of Euler's equation in this problem?
2. The Pure Resource Exhaustion Problem. Imagine an (unchanging) population of people who are "lost in space." They have a fixed stock of consumer goods (K) aboard their spacecraft, which they plan to consume ($C = -\dot{K}$) for T years, at which time the universe will end. They decide to maximize their (discounted) utilities between now and T years from now.

$$\text{MAX } J(K) = \int_0^T u(C) e^{-\rho t} \, dt$$

---

[19] More rigorously, if $r = \rho + \epsilon m < g + m$, the integral of the objective functional does not converge for an infinite program. Recall that $F = u(c) \exp -(\rho - g)t$. Let $u = c^{(1-\epsilon)}/(1 - \epsilon)$ so that $(du/\mu)/(dc/c) = -\epsilon$. Then as the economy approaches a Golden Age, F^* is approximated by $(1 - \epsilon)m - (\rho - g)$. The integral will not converge if F^* is positive. Put another way, as the economy approaches a Golden Age, the discounted value of capital stock must vanish. The discounted price of capital is $\exp -(\rho - g) \cdot \mu$. Thus, the right-hand transversality condition is $\lim_{t \to \infty} \exp -(\rho - g) \cdot \mu \cdot k = 0$. Approaching the Golden Age, we have $-(\rho - g) - \epsilon m + m$. The discounted value of the capital stock is increasing if $\rho + \epsilon m < m + g$ as the Golden Age is approached, and the transversality condition cannot be satisfied.

254 An Introduction to the Theory of Optimal Economic Growth

What should be the time path of consumption? Hint: first find $\dot{\mu}/\mu = \mu^*$. Then use the relation $\mu^* = -\epsilon \cdot C^*$.

3. Assume that production conditions are Cobb-Douglas $X = K^{1-a}L^a$, and that the utility of consumption is given by $u = c^\gamma$, $\gamma < 1$. Use the Euler equation to find a system of differential equations in per capita consumption (c) and the capital-labor ratio (k) when the objective functional is

$$J(k) = \int_{t=0}^{t=T} F\, dt, \qquad F = u(c)$$

Sketch a phase diagram of the system similar to Figure 9.7. What is the elasticity of the marginal utility of consumption curve? How is the equilibrium value of k related to g?

4. Select the saving ratio (s) as the control variable in an optimal control problem. Show that the Hamiltonian is:

$$H = u(c) + P \cdot \dot{k}$$
$$c = (1 - s) \cdot f(k)$$
$$\dot{k} = f(k) - gk - (1 - s) \cdot f(k)$$

Find the corresponding Hamiltonian system.

REFERENCES AND SUGGESTIONS FOR FURTHER READING

1. Allen, R. D. G., *Mathematical Analysis for Economists*. London: Macmillan, 1960. Chapter XX.
2. Arrow, K. J., "Discounting and Public Investment Criteria." In A. V. Kneese and S. C. Smith (Eds.), *Water Resources Research* (Washington: Resources for the Future, 1967).
3. Cass, D., "Optimum Growth in an Aggregative Model of Capital Accumulation." *Review of Economic Studies*, July 1965.
4. Courant, R., *Differential and Integral Calculus*. Volume II. New York: Interscience, 1936. Chapter VII.
5. Gelfand, I. M. and S. V. Fomin, *Calculus of Variations*. Englewood Cliffs: Prentice-Hall, 1963.
6. Hansen, J. A. and P. A. Neher, "The Neoclassical Theorem Once Again." *American Economic Review*, September 1967.

7. Koopmans, T. C., "Intertemporal Distribution and 'Optimal' Aggregate Economic Growth." In W. Fellner, *et al.*, *Ten Economic Studies in the Tradition of Irving Fisher*. New York: Wiley, 1967.
8. Koopmans, T. C., "On the Concept of Optimal Economic Growth." In *Semaine d' Etude sur le Role de l'Analyse Econometrique dans la Formulation de Plans de Développement*. Vatican City: Pontifical Academy of Science, 1965.
9. Marty, A. L., "The Neoclassical Theorem." *American Economic Review*, December 1964.
10. Phelps, E. S., *Golden Rules of Economic Growth*. New York: Norton, 1966.
11. Phelps, E. S., "Second Essay on the Golden Rule of Accumulation." *American Economic Review*, September 1965.
12. Pontryagin, L. S., *et al.*, *The Mathematical Theory of Optimal Processes*. New York: Interscience, 1962.
13. Ramsey, F. P., "A Mathematical Theory of Saving." *Economic Journal* December 1928.
14. Samuelson, P. A., "A Catenary Turnpike Theorem Involving Consumption and the Golden Rule." *American Economic Review*, June 1965.
15. Shell, K. (Ed.), *Essays on the Theory of Optimal Economic Growth*. Cambridge: M.I.T. Press, 1967.

Chapter Ten

GROWTH IN AN OPEN ECONOMY

The Balance of Payments
Growth in the Domestic Economy
Growth of National Wealth
Growth with Capital Movements
An Explicit Solution
Foreign Aid
Exercises
References and Suggestions for Further Reading

THE BALANCE OF PAYMENTS

Models of growth become much more complex when international economic intercourse is allowed for. Yet we must try to construct models of open economies because many of the advanced economies, and many less developed countries as well, have important economic links with the outside world. Their growth and development is influenced by conditions and events in other countries, and we ought to be able to take these into account.

The transmission links between an economy and the outside world can be identified by looking at the country's external accounts (the components of its balance of payments).

If trade were carried out on a strictly barter basis, then all exports would have to be paid for by an equal value of imports. In strictly barter trade, there is only one balance of payments account: the current trade account. It is *always* in balance. Exports (*E*) *always* equal imports (*M*) in value.

$$B_C = E - M = 0$$

Most modern economies use "international money" and trade "securities" with one another. A country that exports more than it imports on current account must be compensated by importing "international money" or "securities," just as an individual who sells more goods and services than he buys must be compensated in cash or I.O.U.'s. Conversely, a country that imports more than it exports on current account must pay for the difference by exporting "international money" or "securities," just as an individual who buys more goods and services than he sells must pay out cash or issue I.O.U.'s.

"International money" is loosely defined as noninterest-bearing money that is acceptable as a means of payment by a number of countries. Traditionally, gold has played this role, but English pounds, American dollars, and International Monetary Fund "paper gold" have qualified as international money in the post gold-standard period.

Broadly construed, "securities" are promises to settle accounts later—to "pay" later with either "international money" or an excess of exports over imports. These securities can take many forms in practice: *bonded debt* can be issued by governments, corporations, or individuals who promise to repay at some stipulated date in the future, and to pay a rate of interest in the meantime; *equities* are usually issued by public or private corporations, which regard them as liabilities, and entitle the owner to a *pro rata* share in the corporation's earnings; countries that receive *foreign aid* or unilateral payments can be thought of as making payment in "securities" that bear no interest and never mature.

When a security is issued to a foreigner, we say that a security is exported. When a security is received from a foreigner, we say that a security is imported. Thus, if a country exports more than it imports on current trade account, it may take payment in an excess of security imports over security exports. If there were no "international money," an excess of security exports would have to offset exactly an excess of imports over exports on current trade account. As a matter of terminology, we say that a country that has an *excess of security exports over security imports* has a *positive balance on capital account*, or is *importing capital*, or is *exporting securities* on net. Conversely, a country that has an *excess of security imports over exports* has a *negative balance on capital account*, or is *exporting capital*, or is *importing securities* on net.

If we call B_K the balance on capital account, then

$$B_K = M - E = -B_C$$

or

$$B_C + B_K = 0$$

is always true if there is no "international money." An excess of imports over exports on current trade account ($B_C < 0$) must be matched by an excess of security exports over security imports ($B_K > 0$).

If we allow "international money" to enter the picture, then a negative balance on current trade account can be "paid for" by exporting securities *or* by running down accumulated balances of internationally acceptable money. If a country pays for an excess of imports over exports on combined current and capital account with international money, then we say that the country exports the money. Let us call the "international money" account the "gold" account, for short, and its balance B_G. Then

$$B_C + B_K + B_G = 0$$

A country can lose international money ($B_G > 0$) only if its combined purchases of goods and securities exceed its combined sales of goods and securities.

$$B_G = -B_C - B_K$$

A country can export gold ($B_G > 0$) *only* if it is buying more goods and securities, taken together, than it is selling.

Clearly, if any *two* of these *three* external accounts is in equilibrium, the third must be as well. Thus, if we are interested in equilibrium growth paths, it is sufficient to discover equilibrium growth conditions for any two of the three accounts.

In this chapter we shall concentrate on the *long-run* growth properties of an open economy. Over long periods of time, a country's "gold" account must balance out to nearly zero, since a country cannot lose more than a finite accumulated stock of international money, nor is it rational for a country to absorb international money indefinitely.[1] This assumption simplifies our task considerably. With B_G *assumed* equal to zero, then $B_C + B_K = 0$ in equilibrium.

---

[1] There are exceptions. Countries that print international reserve currencies can export them indefinitely, as long as other countries are willing to absorb them for international liquidity or other purposes. Gold-producing countries can be continuous exporters of gold. We take these exceptions to be minor relative to equilibrium flows on the other two international accounts.

GROWTH IN THE DOMESTIC ECONOMY

The term "domestic" refers to events that occur within a country's borders. Thus, *domestic product* is the output of resources employed within a country. In the spirit of the analysis in preceding chapters, we continue to assume that one composite good is produced within the country, using homogeneous capital and labor. The domestic production function is assumed to have the usual property of constant returns to scale, so that

$$X = F(K, L)$$

can be written

$$X = L \cdot f(k), \qquad k \equiv \frac{K}{L}$$

where, in addition,

$$f'(k) > 0 \quad \text{and} \quad f''(k) < 0$$

We assume for now that there is no technological progress.[2]

Labor growth is demographically determined. It grows at a constant proportional rate (g), which includes international migration as well as natural increase.

$$L^* = g$$

By taking g to be exogenous, we ignore the possible links between migration and international differences in per capita incomes or wage levels. Moreover, any relationship between natural increase and material welfare is ignored.[3]

As before, with but one good being produced under competitive conditions, the rate of interest is identified with the marginal product of capital.

$$r = f'(k)$$

---

[2] Alternatively, one could allow for Harrod-neutral technological progress here by letting labor be measured in efficiency units.

[3] Population increase could depend on the wage level. In that case, the L^* line in Figure 10.1 would slope upward if population grows faster at higher wage levels.

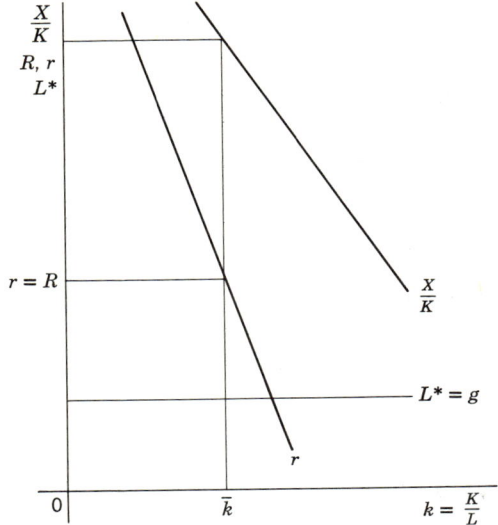

Figure 10.1 The growth of the domestic economy.

But now, r is equal to borrowing and lending rates in international capital markets. Let us assume that the (combined public and private) international lending or borrowing activities of the country do not affect the international rate of interest,[4] and that the rate is otherwise constant. Then international capital flows will ensure that the return on capital in the country (r) cannot deviate from an exogenous and constant world-rate of interest (R) in equilibrium.[5] This means that the equilibrium capital-labor ratio in the domestic economy is locked in by exogenous force.

The domestic economy is illustrated in Figure 10.1. The average and marginal products of capital are shown as declining functions of the capital-labor ratio. The international interest rate is $0R$ which, given domestic technology, determines the equilibrium capital-labor ratio ($\bar{k}$). With this ratio constant in equilibrium, capital must grow at the same rate as labor ($K^* = L^* = g$).

Along any equilibrium growth path, constant-returns technology guarantees that domestic product will grow apace with capital and labor.

Recall that output growth is the weighted average of input growth rates, the weights being the respective shares of domestic product imputed to the

---

[4] This is nearly true for all countries except the United States and perhaps some Western European nations.

[5] The well-known imperfections in international-capital markets cannot be analyzed here. But it is clear that uncertainties, lack of information, exchange risks, and political considerations can pause prolonged inefficiencies in international-capital allocation.

two domestically employed imputs.

$$X^* = \frac{rK}{X} K^* + \frac{wL}{X} L^*$$

$$X^* = (1-a)K^* + aL^*$$

With

$$K^* = L^* = g$$

$$X^* = g$$

along any equilibrium growth path. This is the same rate of growth achieved by the closed economy.

GROWTH OF NATIONAL WEALTH

In an economy that is linked to the rest of the world through capital markets, saving out of national income can be invested either at home or abroad. Moreover, national income is composed of wage income earned at home plus the earnings of nationally owned capital employed in the domestic economy and in other countries.

Define C as capital owned by resident nationals. In this simple model, all nationals are resident workers, and capital is the only form of wealth. National saving increases national wealth. If a constant proportion of national income (Y) is saved, then

$$\frac{d}{dt} C \equiv \dot{C} = sY$$

where national income is domestically earned wage income plus the earnings of capital, wherever employed.

$$Y = wL + rC$$

Note that capital flows guarantee the same interest rate on capital, wherever employed. Thus, we can apply the international rate (R), equal to the domestic rate (r), to all capital owned by nationals (C) irrespective of its location of employment. Note also that the model has nothing to say about precisely *where* nationals employ their capital, although most countries employ more of their capital at home than abroad.

Combining equations, we have

$$\dot{C} = s(wL + rC)$$

or

$$\dot{C} = swL + srC$$

Dividing by C, we express the growth of national wealth in proportional terms.

$$C^* = sw\frac{L}{C} + sr$$

Define c as nationally owned capital per worker.

$$c \equiv \frac{C}{L}$$

Then

$$C^* = sr + sw \cdot \frac{1}{c}$$

Recall that wages and the interest rate are both functions of the capital-labor ratio. If the domestic rate of return on capital is locked onto the international interest rate, then the wage rate is also determined. This is clear in Figure 5.5. The wage is inversely related to interest rate. Let us denote the wage corresponding to $R = r$ as $\bar{w}$. Now we can write

$$C^* = sr + s\bar{w} \cdot \frac{1}{c} \tag{10.1}$$

The growth of national wealth depends positively upon the saving ratio, negatively upon the international interest rate, and negatively upon the ratio of wealth to workers.

This equation is plotted in Figure 10.2, along with the growth of labor. Given $R = 0R$ and s, the growth of C declines as c rises. On the assumption that the C^* line intersects the L^* line, an equilibrium (particular solution) $c \equiv C/L$ is established at a point like $\bar{c}$. That the equilibrium is stable can be established in the usual way.

However, it is possible that no equilibrium $c \equiv C/L$ exists. This will occur if the C^* and L^* lines do not intersect. If that occurs, C and L can never grow at the same rate, so that their ratio (c) can never stabilize.

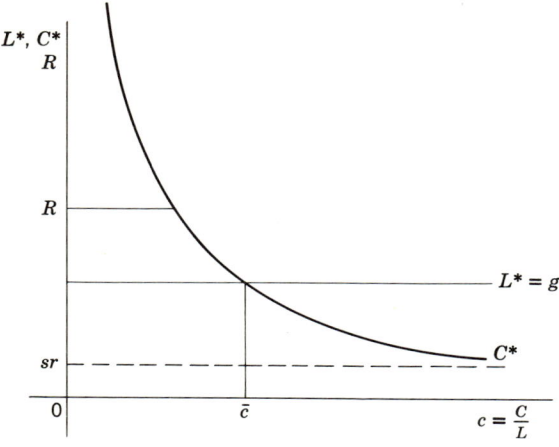

Figure 10.2 The growth of national capital ownership.

Note first that the growth of labor can never be so *large* that equilibrium is impossible. From (10.1),

$$\lim_{c \to 0} C^* = \infty$$

No matter how great $L^* = g$ is, there is always a sufficiently large C^* so that an equilibrium c will eventually be established. On the other hand, L^* might be too *small*. Turning again to (10.1),

$$\lim_{c \to \infty} C^* = sr$$

As c becomes larger, the growth of C approaches a lower limit equal to the product of the saving ratio and the international interest rate. This is shown by the horizontal dotted line in Figure 10.2. If $L^* = g < sr$, the growth of C will forever outstrip the growth of L, and c will continually rise.

The lower limit on C^* as c increases has the following meaning. As c becomes larger, the interest portion of national income becomes greater relative to wage income. When c is infinitely large, all income is from capital ownership.

$$Y = rC$$

With a constant proportion saved of income,

$$\dot{C} = sY$$

Growth of National Wealth

Thus, by substitution

$$\dot{C} = srC$$

or

$$C^* = sr$$

The growth of C cannot fall short of this value.

Another view of the problem is obtained by converting (10.1) into a differential equation in $c \equiv C/L$. Subtract $L^* = g$ from both sides of (10.1).

$$C^* - L^* = (sr - g) + s \cdot \bar{w} \cdot \frac{1}{c}$$

But

$$C^* - L^* = \frac{d}{dt}\frac{C}{L} \cdot \frac{L}{C} = \frac{\dot{c}}{c}$$

so that

$$\frac{\dot{c}}{c} = (sr - g) + s \cdot \bar{w} \cdot \frac{1}{c}$$

or

$$\dot{c} + (g - sr)c = s \cdot \bar{w} \tag{10.2}$$

The constant on the left-hand side is positive if $g > sr$. We saw in Chapter Seven that this term must be positive if the variable is to converge to an equilibrium value. In that case, *higher* values of c must be matched by *lower* values of its growth rate to maintain the equality, and an equilibrium c is eventually established. But if $sr > g$, then *higher* values of c are matched by *higher* values of its growth rate, and c grows forever larger.

The equilibrium c, if it exists, is readily found by setting $C^* = L^* = g$ in (10.1) or $\dot{c} = 0$ in (10.2). Letting $\bar{c}$ equal the *equilibrium* value of $c \equiv C/L$,

$$\bar{c} = \frac{s \cdot \bar{w}}{g - sr} \tag{10.3}$$

Equation 10.3 shows the dynamic equilibrium value of c. With labor growing at the constant proportional rate (g), the national ownership of capital is growing at the same constant proportional rate. But how does the *equilibrium* value of c change in response to changes in g or s? This is a problem in *comparative dynamics*.

If g should rise, it is clear that national wealth per worker will fall. As in the closed economy case, more rapid growth lowers per capita wealth.

One would suspect that a higher saving ratio would correspond to a higher equilibrium value of $\bar{c}$. This is the case. Differentiating (10.3) with respect to the saving ratio,

$$\frac{d\bar{c}}{ds} \cdot \frac{1}{\bar{c}} = \frac{g}{s}(g - sr)$$

It has just been argued that the denominator must be positive for an equilibrium c to exist. Thus, the entire expression is positive for positive labor-growth rates.

GROWTH WITH CAPITAL MOVEMENTS

It is now possible to combine the analysis of (1) domestic economic growth with (2) the growth of national wealth, to obtain a more complete view of growth in an open economy.

Figures 10.1 and 10.2 portrayed, respectively, the growth of the domestic economy and the growth of national wealth. These two figures are superimposed in Figure 10.3. The constant interest rate ($R = 0R$ on the vertical axis) and the domestic production function determine the equilibrium capital-labor ratio ($\bar{k} = 0\bar{k}$ on the horizontal axis). At the same time, the equilibrium value of per capita wealth ($\bar{c} = 0\bar{c}$ on the horizontal axis) is determined by the intersection of the C^* function and the L^* line at point Q. The value of a country's international debt (or credit) is determined by comparing $\bar{k}$ with $\bar{c}$. The country is an international debtor if it employs more capital in its domestic economy (K) than it owns (C). Letting D denote international debt,

$$D = K - C$$

or

$$d = k - c$$

where d is international debt per worker.[6] In Figure 10.3, the country is a debtor in equilibrium because $\bar{k}$ exceeds $\bar{c}$.

It is not difficult to discover if a country is an equilibrium debtor or creditor once we know:

1. The growth rate of labor.
2. The proportion of domestic product imputed to domestically employed capital according to its marginal productivity $(1 - a)$.

[6] The debt is a net figure. It is possible, of course, for a country to be a net creditor ($C > K$), yet all its domestically employed capital be foreign owned (all its nationally owned capital employed abroad).

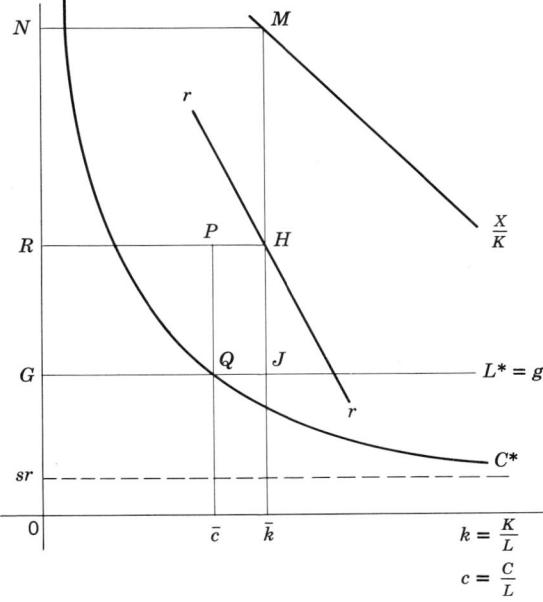

Figure 10.3 Growth and capital movements.

3. The proportion of national income that is saved and invested (s).
4. The international rate of interest $R = r$.

We already have an expression for $\bar{c}$ (10.3) in terms of these variables. A corresponding equation for $\bar{k}$ is required to compare with it.

Recall the definitions of relative shares.

$$a \equiv \frac{wL}{X}$$

$$1 - a \equiv \frac{rK}{X}$$

Thus

$$\frac{a}{1-a} = \frac{wL}{rK}$$

or

$$\frac{K}{L} \equiv k = \frac{1-a}{a} \cdot \frac{w}{r}$$

But the wage rate is locked in by the international interest rate and the domestic production function.

$$w = \bar{w}$$

Thus

$$\bar{k} = \frac{1-a}{a} \cdot \frac{\bar{w}}{r} \qquad (10.4)$$

is the expression for $\bar{k}$ to compare with

$$\bar{c} = \frac{s \cdot \bar{w}}{g - sr} \qquad (10.3)$$

which expresses the equilibrium value of c.

If the country is a debtor, then $\bar{k}$ exceeds $\bar{c}$. For a debtor,

$$\frac{1-a}{a} \cdot \frac{\bar{w}}{r} > \frac{s \cdot \bar{w}}{g - sr}$$

or

$$g(1-a) > sr$$

A country is neither a debtor nor a creditor if

$$g(1-a) = sr$$

and is a creditor if

$$g(1-a) < sr$$

A country is more likely to be a debtor if it uses more capital-intensive techniques, is growing more rapidly, saves a smaller proportion of its income, and faces a lower international interest rate.

If $k - c$ is per capita international debt, then the interest payments to foreigners can be read directly off the figure. In per capita terms,

$$\frac{rD}{L} = r(\bar{k} - \bar{c}) = \bar{c}\bar{k}HP$$

We already know that per capita domestic product is

$$\frac{X}{L} \equiv \frac{X}{K} \cdot \frac{K}{L} \equiv \frac{X}{K} \cdot \bar{k} = 0\bar{k}MN$$

National income is domestic product minus interest payments to foreigners.

$$Y = X - rD$$

In per capita terms,

$$\frac{Y}{L} = \frac{X}{L} - \frac{rD}{L}$$

Graphically,

$$\frac{Y}{L} = 0\bar{k}MN - \bar{c}\bar{k}HP$$

Put another way, national income is domestically earned wage income plus the earnings of nationally owned capital.

$$Y = wL + rC$$

In per capita terms,

$$\frac{Y}{L} = w + r\bar{c}$$

The wage is the average product of labor minus the earnings per worker of domestically employed capital.

$$w = \frac{X}{L} - \frac{rK}{L} = \frac{X}{L} - r\bar{k}$$

We already know that

$$\frac{X}{L} = 0\bar{k}MN$$

Moreover,

$$r\bar{k} = 0\bar{k}HR$$

Thus

$$w = 0\bar{k}MN - 0\bar{k}HR$$

or

$$w = RHMN$$

270 Growth in an Open Economy

Adding this to $r\bar{c}$,

$$\frac{Y}{L} = w + r\bar{c}$$

$$\frac{Y}{L} = RHMN + 0\bar{c}PR$$

This is exactly the same area that was obtained before.

Saving out of national income is invested and increases nationally owned capital.

$$S = \dot{C}$$

In per capita terms,

$$\frac{S}{L} = \frac{\dot{C}}{L}$$

or

$$\frac{S}{L} = \frac{\dot{C}}{C} \cdot \frac{C}{L} = C^* \cdot \bar{c}$$

In equilibrium, $C^* = L^* = g$. Thus

$$\frac{S}{L} = g \cdot \bar{c}$$

Graphically,

$$\frac{S}{L} = 0\bar{c}QG$$

Domestic investment per worker is

$$\frac{\dot{K}}{L} = \frac{\dot{K}}{K} \cdot \frac{K}{L} = K^* \cdot \bar{k}$$

In equilibrium, the capital stock must grow apace with the labor force to maintain the domestic return on capital in equality with the constant international interest rate. Thus

$$\frac{\dot{K}}{L} = g \cdot \bar{k}$$

In terms of Figure 10.3,

$$\frac{\dot{K}}{L} = 0\bar{k}JG$$

The difference between domestic investment and national saving must be financed by foreigners. Domestic investment creates securities that are purchased by saving out of national income or are absorbed by foreigners. Foreign capitalists will snap up investment opportunities, created at the international interest rate, that nationals fail to exploit because of insufficient saving. Since the country is small, it faces an infinitely elastic (horizontal) supply curve of capital at the international interest rate, R. Securities are exported if domestic investment exceeds national saving.

$$B_K = \dot{K} - S$$

or

$$\frac{B_K}{L} = \frac{K}{L} - \frac{S}{L}$$

Graphically,

$$\frac{B_K}{L} = 0\bar{k}JG - 0\bar{c}QG$$

or

$$\frac{B_K}{L} = \bar{c}\bar{k}JQ$$

In the figure, the country is not only a debtor, but is importing capital as well.

It was argued in the first section of this chapter that the current account and the capital account must add up to zero, on the assumption that there are no sustained flows of international money.

$$B_C + B_K = 0$$

or

$$\frac{B_C}{L} + \frac{B_K}{L} = 0$$

Thus

$$\frac{B_C}{L} = -\bar{c}\bar{k}JQ$$

272 Growth in an Open Economy

for the model economy in Figure 10.3. The country has a negative balance of payments on current account. If

$$B_C = E - M$$

then

$$M - E = \bar{c}\bar{k}JQ$$

There is an excess of imports over exports in this model economy. Imports consist of imported goods *plus the import of capital services*. The use of foreign capital in the domestic economy gives rise to current payments to foreigners, just as do conventional imports. The current trade balance consists of the balance of trade of goods and noncapital services (V) plus the balance of trade in capital services ($-rD$).

$$E - M = V - rD$$

If the country is a net debtor ($D > 0$), it has a negative balance of payments on capital services account. Solving for V,

$$V = E - M + rD$$

or

$$\frac{V}{L} = -\frac{M - E}{L} + \frac{rD}{L}$$

Graphically,

$$v \equiv \frac{V}{L} = -\bar{c}\bar{k}JQ + \bar{c}\bar{k}HP$$

In this example, $E - M$ exceeds rD, so the country is a net exporter of goods and noncapital services (V). Although current-account imports exceed current-account exports, current-account imports of capital services are sufficiently great to compel net exports of goods and noncapital services.

We have just examined a model economy which, in equilibrium is:

1. A debtor, and therefore importing capital services.
2. A net exporter of securities.
3. A net exporter of goods and noncapital services.

It is easy to contrive other configurations in Figure 10.3 by changing the saving ratio (raising s shifts the C^* line up) or by changing the growth rate (raising g shifts the L^* line up and the C^* line down). A higher saving ratio or a lower growth rate will make a debtor less of a debtor, convert it into a creditor, or make a creditor more of a creditor.

Continuous technological change of the labor-augmenting variety can be incorporated, as before in Chapter Three, by redefining labor as labor measured in efficiency units, and allowing labor efficiency to grow at a constant proportional rate. A higher rate of technological change will make a debtor more of a debtor, convert a creditor into a debtor, or make it less of a creditor. Continuous technological change permits the open economy to increase per capita incomes over the long haul. This is a crucial feature that the open economy shares with the closed economy.

Other points deserve emphasis. A saving campaign will not raise the domestic capital-labor ratio or per capita domestic product, as the increased saving flow will be shunted abroad. More saving *per se* will not increase the flow of investment opportunities created at the international rate of interest. Similarly, a reduction in population growth will not raise the domestic capital-labor ratio, or product per capita. Slower population growth lowers the rate at which investment opportunities are created at the international interest rate, and the rate of domestic capital formation will fall off concomitantly. However, more saving and lower population growth will raise national *income* per capita, while leaving domestic capital and *product* unchanged. Only if there is official intervention in the international capital market, blocking the export of capital that cannot find domestic employment at going world rates, can a small, open economy promote capital deepening and higher domestic product.

Finally, in this one-good model, there is no room for "terms of trade" effects or the development of "leading export sectors." The reader is referred to more complex multisector models, where these important events can be analyzed.[7]

AN EXPLICIT SOLUTION

An expression to describe the time path of national wealth can be obtained by solving the differential equation

$$\dot{c} + (g - sr)c = s\bar{w} \tag{10.2}$$

This equation is in the standard form of (7.45), which has already been solved in Chapter Seven.

$$\dot{x} + hx = j \tag{7.45}$$

---

[7] George H. Borts, "A Theory of Long-Run International Capital Movements," *Journal of Political Economy* (August 1964).

Growth in an Open Economy

has the solution

$$x = \frac{j}{h} + \left[x(0) - \frac{j}{h}\right]e^{-ht} \tag{7.48}$$

Thus, the solution of (10.2) is

$$c = \frac{s\bar{w}}{g - sr} + \left[c(0) - \frac{s\bar{w}}{g - sr}\right]e^{-(g-sr)t} \tag{10.5}$$

But (10.2) is based on a constant wage ($\bar{w}$) determined by the constant international interest rate and unchanging technology. If there is technological improvement, the wage will not be constant. We can allow for technological change by assuming that it is Harrod neutral and proceeds at a constant proportional rate, m.

In that case, and with a constant international interest rate, capital deepening must be occurring at the rate m. Referring to Table 6.2,

$$r^* = -\frac{a}{\sigma}k^* + \frac{a}{\sigma}m \tag{6.25}$$

With $r^* = 0$,

$$k^* = m$$

Captial deepening at this rate means that wages are rising at the rate m. This is evident in (6.26).

$$w^* = \frac{1-a}{\sigma}k^* + \left(\frac{a}{\sigma} - \frac{1-\sigma}{\sigma}\right)m \tag{6.26}$$

With

$$k^* = m$$
$$w^* = m$$

Now we can replace the constant wage ($\bar{w}$) in (10.2) with a wage that grows at a constant proportional rate m.

$$\dot{c} + (g - sr)c = sw(0)e^{mt} \tag{10.6}$$

This is a linear, nonhomogeneous equation with a nonconstant coefficient on the right-hand side. This coefficient is in a particularly manageable

An Explicit Solution

form: an exponential function of time to the base e. The general form of (10.6) is

$$\dot{x} + hx = je^{gt} \tag{10.7}$$

Note that the standard-form equation explored in Chapter Seven,

$$\dot{x} + hx = j \tag{7.45}$$

is a special case of (10.7), with $g = 0$.

Since we already know how to solve (7.45), it might be a good idea to try to transform (10.7) in order to eliminate the e^{gt} term. This term "drives" the right-hand side of (10.7) and "forces" ever greater values of x and/or $\dot{x}$ as time goes on. We might suspect, then, that there is a systematic "trend" in the time path of x, and that the growth rate along this growth equilibrium path is g. If this is true, then we can decompose the value of x at any point in time into two components:

1. the trend value of x

$$\bar{x} = \bar{x}(0)e^{gt}$$

2. the displacement, z, from the trend.

Thus

$$x = \bar{x} + z$$

or

$$x = \bar{x}(0)e^{gt} + z \tag{10.8}$$

If we can find a differential equation for z, which we can solve, then we know all we have to about the behavior of x. Differentiating (10.8), we obtain an expression for $\dot{x}$.

$$\dot{x} = g \cdot \bar{x}(0)e^{gt} + \dot{z} \tag{10.9}$$

Substituting (10.8) and (10.9) into (10.7) yields

$$g \cdot \bar{x}(0)e^{gt} + \dot{z} + h[\bar{x}(0)e^{gt} + z] = je^{gt}$$

or

$$\dot{z} + hz = [j - g\bar{x}(0) - h \cdot \bar{x}(0)]e^{gt} \tag{10.10}$$

It would be convenient if the right-hand side of this equation could disappear. Perhaps it will, if an expression for $\bar{x}(0)$ can be found.

$$\bar{x} = \bar{x}(0)e^{gt}$$

$$\dot{\bar{x}} = g \cdot \bar{x}(0)e^{gt}$$

Substituting into (10.7),

$$g \cdot \bar{x}(0)e^{gt} + h \cdot \bar{x}(0)e^{gt} = je^{gt}$$

or

$$\bar{x}(0) = \frac{j}{g+h} \tag{10.11}$$

Returning with this to (10.10), we find that the right-hand side of (10.10) indeed disappears, and we are left with

$$\dot{z} + hz = 0$$

which we know solves to

$$z = z(0)e^{-ht}$$

where

$$z(0) = x(0) - \bar{x}(0)$$

or

$$z(0) = x(0) - \frac{j}{g+h}$$

Now we have an expression for the trend of x

$$\bar{x} = \frac{j}{g+h} e^{gt}$$

and an expression for deviations from that trend.

$$z = \left[x(0) - \frac{j}{g+h} \right] e^{-ht}$$

The time path of x is the sum of the trend and deviations from the trend.

$$x = \bar{x} + z$$

$$x = \frac{j}{g+h} e^{gt} + \left[x(0) - \frac{j}{g+h} \right] e^{-ht}$$

or

$$x = x(0)e^{-ht} + (e^{gt} - e^{-ht}) \frac{j}{g+h} \tag{10.12}$$

Equation (10.12) is the general solution of the differential equation (10.7). As before, the initial value of the variable loses its influence over the variable itself as time goes on. The value of x will be dominated by the exponential terms containing g and h. If g and h are both positive, the value of x is eventually dominated by g. As time goes on, x approaches the exponential trend path, with a proportional rate of growth equal to g.

We can solve the differential equation for the growth of per capita wealth (Equation 10.6) by using (10.12) and letting:

$$x = c$$
$$h = (g - sr)$$
$$j = sw(0)$$
$$m = g$$

Then

$$c = c(0)e^{-(g-sr)t} + \left[e^{mt} - e^{-(g-sr)t}\right]\frac{sw(0)}{(g+m) - sr} \qquad (10.13)$$

is the solution of (10.6).

Recalling that labor efficiency is growing at the rate m, we can convert (10.13) into an expression for the growth of wealth per efficiency worker. If

$$c = \frac{C}{L}$$

and

$$\hat{L} = e^{mt} L$$

then

$$\hat{c} = \frac{C}{L} e^{-mt} = c e^{-mt}$$

and (10.13) becomes

$$\hat{c} = c(0)^{-(g+m-sr)t} + \left[1 - e^{-(g+m-sr)t}\right]\frac{sw(0)}{(g+m) - sr}$$

So long as the growth of efficiency labor $(g + m)$ exceeds the saving ratio multiplied by the international interest rate (sr), wealth per efficiency worker will converge toward an equilibrium value equal to

$$\frac{sw(0)}{(g+m) - sr}$$

FOREIGN AID

It was suggested in the first section of this chapter that foreign aid could be viewed as a capital transfer: the receiving country "pays for" an excess of imports over exports on current account with a "security" that bears no interest and never matures. Foreign aid of this kind is a unilateral transfer, an unrequited loan.[8] In this section, we shall ask two questions: (1) will aid of this nature raise the domestic capital-labor ratio, wages, or per capita domestic product, and (2) will it raise per capita incomes?

To answer the first question, let us assume at first that the domestic economy of the recipient country is initially in equilibrium: that the rate of return is equal on all domestically employed capital, and that the domestic return on capital is equal to its opportunity cost (the return from employing the capital abroad). In Figure 10.4, the opportunity cost of investing in the domestic economy is the international interest rate, $0R_0$. The equilibrium ratio of capital to efficiency labor, corresponding to $0R_0$, is $0\hat{k}_0$. If efficiency labor is growing at the rate $g + m$ (the growth of labor itself, plus the growth of its efficiency), then investment opportunities are being created in the domestic economy (at the international interest rate) at the rate $g + m$. The *absorptive capacity* of the economy is growing at the rate $g + m$. Any

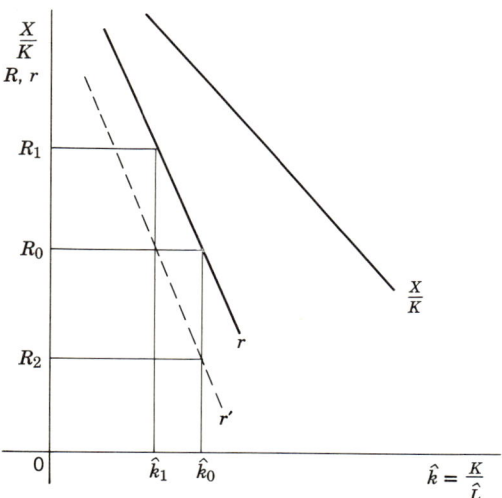

Figure 10.4 The equilibrium ratio of capital to efficiency labor.

[8] In practice, aid can assume a variety of forms: gifts of commodities like military equipment and food, and loans at varying rates of interest, relative to the opportunity cost of capital. A loan at subsidized interest rates can be thought of as a gift in part, and the remainder as an ordinary loan.

attempt to force capital into the domestic economy at a rate in excess of $g + m$ will be thwarted by an expulsion of surplus capital through the international capital market. If the source of surplus capital is foreign aid, which is invested by the recipient government, it will be matched by an export of private capital. Wages and per capita product are unchanged.

It is possible for the social return on capital to exceed the rate that private investors perceive. For example, because of ignorance, institutional barriers, or the inability to capture external benefits, private investors might behave as if the dotted line labeled r' represented the domestic return on capital, while the true social return on investment lies above it on the line labeled r. In that case, private investors will carry capital deepening only up to $0\hat{k}_1$, where the social return $0R_1$ exceeds the apparent private $0R_0$. The government could carry forward with public investment schemes and promote capital deepening up to $0\hat{k}_0$, without driving the social return below the international rate $0R_0$. However, at $0\hat{k}_0$, all private capital has gone elsewhere, for the privately perceived return at $0\hat{k}_0$, equal to $0R_2$, falls short of the corresponding private opportunity cost ($0R_0$).[9]

So long as the borrowing rate exceeds the social return on domestic capital, it pays the government to borrow. Of course, if it can attract aid at a zero interest rate, it is just that much better off.

The situation is very much changed if effective controls can be imposed on capital exports. In that case, aid capital can be forced in without replacing private capital, and "hothouse" development is possible. A continuously increasing flow of aid can keep the domestic return on capital permanently below the international interest rate. The wage rate and per capita domestic product can be made permanently higher through foreign aid programs.

Note, however, that a sustained rise in per capita product will not occur as a consequence of aid alone. If the flow of aid is just sufficient to maintain a constant domestic return on capital, per capita product will still rise at the rate of labor augmentation. We argue as follows: a country receiving aid has two sources of capital, aid and its own saving. Assume that all aid is invested, and that a constant proportion of domestic product (equal to national income) is saved. Then

$$\dot{K} = sX + A$$

In proportional terms, capital formation is

$$K^* = \frac{sX}{K} + \frac{A}{K}$$

---

[9] We still assume homogeneity of capital. Thus, public investments are perfect substitutes for private investments. In another model, where public and private capital are distinguished and are complements, a larger stock of public capital will *raise* the equilibrium stock of private capital.

The share of product imputed to capital is a constant in equilibrium.

$$(1 - a) = \frac{rK}{X}$$

or

$$\frac{X}{K} = \frac{r}{1 - a}$$

where r is the (constant) return on domestic capital. Thus

$$K^* = \frac{sr}{1 - a} + \frac{A}{K}$$

in equilibrium. But capital must be growing as fast as efficiency labor to hold a constant interest rate

$$K^* = g + m$$

Substituting, and solving for the *flow* of aid as a proportion of the capital stock,

$$\frac{A}{K} = g + m - \frac{sr}{1 - a}$$

All the terms on the right-hand side are constants in equilibrium. Thus, aid must grow at the rate $g + m$ to keep A/K constant. With capital and efficiency labor growing at the rate $g + m$,

$$X^* = g + m$$

With labor growing at the rate g,

$$X^* - L^* = m$$

Per capita product (and income) grow at the same rate as labor-augmenting technological change. Recall that this same rate of growth was achieved in the closed economy without the benefit of aid.

Does this mean that the aid is given for no effect? No, for the *level* of per capita income would be lower in the absence of aid.

Figure 10.5 portrays the growth of per capita income and product in an economy with blocked capital markets and all nationally owned capital employed at home. Growth without aid is shown by the dotted line. Per capita income rises through time, due to a positive m. At time $t = 0$, a massive infusion of aid capital raises the domestic capital-labor ratio to a higher

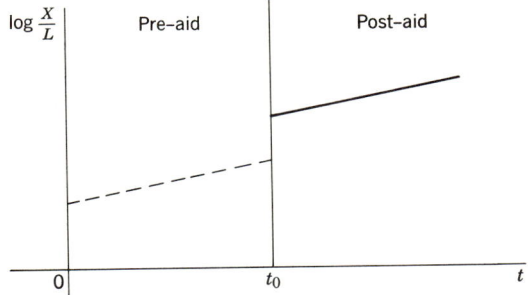

Figure 10.5 The effect of an aid program.

level, corresponding to the higher *level* of per capita income. Thereafter, aid continues growing at the rate $g + m$. For any t subsequent to $t = 0$, per capita income is higher than it would have been in the absence of aid.

If capital exports are not blocked, and the recipient country is initially in equilibrium, it is now clear that aid, if invested, will be diverted abroad. Thus, earned wage income will not be augmented by aid. The incomes of both workers and capitalists will be augmented by aid if it is (1) paid to them as a direct subsidy or as a tax remission; or (2) invested either at home or abroad by the government on their behalf.

EXERCISES

1. Draw a figure similar to 10.3, but let the international interest rate (R) exceed the natural growth rate (g) of the economy. Draw the C^* line so that the country is a creditor. How are the saving ratio(s) and capital's share of income $(1 - a)$ related, if the current-account balance of trade in goods and noncapital services (v) is positive?

2. Using the model in this chapter, how would you account for these "stages" in the balance of indebtedness ($d = k - c$) and the current-account balance of payments (B_C/L)?

    (a) Young debtor: current account negative and falling with the debt rising.
    (b) Adult debtor: current account negative at first but rising and becoming positive.
    (c) Mature debtor: current account positive and constant. The debt position is falling and becoming zero.
    (d) Young creditor: current account positive and constant. The debt position starts at zero and is falling.
    (e) Adult creditor: current account falling and becoming negative. The debt position continues to fall for a while but then rises.
    (f) Mature creditor: the current account stabilizes at a negative value, as does the debt position.

REFERENCES AND SUGGESTIONS FOR FURTHER READING

1. Borts, G. H., "A Theory of Long-Run International Capital Movements." *Journal of Political Economy*, August 1964.
2. Domar, E. D., "Foreign Investment and the Balance of Payments." *American Economic Review*, December 1950.
3. Hansen, J. A. and P. A. Neher, "The Neoclassical Theorem Once Again: Closed and Open Economies." *American Economic Review*, September 1967.
4. Kindleberger, C. P., *International Economics*, Third Edition. Homewood: Irwin, 1963, pp. 458–465.
5. Little, I. M. D. and J. M. Clifford, *International Aid*. London: Allen and Unwin, 1965, pp. 205–212.

Chapter Eleven

A SIMPLE TWO-SECTOR MODEL OF GROWTH IN AN ADVANCED ECONOMY

The Model
Production Conditions
Resource Constraints
The Factor Markets
National Income Accounting
The Demand for Final Products
A Graphical Solution of the Static Model
The Dynamic Problem
Comparative Statics
The Capital-Labor Ratio and Factor Prices
The Interest Rate and Factor Prices
Relative Shares and Factor Prices
On the Uniqueness and Stability of Growth Equilibrium
Exercises
References and Suggestions for Further Reading

THE MODEL

Production Conditions

Thus far, the discussion of economic growth in an advanced economy has been much simplified by the assumption that there is only one production sector, which produces an all-purpose good that serves equally well as a consumption good and as a capital good in its own production. This simplification is foregone in this chapter, and we move a step closer to reality by distinguishing two different economic goods:

1. A consumption good, produced with labor and capital.
2. A capital good, also produced with labor and capital. This capital good is used in production of the consumption good, and in the production of itself.

This model is significantly more complicated than those encountered before. We shall need, in addition to separate specification of production relations in the two sectors, rules for allocating the available resources between the sectors, and demand conditions for the output of the two sectors. These relations will constitute a two-sector model of economic growth.[1]

The production relations show how output depends on capital and labor inputs. As before, there are constant returns to scale and, to keep matters simple, we shall assume that capital does not depreciate so that gross output equals net output. In addition, we assume that there is no technological change, so that the functions do not shift as time goes on.

The output of consumption goods (X) depends on the capital (K_X) and labor (L_X) allocated to that sector

$$X = F(K_X, L_X)$$

where, as usual, marginal products are positive, but there are diminishing marginal returns to proportions.

To put production conditions in this sector another way, we can write

$$X = L_X \cdot f(k_X), \qquad k_X \equiv \frac{K_X}{L_X} \qquad (11.1)$$

by virtue of the constant returns to scale assumption and

$$f'(k_X) > 0, \qquad f''(k_X) < 0$$

---

[1] The seminal articles that presented the model are H. Uzawa, "On a Two-Sector Model of Economic Growth, I; II," *Review of Economic Studies* (October 1961; June 1963).

Similarly, the output of the capital-goods sector ($\dot{K} = dK/dt$) depends on the resources allocated to that sector, and there are positive but declining marginal products.

$$\dot{K} = H(K_K, L_K)$$

Or

$$\dot{K} = L_K \cdot h(k_K), \qquad k_K \equiv \frac{K_K}{L_K} \qquad (11.2)$$

and

$$h'(k_K) > 0, \qquad h''(k_K) < 0$$

Resource Constraints

At any point in time, there is a given amount of labor and capital available to be allocated between the two production sectors. We assume that both labor and capital are homogeneous and free to move between industries seeking the highest reward. The supply curve of either factor to one industry thus reflects the factor's opportunity cost in the other industry. But for the economy as a whole, both capital (K) and labor (L) are in perfectly inelastic supply.

$$L_X + L_K = L \qquad (11.3)$$
$$K_X + K_K = K \qquad (11.4)$$

The Factor Markets

Labor-market equilibrium requires that labor earn the same money wage irrespective of its sector of employment. Moreover, competition prevails everywhere, so that the money wage equals the value of labor's marginal product in each sector.

$$w_X = MPP_{LX} \cdot P_X$$
$$w_K = MPP_{LK} \cdot P_K$$
$$w_X = w_K = w$$

Or, if we define

$$a \equiv \frac{MPP_{LX} \cdot L_X}{X}$$

and

$$b \equiv \frac{MPP_{LK} \cdot L_K}{\dot{K}}$$

it follows that

$$w = a \cdot \frac{XP_X}{L_X} \qquad (11.5)$$

and

$$w = b \cdot \frac{\dot{K}P_K}{L_K} \qquad (11.6)$$

describe labor-market equilibrium conditions.

Capital-market equilibrium requires that the rate of return on capital be the same everywhere, and that the rental rate on capital equal the value of capital's marginal product in both sectors.

$$R_X = MPP_{KX} \cdot P_X$$
$$R_K = MPP_{KK} \cdot P_K$$

The rental rate (R) is the percent rate of return on capital (the interest rate) multiplied by the supply price of the capital good. For each sector,

$$R = rP_K$$

If capital goods cost $100 each to produce and if the interest rate is five percent, then the rental rate is $5.

We can thus express the rate of return on capital (the interest rate) in the two sectors as

$$r_X = \frac{MPP_{KX} \cdot P_X}{P_K}$$

and

$$r_K = \frac{MPP_{KK} \cdot P_K}{P_K} = MPP_{KK}$$

Moreover,

$$r_X = r_K = r$$

Or, recalling the constant returns to scale assumption, we can define

$$1 - a \equiv \frac{MPP_{KX} \cdot K_X}{X}$$

and

$$1 - b \equiv \frac{MPP_{KK} \cdot K_K}{\dot{K}}$$

so that

$$r = (1 - a)\frac{XP_X}{K_X P_K} \qquad (11.7)$$

and

$$r = (1 - b)\frac{\dot{K} P_K}{K_K P_K} = (1 - b)\frac{\dot{K}}{K_K} \qquad ^2 \qquad (11.8)$$

are alternate expressions for capital market equilibrium.

National Income Accounting

Taken together, the factor-market equilibrium conditions reveal the national accounting framework for the simple two-sector model economy. Rewriting (11.5), (11.6), (11.7), and (11.8),

$$wL_X = aXP_X$$
$$wL_Y = b\dot{K}P_K$$
$$rK_X P_K = (1 - a)XP_X$$
$$rK_K P_K = (1 - b)\dot{K}P_K$$

we can see that gross (equals net) national product (Y) is the sum of factor rewards. For the consumption-goods sector, value added is equal to income originating in that sector

$$XP_X = wL_X + rK_X P_K$$

and for the investment-goods sector, value added is equal to income originating there.

$$\dot{K}P_K = wL_K + rK_K P_K$$

These add up to income and total value added.

$$Y = w(L_X + L_K) + rP_K(K_X + K_K) = XP_X + \dot{K}P_K$$

Or, in view of the full-employment assumptions, (11.3) and (11.4),

$$Y = wL + rKP_K = XP_X + \dot{K}P_K$$

[2] Note that r is simply the "own rate" of return on capital in producing capital.

The Demand for Final Products

We retain the familiar assumption that a constant proportion of income is saved.

$$S = sY = s(XP_X + \dot{K}P_K)$$

The value of capital-goods output is equal to the value of saving.

$$\dot{K}P_K = sY$$

It follows that

$$XP_X = (1 - s)Y$$

Thus

$$\dot{K}P_K = s(XP_X + \dot{K}P_K)$$

or

$$\dot{K}P = \frac{s}{1-s} XP_X \tag{11.9}$$

A constant saving ratio means that the value of capital formation is proportional to the value of consumption.

A Graphical Solution of the Static Model

The two-sector model is a complete static model as it now stands, and it is amenable to a graphical solution. There are nine equations and nine unknowns: the outputs (X and $\dot{K}$), the factor inputs (K_X, L_X, K_K, and L_K), the wage of labor (w), the return on capital (r), and relative prices (P_K/P_X).[3]

The first eight equations can be used to derive a production-possibilities curve between consumption goods and capital goods. Sometimes called a "guns and butter curve,"[4] the production-possibilities curve shows the maximum amount of one good that can be produced (with available resources), given alternate rates of output of the other good. The ninth equation, the demand equation, then determines the production *point* on the production-possibilities *curve*, and the model is solved.

We begin with the familiar Stolper-Samuelson *production-box diagram*.[5] In Figure 11.1, the resource endowment of the economy at a point in time

---

[3] With no money in the system, absolute prices cannot be determined.

[4] P. A. Samuelson, *Economics*, Sixth Edition (New York: McGraw-Hill, 1964), p. 19.

[5] W. F. Stolper and P. A. Samuelson, "Protection and Real Wages," *Review of Economic Studies* (November 1941). Reprinted in H. S. Ellis, Ed., *Readings in the Theory of International Trade* (Homewood, Illinois: Irwin, 1950). Excellent expositions of the geometry of the production box and derivation of the production possibilities curve are by K. M. Savosnick, "The Box Diagram and the Production Possibilities Curve," *Ekonomisk Tidskrift* (September 1958), and T. M. Rybczynski, "Factor Endowment and Relative Commodity Prices," *Economica* (November 1955). Box diagrams like this are associated with the names of A. L. Bowley and F. Y. Edgeworth.

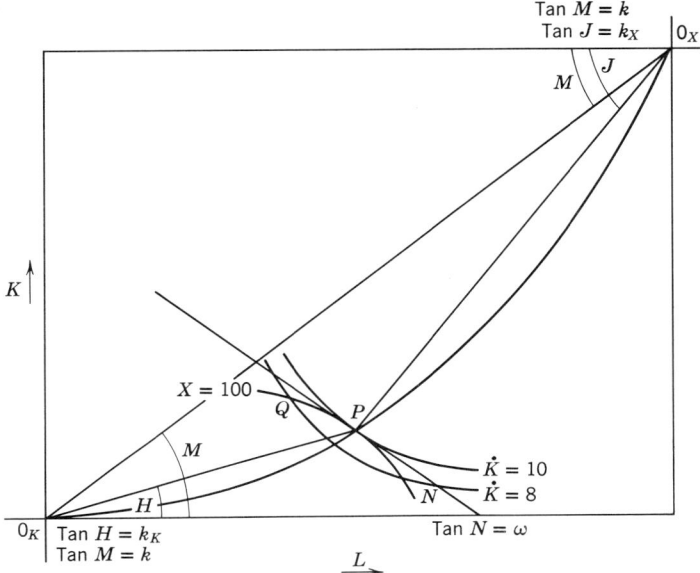

Figure 11.1 A production box diagram for the two-sector economy.

fixes the dimensions of the box; the capital stock determines the vertical dimension, and the supply of labor fixes the horizontal dimension. Production isoquants originate for the capital goods industry at the lower left corner of the box, and those for the consumption goods industry at the upper right corner. These isoquants portray the production relations (11.1) and (11.2).

A point within the box, such as P or Q, determines the allocation of resources between the two sectors according to (11.3) or (11.4). With resources allocated, the production relations determine relative outputs in the two sectors. Graphically, we merely observe the outputs corresponding to the respective isoquants that pass through the point. As examples: at point Q, $\dot{K} = 8$ and $X = 100$; at point P, $\dot{K} = 10$ and $X = 100$.

Clearly, point P corresponds to a "better" allocation of resources than point Q, because more $\dot{K}$ can be had at P than at Q, without any sacrifice of X. Only at points like P, where the isoquants are tangent to one another, is it impossible to get more of one good without giving up some of the other good. The locus of points like P is called a *contract curve*, which is illustrated in Figure 11.1 by the curve $0_K P 0_X$.

We can show that points along the contract curve satisfy the conditions for competitive factor-market equilibrium, Equations 11.5, 11.6, 11.7, and 11.8. We reason as follows. The *slope* of an isoquant in either sector (ω in

Figure 11.1) is the *marginal rate of technical substitution* between the inputs, defined as

$$MRS_{KL} \equiv \omega \equiv \frac{MPP_L}{MPP_K}$$

The $MRS_{KL} \equiv \omega$ in the two sectors is equal where the isoquants are tangent to one another (their slopes are equal).

Looking back to the factor market equilibrium conditions, we see that when wages are equal between the sectors,

$$\frac{aXP_X}{L_X} = \frac{b\dot{K}P_K}{L_X} \qquad (11.5)$$
$$\qquad\qquad\qquad\qquad (11.6)$$

Recalling that

$$a \equiv \frac{MPP_{LX} \cdot L_X}{X}$$

and

$$b \equiv \frac{MPP_{LK} \cdot L_K}{\dot{K}}$$

we have

$$MPP_{LX} \cdot P_X = MPP_{LK} \cdot P_K$$

With the rate of return on capital equal between sectors,

$$(1-a)\frac{XP_X}{K_X P_K} = (1-b)\frac{\dot{K}P_K}{K_K P_K} \qquad (11.7)$$
$$\qquad\qquad\qquad\qquad\qquad (11.8)$$

Recalling that

$$1 - a \equiv \frac{MPP_{KX} \cdot K_X}{X}$$

and

$$1 - b \equiv \frac{MPP_{KK} \cdot K_K}{\dot{K}}$$

we have

$$MPP_{KX} \cdot \frac{P_X}{P_K} = MPP_{KK} \cdot \frac{P_K}{P_K}$$

or

$$MPP_{KX} \cdot P_X = MPP_{KK} \cdot P_K$$

Dividing the first of these new expressions by the second,

$$\omega \equiv \frac{MPP_{LX}}{MPP_{KX}} \equiv \frac{MPP_{LK}}{MPP_{KK}}$$

Or we can write

$$\omega \equiv \frac{w}{rP_K} = \frac{MPP_{LX} \cdot P_X}{MPP_{KX} \cdot P_X} = \frac{MPP_{LK} \cdot P_K}{MPP_{KK} \cdot P_K}$$

so ω can be labeled the *wage-rentals* ratio.

Factor-market equilibrium requires a *common* $\omega = MRS_{KL}$. It requires that the isoquants be tangent to one another, and it prevails only along the contract curve.

As the point P moves along the contract curve to the northeast, resources are released by the X industry and absorbed by the $\dot{K}$ industry; the output of $\dot{K}$ expands and the output of X contracts. In the diagram, the capital-labor ratio in $\dot{K}(k_K)$ is always less than the capital-labor ratio in $X(k_X)$ along the contract curve. The capital-goods industry is relatively labor-intensive.

$$\frac{K_K}{L_K} < \frac{K_X}{L_X}$$

or

$$k_K < k_X \quad ^6$$

As a consequence, as $\dot{K}$ expands and X contracts, relatively more capital and less labor are released by X than will be absorbed by $\dot{K}$ at the existing ratio of labor wages to capital rentals. Wages will rise relative to rentals (ω will rise).

On the other hand, if the capital-goods industry were relatively capital-intensive, an expansion of $\dot{K}$ would require the absorption of more capital relative to labor than is released by X. Rentals will rise relative to wages (ω will fall).

Moreover, if the production of capital goods is relatively capital-intensive, a relatively *higher* rate of investment ($\dot{K}$ greater relative to X) corresponds to *higher* rate of return on capital. Recall that

$$r = MPP_{KK}$$

[6] With constant returns to scale technology, the contract curve cannot cross the diagonal connecting 0_K and 0_X. Suppose a point like P did lie on the diagonal, so that $k_X = k_K$ at the point. Then *every* point like P must also lie on the diagonal; the entire contract curve must be coincident with the diagonal. Thus, if *one* point like P is off the diagonal, on one side, the entire curve must lie to one side of the diagonal.

in the capital-goods industry. A rise in $\dot{K}$ lowers k_K if k_K exceeds k_X. A lower k_K corresponds to a higher MPP_{KK}.

A higher level of investment is associated with more labor working with a unit of capital used to produce capital. The "own rate" of return on capital must rise in the capital-goods sector and, given capital-market equilibrium, the rate of return must rise in the rest of the economy as well.

On the other hand, if the capital-goods industry is relatively labor-intensive, as illustrated in Figure 11.1, a higher level of investment is associated with a higher capital-labor ratio in the capital-goods industry (a higher k_K) and a lower rate of return on capital.[7]

These phenomena are illustrated in the left-hand panel of Figure 11.2. An increase in investment (on the vertical axis) will raise or lower the rate of return on capital (on the horizontal axis) according to whether the capital goods industry is more or less capital-intensive than the consumption-goods industry.

We will see later on that these relative capital-intensity conditions are important in shaping the growth properties of the two-sector model.

The right-hand panel of Figure 11.2 illustrates a production possibilities curve. It is derived from Figure 11.1 by measuring to points like P (on the contract curve) the distances along the rays $0_K P$ and $0_X P$ to find the corresponding outputs of $\dot{K}$ and X. For example, the point P' on the production-possibilities curve corresponds to the point P on the contract curve, where capital goods output equals ten units and one hundred units of consumption goods are being produced.

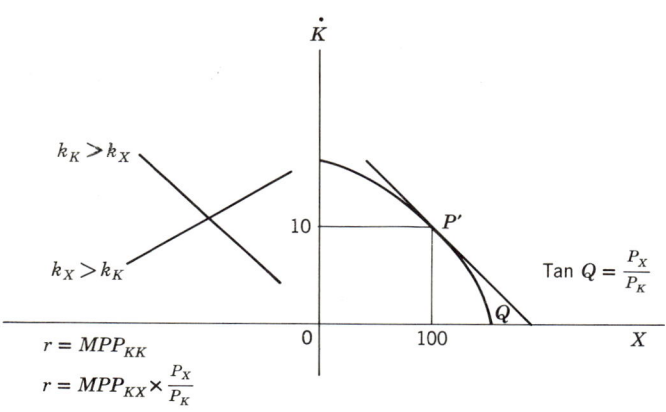

Figure 11.2 A production-possibilities curve and the rate of return on capital as a function of investment.

[7] There is some empirical evidence suggesting that the capital-goods industry is more labor-intensive than the consumption-goods industry. See R. A. Gordon, "Differential Changes in the Prices of Consumers' and Capital Goods," *American Economic Review* (December 1961).

The slope of the production-possibilities curve is (minus) the price of X relative to the price of $\dot{K}$. That is,

$$-\frac{d\dot{K}}{dX} = \frac{P_X}{P_{\dot{K}}} \equiv p$$

The price of one good is the opportunity cost incurred by not producing the other good. If the output of $\dot{K}$ expands relative to that of X, then the point P' moves counterclockwise along the production possibilities curve; the slope of the curve declines; progressively more X has to be given up to get another unit of $\dot{K}$; and the price of $\dot{K}$ rises relative to the price of X.

We have now used (11.1) through (11.8) to move from resource constraints, via production functions and competitive equilibrium conditions in factor markets, to a set of production possibilities and relative prices. These latter data are displayed as a "relative supply" curve, in Figure 11.3. The relative price of consumption goods is plotted on the vertical axis and their relative output on the horizontal axis. The relative quantity supplied of consumption goods increases as their relative price rises.

The model is closed by adding the demand conditions, Equation 11.9.

$$\frac{P_X}{P_{\dot{K}}} = \frac{1-s}{s} \cdot \frac{\dot{K}}{X}$$

or

$$\frac{P_X}{P_{\dot{K}}} = \frac{1-s}{s} \cdot \frac{1}{(X/\dot{K})}$$

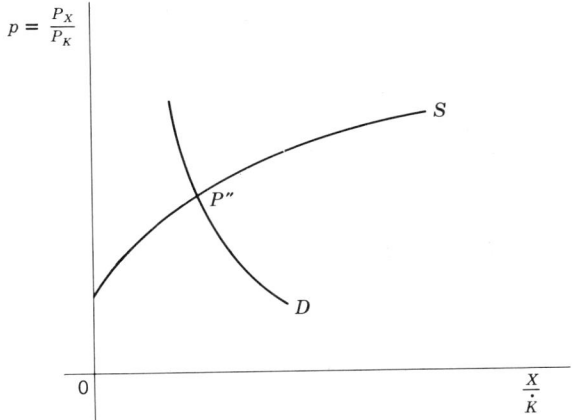

Figure 11.3   Supply and demand curves for the two-sector model.

The "relative-demand" curve is a rectangular hyperbola. The constant saving ratio means that relative prices multiplied by relative outputs is a constant.

Equilibrium in the product market is established where the "relative supply" and "relative demand" curves intersect, at a point like P'', where relative outputs and prices are determined.

Point P'' in Figure 11.3 corresponds to point P' in Figure 11.2, which, in turn, corresponds to point P in Figure 11.1. The reader can trace through the consequences of a disturbance, say a fall in the saving ratio, from Figure 11.3 back through the system to Figure 11.1 and ask himself what happens to relative outputs ($X/\dot{K}$), relative prices (p), resource allocation (the k's), relative factor prices (the wage-rental ratio $= \omega$), and the return on capital (r).

The Dynamic Problem

So far, in the static model, we have allowed for investment, but not for capital accumulation; we have specified that labor be used in production, but we have not allowed for its growth. As before, we will assume that labor grows at a constant proportional rate, g

$$L = L(0)e^{gt} \qquad (11.10)$$

so that

$$\frac{\dot{L}}{L} = L^* = g$$

As before, we may try to obtain a differential equation in the capital-labor ratio. With the net increase in the value of capital equal to a proportion, s, of net national income,

$$\dot{K}P_K = sY$$

it follows that the proportional increase in capital is

$$\frac{\dot{K}}{K} = s\frac{Y}{KP_K}$$

so that

$$\frac{\dot{K}}{K} - \frac{\dot{L}}{L} = K^* - L^* = s\frac{Y}{KP_K} - g$$

or

$$\frac{\dot{k}}{k} = s\frac{Y}{KP_K} - g \qquad (10.11)$$

where k is the economy's capital-labor ratio at a point in time. This is the fundamental differential equation for the two-sector economy.

Recall that for the single-sector economy (Chapter Three), a rise in the capital-labor ratio was associated with a fall in the ratio of product to capital

$$\frac{X}{K} = \frac{f(k)}{k} \tag{5.3}$$

$$X^* - K^* = -ak^* \tag{5.31}$$

Can we show, for the two-sector economy, that a rise in the overall capital-labor ratio is associated with a fall in the ratio of the *value* of national income to the *value* of the capital stock when the saving ratio is constant? That is, can we show that

$$\frac{Y}{KP_K} = J(k)$$

and

$$J'(k) < 0$$

when s is constant?

If so, then a *higher* value of k is associated with a *lower* value of its growth rate in (10.11), and there is some assurance that k will approach an equilibrium value from any starting position.

The next step is to try to find out if Y/KP_K falls when k rises.

COMPARATIVE STATICS

The Capital-Labor Ratio and Factor Prices

There are a number of important comparative statics propositions that can be derived for the two-sector economy.[8] We shall concentrate in this section on those propositions most directly related to the relation between capital deepening and changes in the economy-wide capital-output ratio.

A fundamental relation in the two sector model is between the *economy-wide* ratio of wages to capital rentals and the *aggregate* capital-labor ratio. For the single-sector model, change in the wage-rental ratio was linked to capital deepening by the elasticity of substitution,

$$\sigma = \frac{dk/k}{dw/w - dr/r} \tag{5.15}$$

---

[8] For a more detailed exploration of comparative statics in the two-sector model, see the appendix of Karl Shell's "A Model of Inventive Activity and Capital Accumulation," in Karl Shell (Ed.), *Essays on the Theory of Optimal Economic Growth* (Cambridge, The M.I.T. Press, 1967), pp. 79–84.

Or, since $\omega = w/r$, we can write

$$\frac{dk}{k} = \sigma \frac{d\omega}{\omega}$$

because

$$\frac{d\omega}{\omega} = \frac{dw}{w} - \frac{dr}{r}$$

in the single-sector model. That the elasticity of substitution is positive was a consequence of assumed diminishing returns to factor proportions in the single-production sector.

In the two-sector model, the relationship is more complex. It will be influenced by the elasticities of substitution in the two-production sectors, but other facts will bear as well. Moreover, we must specify demand conditions for final output to maintain a determined model. We will assume throughout that a constant proportion of income is invested. Under these conditions, we wish to find σ for the economy as whole where

$$\sigma = \frac{dk/k}{d\omega/\omega}, \quad k = \frac{K}{L}, \quad \omega = \frac{MPP_L}{MPP_K} = \frac{w}{rP_K}$$

We begin with our resource constraints to derive an expression for the economywide capital-labor ratio.

$$K = K_X + K_K \tag{11.4}$$

$$k = \frac{K}{L} = \frac{K_X}{L} + \frac{K_K}{L}$$

$$k = \frac{L_X}{L} \cdot \frac{K_X}{L_X} + \frac{L_K}{L} \cdot \frac{K_K}{L_K}$$

$$k = \frac{L_X}{L} \cdot k_X + \frac{L_K}{L} \cdot k_K$$

We wish to find out how k changes when ω changes, so let us differentiate this expression for k, hoping to be able to substitute into it expressions in terms of changes in ω.

$$dk = \frac{L_X}{L} \cdot dk_X + k_X \cdot d\frac{L_X}{L} + \frac{L_K}{L} \cdot dk_K + k_K \cdot d\frac{L_K}{L}$$

In terms of proportional changes,

$$\frac{dk}{k} = \frac{L_X}{L} \cdot \frac{L}{K} \cdot \frac{K_X}{L_X} \cdot \frac{dk_X}{k_X} + \text{etc.}$$

Simplifying,

$$\frac{dk}{k} = \frac{K_X}{K}\left[\frac{dk_X}{k_X} + d\left(\frac{L_X}{L}\right) \cdot \frac{L}{L_X}\right] + \frac{K_K}{K}\left[\frac{dk_K}{k_K} + d\left(\frac{L_K}{L}\right) \cdot \frac{L}{L_K}\right]$$

But for the individual sectors, we have, from the definition of the elasticity of substitution within sectors, that

$$\frac{dk_X}{k_X} = \sigma_X \frac{d\omega}{\omega}$$

and

$$\frac{dk_K}{k_K} = \sigma_K \frac{d\omega}{\omega}$$

Substituting,

$$\frac{dk}{k} = \frac{K_X}{K}\left[\sigma_X \cdot \frac{d\omega}{\omega} + d\left(\frac{L_X}{L}\right) \cdot \frac{L}{L_X}\right] \quad (11.12)$$
$$+ \frac{K_K}{K}\left[\sigma_K \cdot \frac{d\omega}{\omega} + d\left(\frac{L_K}{L}\right) \cdot \frac{L}{L_K}\right]$$

This represents progress, but how is the proportion of labor employed in the two sectors related to ω? We suspect that the employment split is related to demand conditions

$$\frac{\dot{K}P_K}{XP_X} = \frac{s}{1-s} \quad (11.9)$$

and to equilibrium conditions in the labor market. Equating the wage in (11.5) and (11.6) yields

$$\frac{\dot{K}P_K}{XP_X} = \frac{a}{b} \cdot \frac{L_K}{L_X}$$

Combining these expressions,

$$\frac{L_K}{L_X} = \frac{b}{a} \cdot \frac{s}{1-s}$$

With the saving ratio constant,

$$d\frac{L_K}{L_X} \cdot \frac{L_X}{L_K} = \frac{db}{b} - \frac{da}{a}$$

But changes in labor's relative share in each sector depend on changes in the capital-labor ratio in the respective sector. From Table 5.1, we have, for example,

$$\frac{da}{a} = \frac{1-\sigma_X}{\sigma_X}(1-a)\frac{dk_X}{k_X}$$

Recalling the definition of σ for a single sector, we can write

$$\frac{da}{a} = (1-\sigma_X)(1-a)\frac{d\omega}{\omega}$$

and, by similar reasoning,

$$\frac{db}{b} = (1-\sigma_K)(1-b)\frac{d\omega}{\omega}$$

Now we have

$$d\left(\frac{L_K}{L_X}\right)\frac{L_X}{L_K} = [(1-\sigma_K)(1-b) - (1-\sigma_X)(1-a)]\frac{d\omega}{\omega} \quad (11.13)$$

But (11.12) requires that we have expressions for changes in L_X/L and L_K/L. However,

$$d\left(\frac{L_X}{L}\right) \cdot \frac{L}{L_X} = \frac{dL_X}{L_X} - \frac{dL}{L}$$

$$= \frac{dL_X}{L_X} - \frac{L_X}{L} \cdot \frac{dL_X}{L_X} - \frac{L_K}{L} \cdot \frac{dL_K}{L_K}$$

$$= \frac{L_K}{L} \cdot \frac{dL_X}{L_X} - \frac{L_K}{L} \cdot \frac{dL_K}{L_K}$$

$$d\left(\frac{L_X}{L}\right) \cdot \frac{L}{L_X} = -\frac{L_K}{L} \cdot d\left(\frac{L_K}{L_X}\right) \cdot \frac{L_X}{L_K}$$

In the same way, it can be shown that

$$d\left(\frac{L_K}{L}\right) \cdot \frac{L}{L_K} = \frac{L_X}{L} \cdot d\left(\frac{L_K}{L_X}\right) \cdot \frac{L_X}{L_K}$$

Thus

$$d\left(\frac{L_X}{L}\right) \cdot \frac{L}{L_X} = -\frac{L_K}{L}[(1 - \sigma_K)(1 - b)$$
$$- (1 - \sigma_X)(1 - a)]\frac{d\omega}{\omega}$$

and

$$d\left(\frac{L_K}{L}\right) \cdot \frac{L}{L_K} = -\frac{L_X}{L}[(1 - \sigma_K)(1 - b)$$
$$- (1 - \sigma_X)(1 - a)]\frac{d\omega}{\omega}$$

We can substitute these expressions back into (11.12) to obtain an expression for the change in k with respect to a change in ω. After simplifying,

$$\frac{dk}{k} = \left\{\frac{K_X}{K}\sigma_X + \frac{K_K}{K}\sigma_K + \left(\frac{K_X}{K} \cdot \frac{L_X}{L} - \frac{K_K}{K} \cdot \frac{L_K}{L}\right)\right.$$
$$\left.[(1 - \sigma_K)(1 - b) - (1 - \sigma_X)(1 - a)]\right\}\frac{d\omega}{\omega} \quad (11.14)$$

It is still not clear what algebraic sign we should assign to the expression in braces. But clearly, this expression { } is the elasticity of substitution (σ) which we seek for the two sector economy. We should press on and try to find values for K_X/K, K_K/K, L_X/L, and L_K/L, since these ratios cannot be arbitrary in view of the factor-market equilibrium conditions. We have just noticed that labor-market equilibrium implies

$$\frac{L_K}{L_X} = \frac{b}{a} \cdot \frac{s}{1-s}$$

In the same way, one can show that capital-market equilibrium implies

$$\frac{K_K}{K_X} = \frac{1-b}{1-a} \cdot \frac{s}{1-s}$$

Then, given the resource constraints ($K = K_X + K_K$ and $L = L_X + L_K$),

$$\frac{K_K}{K} = \frac{(1-b)s}{(1-a)(1-s) + (1-b)s}$$

$$\frac{K_X}{K} = \frac{(1-a)(1-s)}{(1-a)(1-s) + (1-b)s}$$

$$\frac{L_K}{L} = \frac{bs}{a(1-s) + bs}$$

$$\frac{L_X}{L} = \frac{a(1-s)}{a(1-s) + bs}$$

Substituting these expressions back into (11.14) and simplifying we have, finally,

$$\frac{dk}{k} = \sigma \cdot \frac{d\omega}{\omega} \qquad (11.15)$$

where

$$\sigma = \frac{a(1-a)(1-s)\sigma_X + b(1-b)s\sigma_K + s(1-s)(a-b)^2}{[(1-a)(1-s) + (1-b)s] \cdot [a(1-s) + bs]}$$

The elasticity of substitution in the two-sector economy is clearly positive. Capital deepening is associated with a rise in the ratio of labor wages to capital rentals.

The two-sector economy also displays diminishing marginal returns to proportions.

The Interest Rate and Factor Prices

Recall from the graphic solution of the static model that the rate of return on capital, or the interest rate, is simply the "own rate" of return on capital employed in the capital-goods sector. How is the interest rate related to the ratio of labor wages to capital rentals (ω)?

From Table 5.1, we know that

$$\frac{dr}{r} = -\frac{b}{\sigma_K} \cdot \frac{dk_K}{k_K}$$

But

$$\frac{dk_K}{k_K} = \sigma_K \cdot \frac{d\omega}{\omega}$$

Consequently,

$$\frac{dr}{r} = -b\frac{d\omega}{\omega} \tag{11.16}$$

The elasticity of the interest rate (r) with respect to the wage-rentals ratio (ω) is the share of output imputed to labor in the capital-goods sector.[9]

Relative Shares and Factor Prices

We saw in the single-sector economy that the share of income imputed to labor, relative to that imputed to capital, would rise with capital deepening if the elasticity of substitution was less than one. Or, since capital deepening raises wages relative to capital rents, we could say that higher wages (relative to rents) were associated with a higher labor share (relative to capital share) if the elasticity of substitution were less than one.

Here we are looking for the corresponding relationship in the two-sector economy. Wage payments are equal to

$$wL = aXP_X + b\dot{K}P_K$$

Moreover, since

$$XP_X = (1-s)Y$$

and

$$\dot{K}P_K = sY$$

we can write

$$wL = a(1-s)Y + bsY$$

or

$$c \equiv \frac{wL}{Y} = a(1-s) + bs$$

where c is the share of national income imputed to labor.

---

[9] Equation 11.15 tells us that *economy-wide* capital deepening raises the wage-rentals ratio. Now we know that the interest rate falls if the wage-rentals ratio rises. Since a higher wage-rentals ratio is associated with capital deepening in *each sector*, we can infer that economy-wide capital deepening lowers the interest rate and induces capital deepening in *each sector*. This model economy will not "switch" from more to less capital-intensive techniques as the interest rate falls. The phenomenon of "reswitching" cannot occur here, but it can in other models. The "reswitching" controversy is reviewed by G. C. Harcourt, "Some Cambridge Controversies," *Journal of Economic Literature* (June 1969), pp. 386–395.

The variation of c can be written as

$$dc = (1-s)da + s\,db$$

Or, in terms of proportional variation,

$$\frac{dc}{c} = \frac{1}{c}\left[(1-s)a\frac{da}{a} + sb\frac{db}{b}\right]$$

This tells us how labor's overall share (c) varies with respect to its individual industry shares (a and b). Table 5.1 tells us how the individual industry shares vary with respect to the k in each industry.

$$\frac{da}{a} = \frac{1-\sigma_X}{\sigma_X}(1-a)\frac{dk_X}{k_X}$$

and

$$\frac{db}{b} = \frac{1-\sigma_K}{\sigma_K}(1-b)\frac{dk_K}{k_K}$$

Moreover, the k in *each* industry is linked to the *common* ω by

$$\frac{dk_X}{k_X} = \sigma_X \frac{d\omega}{\omega}$$

and

$$\frac{dk_K}{k_K} = \sigma_K \frac{d\omega}{\omega}$$

so that by substitution we obtain

$$\frac{dc}{c} = \frac{1-c}{c}\gamma\frac{d\omega}{\omega} \qquad (11.7)$$

where

$$\gamma = \frac{1}{1-c}\left[a(1-a)(1-s)(1-\sigma_X) + b(1-b)(1-\sigma_K)\right]$$

Labor's overall share will rise ($dc/c > 0$) if there is capital deepening ($dk/k > 0$), raising the wage-rentals ratio ($d\omega/\omega > 0$), *if* the elasticity of substitution in *both* sectors is less than one ($\sigma_X < 1; \sigma_K < 1$), and conversely. If there is Cobb-Douglas technology in both sectors ($\sigma_X = \sigma_K = 1$), capital deepening raises ω but does not affect c. However, if the elasticity of substitution is greater than one in one sector, and less than one in the other, the direction of the effect on c of capital deepening may depend on the values of s, a, and b.

Naturally, if labor's overall share (c) moves in one direction, capital's overall share moves in the other direction. The reader can show that

$$\frac{d(1-c)}{1-c} = -\gamma \frac{d\omega}{\omega} \tag{11.18}$$

where

$$\gamma = \frac{1}{1-c}[a(1-a)(1-s)(1-\sigma_X) + b(1-b)(1-\sigma_X)]$$

and interpret the result in the same manner.

ON THE UNIQUENESS AND STABILITY OF GROWTH EQUILIBRIUM

The comparative-statics results just obtained can now be used to ask if the fundamental differential equation

$$\frac{\dot{k}}{k} = s\frac{Y}{KP_K} - g \tag{10.11}$$

$$= s \cdot J(k) - g$$

implies a unique and stable equilibrium value for k. Recalling our discussion in Chapter Eight, a necessary and sufficient condition for uniqueness and stability is that (10.11) cross the horizontal axis only once and be falling from left to right at that point of intersection. A unique and stable equilibrium is illustrated in Figure 11.4, where the equilibrium k is denoted by $\bar{k}$.

In what follows, we *assume* that there is an intersection with the horizontal axis at some $k > 0$ and search for conditions such that $\dot{k}/k$ is a declining function of k everywhere. These will be *sufficient* conditions for $\bar{k}$ to be unique.[10]

---

[10] The function may take the dotted excursion illustrated in Figure 11.4. In that case, $\dot{k}/k$ is not *everywhere* a declining function of k but, as illustrated, $\bar{k}$ is still unique. Hence, it is not necessary that $\dot{k}/k$ be *everywhere* a declining function of k for $\bar{k}$ to be unique. However, if the dotted excursion dipped somewhat lower, $\bar{k}$ would not be unique because there would be more than one k where $\dot{k}/k = 0$.

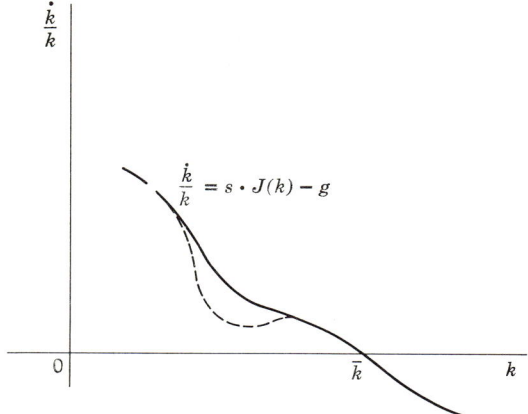

Figure 11.4 A unique and stable equilibrium for the two-sector model.

To begin, we note that the expression

$$J(k) = \frac{Y}{KP_K}$$

can be written

$$J(k) = r \cdot \frac{Y}{rKP_K}$$

or

$$J(k) = \frac{r}{1-c}$$

In terms of proportional changes,

$$\frac{dJ(k)}{J(k)} = \frac{dr}{r} - \frac{d(1-c)}{1-c}$$

In view of (11.15), (11.16), and (11.18), we can write

$$\frac{dJ(k)}{J(k)} = -b\frac{d\omega}{\omega} + \gamma\frac{d\omega}{\omega} = -(b-\gamma)\frac{d\omega}{\omega}$$

$$\frac{dJ(k)}{J(k)} = -\left(\frac{b-\gamma}{\sigma}\right)\frac{dk}{k}$$

On the Uniqueness and Stability of Growth Equilibrium

Recall that $J(k) = Y/KP_K$ (the output-capital ratio in value terms). Thus, the term in brackets can be thought of as the elasticity of the output-capital ratio with respect to the capital-labor ratio. A sufficient condition for $\bar{k}$ to be unique is that this elasticity be positive.

Recall that labor's share in the capital-goods industry (b) and the elasticity of substitution (σ) are always positive. Also, the elasticity of capital's overall share with respect to $\omega(\gamma)$ is negative if both σ_X and σ_K exceed one. It is zero if $\sigma_X = \sigma_K = 1$. Consequently, we can state that *one* sufficient condition for $\bar{k}$ to exist is

$$\sigma_X \geq 1$$

and

$$\sigma_K \geq 1$$

We can call this the *elasticity of substitution condition*, and an intuitive interpretation of it might go like this: We have defined

$$c \equiv \frac{wL}{Y}$$

so that with constant returns to scale,

$$1 - c = \frac{rKP_K}{Y}$$

or

$$KP_K = \frac{(1-c)Y}{r}$$

That is, the value of the capital stock is the capitalized value of payments to capital, the capitalization factor being the rate of interest. If capital deepening occurs (k rises), the interest rate (r) will fall, tending to increase the value of capital (KP_K). At the same time, with the elasticity of substitution greater than one everywhere, capital's share of output is rising in both sectors [$(1 - a)$ and $(1 - b)$ are rising], so that $(1 - c)$ must be rising. This effect tends to raise the value of capital also. Hence

$$\frac{Y}{KP_K} = \frac{r}{1-c}$$

must be falling with capital deepening, thus slowing down the growth of k.

306   A Simple Two-Sector Model of Growth in an Advanced Economy

Graphically, the growth line of k slopes everywhere downward in Figure 11.4. Higher values of k are always associated with lower values of its growth, so equilibrium is eventually established.

Can we say more? Can additional sufficient conditions be found? The elasticity $(b - \gamma)/\sigma$ is positive so long as b exceeds γ. The value of b will exceed that of γ if

$$b > \frac{1}{1 - c} [a(1 - a)(1 - s)(1 - \sigma_X) + b(1 - b)s(1 - \sigma_K)]$$

It is not at once obvious that this inequality holds under conditions that have economic meaning. Perhaps we can find an interpretation after a little manipulation. The expressions $(1 - a) \cdot (1 - s)$, and $(1 - b)s$ look familiar when we recall that

$$XP_X = (1 - s)Y$$

and

$$rK_X P_K = (1 - a)XP_X$$

so that

$$rK_X P_K = (1 - a)(1 - s)Y$$

or

$$(1 - a)(1 - s) = \frac{rK_X P_K}{Y}$$

Similarly,

$$(1 - b)s = \frac{rK_K P_K}{Y}$$

Recalling that

$$(1 - c) = \frac{rKP_K}{Y}$$

we can substitute into the inequality to obtain

$$b > \frac{Y}{rKP_K} \left[a(1 - \sigma_X) \frac{rK_X P_K}{Y} + b(1 - \sigma_K) \frac{rK_K P_K}{Y} \right]$$

or

$$b > a(1 - \sigma_X)\frac{K_X}{K} + b(1 - \sigma_K)\frac{K_K}{K}$$

But we also recall that the capital allocation between the two industries is linked to relative capital shares within sectors and to the saving ratio.

$$\frac{K_X}{K_K} = \frac{1-a}{1-b} \cdot \frac{XP_X}{\check{K}P_K} \qquad (11.7)$$
$$\qquad\qquad\qquad\qquad\qquad (11.8)$$

$$\frac{XP_X}{\check{K}P_X} = \frac{1-s}{s} \qquad (11.9)$$

Thus

$$\frac{K_K}{K_X} = \frac{1-b}{1-a} \cdot \frac{s}{1-s}$$

We found in an earlier section that this means:

$$\frac{K_K}{K} = \frac{(1-b)s}{(1-a)(1-s) + (1-b)s}$$

$$\frac{K_X}{K} = \frac{(1-a)(1-s)}{(1-a)(1-s) + (1-b)s}$$

Substituting these expressions into the inequality and simplifying we obtain at last

$$a(1-a)(1-s)\sigma_X + b(1-b)s\sigma_K > -(1-a)(1-s)(b-a)$$

The left-hand side is always positive, so we can be sure that the inequality holds if b exceeds a.[11] It holds if the capital-goods industry is more labor-intensive relative to the consumer-goods industry. We can call this the *capital-intensity condition*.

It is not intuitively clear why the capital-intensity condition is sufficient. However, we may think back to the graphic solution of the two-sector model. In that static context, it was found that higher rates of investment led to a lower interest rate *only* if the consumer-goods industry were more capital intensive—if the capital-intensity condition was satisfied. Since many

---

[11] It also holds if a equals b. But then the two-sector model is reduced to a single-sector model.

economists would view this as a "normal" relation between the interest rate and investment, the capital intensity condition might be thought of as "normally" satisfied; the relations between investment and the interest rate are "normal," and $\bar{k}$ is "normally" unique and stable. However, the world is what it is and no sufficient condition for uniqueness and stability of long-run equilibrium may be satisfied as an empirical matter. "Perverse" behavior is possible. But if "perverse" growth is ruled out, the two-sector model behaves very much like the one-sector model (Chapter Three).

EXERCISES

1. Suppose the saving ratio (s) were to fall. Using diagrams like Figures 11.1, 11.2, and 11.3, trace through the comparative statics effects on
    (a) Relative outputs ($X/\dot{K}$).
    (b) Relative prices (p).
    (c) Resource allocation (k_X and k_K).
    (d) The wage-rental ratio (ω).
    (e) The return on capital (r).

    Are your results sensitive to your assumption about relative capital intensities in the two sectors?

2. Derive Equation 11.18.

3. In this model, P_X is the price of consumer goods, so that w/P_X is the "real wage" from the point of view of workers. What would be the comparative-statics effects on the real wage if the saving ratio were to rise?

4. As a comparative dynamics proposition, what would happen to the economy-wide share of labor if the growth rate of labor were to increase? (Assume that the equilibrium is stable and unique.)

REFERENCES AND SUGGESTIONS FOR FURTHER READING

1. Gordon, R. A., "Differential Changes in the Prices of Consumers' and Capital Goods." *American Economic Review*, December 1961.
2. Harcourt, G. C., "Some Cambridge Controversies in the Theory of Capital." *Journal of Economic Literature*, June 1969.
3. Rybczynski, T. M., "Factor Endowment and Relative Commodity Prices." *Economica*, November 1955.

4. Savosnick, K. M., "The Box Diagram and the Production Possibilities Curve." *Ekonomisk Tidskrift*, September 1958.
5. Shell, K. (Ed.), *Essays on the Theory of Optimal Economic Growth*. Cambridge: The M.I.T. Press, 1967, pp. 79–84.
6. Stolper, W. F., and P. A. Samuelson, "Protection and Real Wages." *Review of Economic Studies*, November 1941. Reprinted in H. S. Ellis (Ed.), *Readings in the Theory of International Trade*, Homewood, Illinois: Irwin, 1950.
7. Uzawa, H., "On a Two-Sector Model of Economic Growth, I; II." *Review of Economic Studies*, October, 1961; June, 1963.

Chapter Twelve

UNDERDEVELOPMENT AND ECONOMIC DUALISM

An Interpretation of Economic Dualism
The Dynamic Core of a Developing Economy
The Setting
Growth with Constant Technology
A Single Technological Improvement
Continuous Technological Improvement
Exercises
References and Suggestions for Further Reading

AN INTERPRETATION OF ECONOMIC DUALISM

The term "dualism" has been given different meanings by various authors. Here, we adopt a particularly simple interpretation that partakes of meanings common in the literature and yet has analytic content.

Imagine a model economy composed of two sectors:

1. A primitive sector where primarily agricultural economic activity is chiefly organized along traditional lines, within extended family units. The product is distributed so that each worker receives a traditional real wage that is in excess of his marginal product and is equal to his average product.

2. A relatively modern sector where agricultural and manufacturing economic activity is dominated by profit maximizing, competitive firms. Consequently, the factors of production, including labor, are paid the value of their marginal products.

In the primitive sector, a laborer has a claim on the earnings of nonlabor inputs *by virtue of family membership*. If he migrates to the modern sector, he normally loses claim on nonlabor income that he would have received if he had remained in the primitive sector. As a consequence, the opportunity earnings of a prospective migrant exceed his marginal contribution in the primitive sector by the amount that his average product exceeds his marginal product.

Profit maximizing entrepreneurs in the modern sector will hire labor up to the point where the wage equals the value of labor's marginal product. Thus, the prospective migrant from the primitive sector chooses between the value of his *average* product in the primitive sector and the value of his potential *marginal* product in the modern sector.[1]

The two labor markets are illustrated in Figure 12.1. The product of the primitive sector (Y) is produced with land (N) and labor (L_Y). The marginal product of labor (w_Y) and the average product of labor ($\bar{w} = Y/L_Y$) fall as the ratio of labor to land rises. The product of the modern sector (X) is produced with capital (K) and labor (L_X). The marginal product (w_X) and average product (X/L_X) of labor fall as the labor-capital ratio rises.

If measurement units for X and Y are chosen so that the price of each equals one, and migration costs are disregarded, then the labor market is in equilibrium when the average product of labor in $Y(\bar{w})$ equals the marginal product of labor in $X(w_X)$. In this configuration, the marginal products are unequal ($w_Y < w_X$). If a worker were reallocated from Y to X, society's income would fall by w_Y in Y but rise by w_X in X, so that the *net* change in

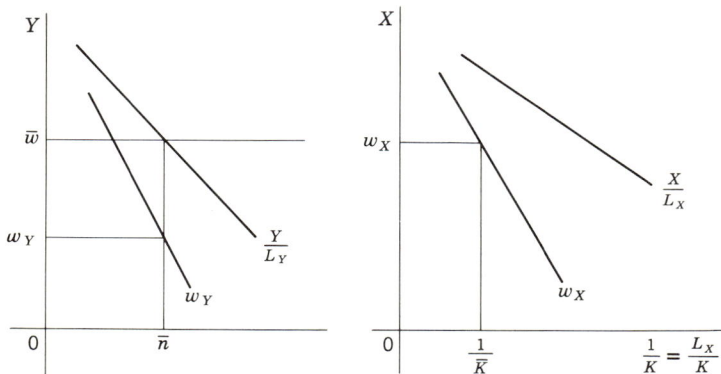

Figure 12.1   Labor markets in a dual economy.

---

[1] The choice may not be reversible. That is, a prospective migrant from the modern sector to the primitive sector may not be able to lay claim on a share of nonlabor earnings. Since developing countries normally experience net migration from the primitive to the modern sectors, this is not an important qualification.

income would be $w_X - w_Y$, which is positive.[2] This event could be interpreted as a once-and-for-all technological improvement in the aggregate production function. That is, greater output is obtained from society's land, capital, and labor.

Government policy could be aimed at equalizing social and private opportunity costs of labor through appropriate tax and subsidy schemes. Alternatively, institutional reform could be implemented that would permit the prospective migrant in the primitive sector to sell the income stream from his nonlabor income sources for its capitalized value to those who remain.

In the absence of these schemes, the overall efficiency of labor allocation can be improved through the relative expansion of the modern sector. As it grows in relative size, the proportion of workers "misallocated" in the primitive sector becomes relatively smaller. We now turn to an analysis of growth in the modern sector.

THE DYNAMIC CORE OF A DEVELOPING ECONOMY

The Setting

The modern sector is marked by profit maximizing, competitive firms that employ capital along with labor in productive processes. We assume that labor is furnished to this sector with perfect elasticity at a constant institutionally determined wage, measured in terms of the product of the modern sector.

This constant institutional wage is linked to the average product of labor in the primitive sector,[3] whose chief role is to furnish labor to the modern sector. If workers are thought to consume "wage goods," consisting mainly of agricultural commodities, then we can specify that the real *marginal* product of labor in the modern agricultural sector is equal to the *average* product of labor in the primitive sector. Moreover, we may assume, for a closed economy, that production conditions in modern agricultural production are identical to production conditions in modern nonagricultural activity, in the sense that the capital-labor ratios are always identical when the marginal rate of substitution between capital and labor is equal between the two sectors.[4] This condition assures that the price of nonagricultural

---

[2] Assume no change in the relative price of X and Y. For example, P_X and P_Y may be set in international markets.

[3] The average product is determined in that sector according to the principles outlined in Chapter Four. Since a constant rate of out-migration can be construed as an increase in the death rate (D), raising per capita product, we must imagine that this effect is small or that the rate of migration (in proportional terms) is constant.

[4] Put another way, the production functions differ at most by a scale factor. By an appropriate choice of measurement units for the respective outputs, they *are* identical.

goods is a constant, relative to agricultural goods. Thus, the real wage, expressed in terms of wage goods, is the same among all modern sectors and equal to the constant average product of labor in the primitive sector.

For an open economy, we may assume that internal price ratios are fixed by constant international prices. In this way, international trade assumes that wage goods can be obtained on constant terms of trade for nonwage goods. As an extreme example, it might be supposed that the modern sector does *not* produce wage goods (Y). Workers must be paid with nonwage goods (X) that *are* produced. Letting w' equal the money wage,

$$\frac{w'}{P_X} = MPP_{LX}$$

is the real wage in terms of X. Workers can trade these goods internationally to obtain wage goods on constant terms of trade ($\bar{p}$).[5] Thus,

$$\frac{w'}{P_Y} = \frac{MPP_{LX}}{\bar{p}}$$

is the constant wage, in terms of wage goods, that is equated to the average product of labor in the primitive sector. If we set $\bar{p} = 1$ by an appropriate choice of measurement units for X and Y, and let $\bar{w}$ equal the constant real wage in the primitive sector, then

$$\frac{w'}{P_Y} = \bar{w} = APP_{LX}$$

Growth with Constant Technology

The constant real wage, $\bar{w}$, is the supply curve of labor to the modern sector. It is plotted in Figure 12.2 as a horizontal straight line. The demand conditions are also illustrated. When $MPP_L = MPP_{LX}$ is plotted on the vertical axis and the capital-labor ratio ($k \equiv K/L$) is plotted on the horizontal axis, MPP_L rises as more capital is combined per unit of labor (see Figure 5.5).

The MPP_L function is derived from the production function, assumed to have constant returns to scale in capital and labor, with positive but declining marginal products.

$$X = L \cdot f(k), \quad f' > 0, \quad f'' < 0 \tag{12.1}$$

---

[5] This is also the internal, and constant, terms of trade between wage and nonwage goods in a closed economy, on the assumption of identical production conditions for X and Y.

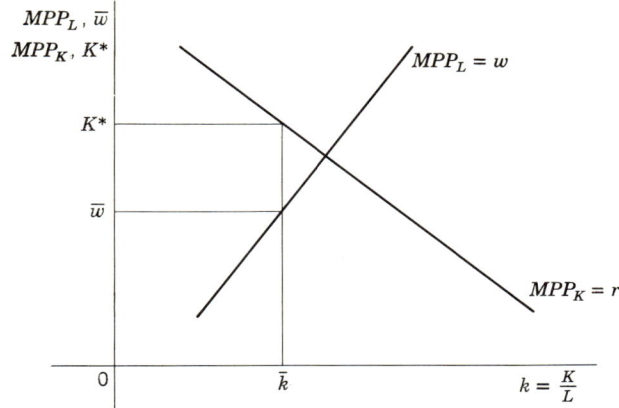

Figure 12.2 Growth in the dynamic core of a dual economy with constant technology.

We know from Chapter Five that

$$MPP_L = w = f(k) - k \cdot f'(k) \tag{5.7}$$

is an increasing function of k.

If the real wage is established at $\bar{w}$, an equilibrium $k = \bar{k}$ is established that satisfies

$$\bar{w} = f(k) - k \cdot f'(k) \tag{12.2}$$

In the absence of technological change, these functions are stable, so $\bar{k}$ is constant as long as $\bar{w}$ is constant. Labor employment will grow apace with capital accumulation.

Note that here there are "unlimited supplies of labor" at the traditional real wage ($\bar{w}$), just as there were "unlimited supplies of capital" at the world interest rate (R) in the open economy model in Chapter Ten. In both cases, a fixed real return to *one* of the inputs fixes the capital-labor ratio and the real return to the *other* input. In the open economy, the model was "driven" by ever-rising population. Here, the model must be "driven" by capital accumulation if it is to grow at all. But how fast is capital growing?

Let us assume that workers consume all their incomes, but that capitalists save and invest all their property income.[6]

$$\dot{K} = MPP_K \cdot K = rK$$

---

[6] Capital goods may be produced domestically or imported, at constant terms of trade with noncapital goods in both cases.

316 Underdevelopment and Economic Dualism

or

$$K^* = MPP_K = r$$

We know from Chapter Five that

$$MPP_K = r = f'(k) \qquad (5.6)$$

is a decreasing function of k. Thus, the proportional rate of capital accumulation is

$$K^* = f'(k) \qquad (12.3)$$

The equilibrium rate of capital accumulation is determined by the equilibrium ratio of capital to labor, which, in turn, is determined by the constant real wage. Note that a higher real wage is associated with a higher capital-labor ratio and lower proportional rate of capital accumulation.

Employment will increase at a proportional rate equal to the rate of return on capital. If this rate exceeds the rate of natural increase in the modern sector, migration from the primitive sector will fill the gap.

A Single Technological Improvement

The effects of a single technological improvement can be analyzed by exploiting Table 6.1 and interpreting the growth equations contained therein as comparative statics relations. For example, the growth in the real wage is now read as

$$w^* = \frac{1-a}{\sigma} k^* + \pi - (1-a)\beta$$

where

$$w^* = \frac{1}{w} \cdot \frac{dw}{dt}$$

$$k^* = \frac{1}{k} \cdot \frac{dk}{dt}$$

$$\pi = \frac{1}{X} \cdot \frac{\partial X}{\partial t}$$

and

$$\beta = \pi_K - \pi_L = \frac{1}{r} \cdot \frac{\partial r}{\partial t} - \frac{1}{w} \cdot \frac{\partial w}{\partial t}$$

Interpreted as a timeless, comparative-statics relation, we have

$$\frac{dw}{w} = \frac{1-a}{\sigma} \cdot \frac{dk}{k} + \pi - (1-a)\beta$$

where π is the proportional change in output due to technological change alone, and β is the relative change in marginal products attributable solely to the improvement.

With the real wage constant ($dw/w = 0$), the proportional change in the capital-labor ratio is

$$\frac{dk}{k} = -\frac{\sigma}{1-a}\pi + \sigma\beta$$

At the moment the change occurs, the capital stock is what it is. Any initial change in k must be due to changes in L. Since

$$\frac{dk}{k} = \frac{dK}{K} - \frac{dL}{L}$$

the initial change in employment must be

$$\frac{dL}{L} = \frac{\sigma}{1-a}\pi - \sigma\beta$$

Initial labor absorption from the primitive sector is greater, the greater is π and the greater labor-using or capital-saving bias is (the greater minus β is). Moreover, if β is negative, a higher elasticity of substitution will unambiguously promote labor absorption.

The initial change in output reflects the *direct* effects of the technological change plus the *induced* increase in employment.

$$\frac{dX}{X} = \pi + (1-a)\frac{dK}{K} + a\frac{dL}{L}$$

With the capital stock momentarily unchanged when the improvement occurs,

$$\frac{dX}{X} = \pi + a\frac{dL}{L}$$

Substituting for the proportional change in employment due to the improvement,

$$\frac{dX}{X} = \pi + a\left(\frac{\sigma}{1-a}\pi - \sigma\beta\right)$$

or

$$\frac{dX}{X} = \left(1 + \frac{a}{1-a}\sigma\right)\pi - a\sigma\beta$$

For any given π, the *initial* change in both output and employment is greater, the more labor-using the improvement is.

Over the longer term, we should ask how the improvement impinges on the rate of growth of capital. Since output and employment grow apace once more with capital after the improvement, we also know how the growth of these variables is affected if we know the impact on capital growth.

But on our assumption that saving is equal to profits, capital growth subsequent to the improvement is equal to the new interest rate. From Table 6.1,

$$\frac{dr}{r} = -\frac{a}{\sigma}\cdot\frac{dk}{k} + \pi + a\beta \tag{6.13}$$

We have just found the change in the capital-labor ratio, on the assumption of a constant real wage.

$$\frac{dk}{k} = -\frac{\sigma}{1-a}\pi + \sigma\beta$$

By substitution,

$$\frac{dr}{r} = \frac{1}{1-a}\pi$$

This is also the proportional rise in the rate of capital accumulation due to the improvement,

$$\frac{dK^*}{K^*} = \frac{1}{1-a}\pi$$

The bias of the technological change has no effect on subsequent capital, labor, and output growth.

It may be that an underdeveloped country, in choosing from a menu of technology developed for more advanced countries, faces a trade-off between π and β.

$$\beta = \beta(\pi), \quad \beta' > 0$$

Greater increases in output due to the change alone (π) may be associated with capital-using bias ($\beta > 0$). In that case, there is a trade-off between short-run and long-run gains in employment and output that can be obtained from a single improvement.

Continuous Technological Improvement

Suppose technological change occurs at a constant labor-augmenting (Harrod-neutral) rate m and that production conditions are Cobb-Douglas.

$$X = e^{amt} K^{1-a} L^a$$

The real wage is

$$\frac{\partial X}{\partial L} = w = e^{amt}\left(\frac{K}{L}\right)^{1-a} = e^{amt} k^{1-a}$$

so that

$$w^* = am + (1-a)(K^* - L^*).$$

But real wages cannot grow, because of unlimited supplies of labor at the traditional wage. Capital shallowing must therefore occur.

$$K^* - L^* = -\frac{a}{1-a} m$$

As before, let us assume that profits are reinvested

$$K^* = r$$

But now the interest rate is not constant.

$$\frac{\partial X}{\partial K} = r = e^{amt}\left(\frac{K}{L}\right)^{-a} = e^{amt} k^{-a}$$

and

$$r^* = am - a(K^* - L^*)$$

From above,

$$r^* = am + a \cdot \frac{a}{1-a} m$$

320 Underdevelopment and Economic Dualism

or

$$r^* = \frac{a}{1-a} m$$

The growth rate of capital is therefore growing.

$$K^{**} = \frac{d}{dt}\left(\frac{\dot{K}}{K}\right) \bigg/ \left(\frac{K}{\dot{K}}\right) = r^*$$

$$K^{**} = \frac{a}{1-a} m$$

This "explosive development" of the modern sector will continue as long as labor remains available at the traditional wage. But eventually the quantity demanded of labor may exceed the quantity supplied at the traditional wage. Wages will start to rise, and a more complicated model is required to describe the subsequent development of the economy.

EXERCISES

1. The dynamic core of a developing economy cannot import (or export) capital at a constant international interest rate, as long as it can hire labor at a constant real wage and production is subject to constant returns to scale. Why?
2. How is the growth of output and labor modified if capitalists save less than all their income and workers save nothing? Assume no technological change.

REFERENCES AND SUGGESTIONS FOR FURTHER READING

1. Fei, J. C. H. and G. Ranis, *Development of the Labor Surplus Economy*. Homewood: Irwin, 1964.
2. Fei, J. C. H. and G. Ranis, "Innovation, Capital Accumulation and Economic Development." *American Economic Review*, June 1963.
3. Jorgenson, Dale W., "The Development of the Dual Economy." *Economic Journal*, June 1961.
4. Meade, J. E., *A Neo-Classical Theory of Economic Growth*. New York: Oxford, 1961, Chap. 5.
5. Ranis G. and J. C. H. Fei, "A Theory of Economic Development." *American Economic Review*, September 1961.

INDEX

Allan, R. D. G., 76n, 85n, 216n

Big push, 191
Boley, A. L., 288n
Borts, G. H., 273n
Boundary conditions, 225
Brachistochrone, 217n

Capital-intensity condition, 307
Catenary, 221
Comparative dynamics, 144–145
Comparative statics, 8, 104, 144–145
Compounding, continuous, 16–17
  discontinuous, 14
Contract curve, 289
Courant, R., 216n

Denison, E. F., 110n
Derivative, of constant, 77
  of function, of a function, 78–79, 112
  of one variable, 72–73
  of logarithm, 21
  partial, 76
  of product, 76–77, 112
  of proportional growth path, 19
  of quotient, 83
  total, 100
Difference equation, first order, 3, 5–7
Differential, 73, 79, 100
Differential Equation, single equation, 160–167, 184–187, 273–276
  systems of equations, 193
Diminishing returns, law of, 27–28
Domar, Evsey, 3n, 133n

Dynamic inefficiency, 249, 253
Dynamic multiplier, 242

Edgeworth, F. Y., 288n
Efficiency labor, 126
Elasticity, average product, of capital, 99–100, 104
  of labor, 98–99, 104
  interest rate, 89, 104, 300
  output, 101
  share, of capital, 102–103, 104, 301–303
    of labour, 102–103, 104, 301–303
  wage, 90, 104
Elasticity of substitution condition, 305
Equilibrium rate of growth, 35, 58–59
Euler's equation, 219, 221

Fisher, F. M., 30n, 110n
Foreign aid, 278–281
Functional notation, 3

Gatmacher, F. R., 199n
Gelfand, I., and S. V. Fomin, 216n, 221n
Golden age, 184
Golden rule, 209–214, 250
Gordon, R. A., 292n

Hamiltonian, 241
Hamiltonian system, 242
Hansen, J. A., and P. A. Neher, 210n
Harcourt, G. C., 301n
Harrod, Sir Roy, 3n, 133n
Hicks, Sir John, 111, 117n

321

Institutional wage, 313
Isochrone, 232
Isokine, 195
Isoquant, 119

Johansen, L., 49n
Johnson, H., 31n
Jones, R. W., 95n, 135n, 139n
Jorgenson, D. W., 52n, and Z. Griliches, 110n

Koopmans, T. C., 251n

Leftwich, R. H., 28n
Low-level equilibrium trap, 191

Malthus, T. R., 52n
Marty, A. L., 210n
Maximum principle, 242
Myint, Hla, 22n
Myrdal, G., 199n

National product, single sector, 36–38
 two sectors, 287
Nelson, R. R., 52n
Nurske, R., 189n, 199n

Olech, C., 198n
Olech conditions, 186

Phase diagram, 162, 184, 189
Phelps, E. S., 210n, 249
Pontryagin, L. S., et al., 216n, 240n, 241n
Production function, Cobb-Douglas, 69, 106–107, 140–141, 167
 fixed proportions, 47–49
 neoclassical, 26–30, 52–53
 product exhaustion, 84–85
Production possibilities curve, 292

Propensity to proliferate, 55, 63–64

Ramsey, F. P., 238n
Ricardo, D., 52n
Routh-Hurwicz conditions, 199n
Rykczynski, T. M., 288n

Samuelson, P. A., 30n, 91n, 144n, 235n, 288n
Savosnick, K. M., 288n
Shell, K., 144n, 199n, 295n
Solow, R. M., 26n, 39n, 49n, 110n
Speed of adjustment, 169
Stability, global, 186, 198
 local, 186
 saddle point, 199, 204
Stages of growth, 3
Stigler, G., 28n, 36n
Stolper, W. F., and P. A. Samuelson, 288n
Swan, T. W., 26n, 168n

Technological change, bias, 111, 117
 continuous improvement, 42–43, 148–156, 177–181
 embodied and disembodied, 39
 Harrod neutral, 133–141
 Hicks neutral, 117–121, 137–141
 labour augmenting, 125, 134–137
 single improvement, 38–42, 60–62, 156–160, 173–177
Time constant, 188
Tobin, J., 31n
Transversality condition, 226
Turnpike, 217, 235

Uzawa, H., 133n, 284n

Yamane, T., 76n